IMAGE BEARERS

IMAGE BEARERS

Restoring our identity and living out our calling

Rachel Atkinson & Michael Lloyd

HODDER &
STOUGHTON

First published in Great Britain in 2023 by Hodder & Stoughton
An Hachette UK company

1

A CIP catalogue record for this title is available from the British Library

Trade Paperback ISBN 978 1 529 31866 1
eBook ISBN 978 1 529 31868 5

Typeset in Ehrhardt by Hewer Text UK Ltd, Edinburgh
Printed and bound in Great Britain by Clays Ltd, Elcograf S.p.A.

Hodder & Stoughton policy is to use papers that are natural, renewable and recyclable products
and made from wood grown in sustainable forests. The logging and manufacturing processes
are expected to conform to the environmental regulations of the country of origin.

Hodder & Stoughton Ltd
Carmelite House
50 Victoria Embankment
London EC4Y 0DZ

www.hodderfaith.com

To the memory of our dear friend and mentor,
Ruth Miller

Contents

Foreword – from N. T. Wright ix
Introduction xv

Part 1: The Theology of Restoration (Michael Lloyd) 1

1 The Image of God – Created 3
2 The Image of God – Broken 25
3 The Image of God – Restored 49

Part 2: Spiritual Practices for Restoration (Rachel Atkinson) 91

4 Listening to God 93
5 Rediscovering Heart Knowing 113
6 Practising Confession 133
7 Forgiving Others 148

Part 3: Emotional Aspects of Restoration (Rachel Atkinson) 167

8 Receiving Mother Love 169
9 Receiving Father Love 194

Part 4: Practising and Sustaining Restoration (Rachel Atkinson) 219

10 Living Well 221
11 Dying Well 242

Appendix 1 Ministering Restoration to Individuals – In
             Conversation with Ruth   263
Appendix 2 Ministering Restoration in the Local Church
             (Hennie Johnston)   275

Acknowledgements   283
Notes   285

Foreword

Most psychiatrists are now agreed that Sigmund Freud, the great guru of psychology a hundred years ago, got it wrong. But that doesn't mean there aren't important questions to be addressed. Why do some things make us angry? Is there a deep root underneath the sadness which sometimes overwhelms us? Why do I find myself doing or saying things that, at other times, I know to be wrong or inappropriate? Why does beauty – in whatever form – move us, sometimes to tears? Why are human relationships so important and yet so difficult? Why do some of us, some of the time, find ourselves in despair, feeling that life has neither meaning nor purpose? And what, if anything, can we do about it?

Addressing such questions has been made harder because our culture as a whole has fenced off areas of human life that, arguably, matter most. In his remarkable book *The Master and his Emissary* Iain McGilchrist, a brain scientist who is also expert in modern culture and literature, argues that the left and right hemispheres of the brain have very different roles, and that the modern Western world has privileged the wrong one. The right hemisphere is designed as the 'master', looking at the big picture, open to the imagination, keenly aware of beauty, sensitive to music, to stories, to love, perhaps even to God. The

left hemisphere is there to work on the details, to fill in the foot-
notes, to add up the figures. The left hemisphere will remind
you to check the tyres and fill up the petrol tank. But it can't
tell you where to go. Western modernity, however, has put the
left hemisphere in charge, only interested (like Dickens' Mr
Gradgrind) in 'Facts, facts, facts', and not bothering about
their meaning. That is why, as an obvious example, a school
board, faced with shrinking budgets, will often cut out art,
music or drama, the very things which add 'meaning' to everything else.

Many people, both Christian and not, find themselves at a
loss in this world. Many solutions are on offer, including a
range of secular therapies. But over the last generation, appear-
ing like an unexpected and beautiful plant in the barren landscape of late modernity, we have seen a remarkable growth in
the ministry of healing – healing, not just for bodies (though
that happens too) but for the whole person: body, mind,
memory, imagination, emotions, hopes and fears. Healing like
this isn't simply about finding a theory to explain *why* things
have gone wrong. It is about exploring ways in which things
can be put right.

Within that, many wise Christians have found within the
Christian tradition resources for understanding and restoration, mostly involving various kinds of prayer. Within that
again, many have discovered that this is difficult to do alone.
Prayer can seem difficult or dry. But a shared journey of spiritual friendship and counselling can make all the difference.

That is where Ruth Miller came in. My wife and I knew
Ruth and her husband Andrew back in student days, and
though our paths had led us apart geographically we were still
in touch. Having myself received from others help and counsel
of the sort in which Ruth became expert, I rejoiced to hear of

her ministry and the ways in which it was providing life-giving help and hope – including to some of my own friends.

In particular, I was, and am, grateful and excited that this ministry was not simply about 'therapy' in the sense of 'making people feel better'. Again and again it was about guiding people into the presence, and within reach of the healing love, of the God made known in Jesus. At that point some therapists get nervous: won't that mean bringing in abstract 'theology', dry, cerebral biblical study, and so on – precisely the sort of thing you might get in the kinds of churches where people have not received the help they so obviously need? In other words, please don't give us a left-brain solution for a right-brain problem.

But the solution – as Ruth was very much aware, and as the present book makes clear – is not to lurch between dry academic analysis and a free-wheeling (and possibly fantasy-inducing) feel-good therapy. The solution is about integration: the whole person addressing the whole problem, and doing so in relation-ship not only with the God in whose image they are made but with fellow members of the body of Christ, and sometimes with one (a wise counsellor) in particular. Within that integra-tion, the academic analysis ceases to be dry, and the therapy, though it reaches into wide areas of the imagination, is firmly anchored to the deep and biblical roots of the Christian tradi-tion. In the present book I specially enjoyed, in quotations from Ruth herself, the moments when she, mostly comfortable within her own broadly evangelical tradition, was eager to discern and celebrate wisdom and value in other branches of historic Christianity. That generosity of spirit, not to be confused with indifference to questions of truth, came from her vision of the capacious generosity of God himself.

At the heart of it all, as the underlying truth at which the best secular psychology is gesturing, is the central biblical theme of humans made in God's image – made to reflect the love and wisdom of God into the world, and to reflect the praises of creation back to God. That God-reflecting vocation is easily disfigured or distorted. That is when we meet the deep personal problems of which we are all uncomfortably aware, and which psychology, not to mention the popular analyses such as the Myers-Briggs Type Indicator, have tried to address. But the good news, as Michael Lloyd shows in the first half of this book, is that the image-bearing vocation can be restored. And the Christian gospel, the good news of what God has done, is doing and will do in Jesus, applied to human hearts and minds through the Holy Spirit, is the means by which this restoration can and does happen. Michael's account of this provides in itself a model of what he is expounding: a thorough and careful exposition of biblical theology in which the pastoral heart is visible all through. Restoration includes re-integration.

The same is true, in reverse as it were, in Rachel Atkinson's account of the spiritual practices and emotional aspects of 'restoration', climaxing in the moving account of 'Living Well' and particularly 'Dying Well'. Rachel's chapters are practical without being merely pragmatic, because they are so obviously rooted in the same biblical theology which was the source of Ruth's lifelong understanding and which Michael so ably expounds. The frequent quotations from some of Ruth's former clients, and from Ruth herself, bring these practical chapters an extra vivid dimension, not least when we are privy to the honest and brave reflections of Ruth herself as her own death drew near.

We live in strange and challenging times. We celebrate in this book the fact that God has raised up ministries like that of Ruth Miller to enable more and more people to find healing and hope at every level of life. My hope and prayer is that the book will encourage many to seek that healing for themselves, in a deeper and personal relationship with the God we know in and through Jesus; and perhaps also to stimulate some towards the same kind of vocation to which Ruth so generously gave herself.

Rt Revd Prof N. T. Wright DD FRSE
Senior Research Fellow, Wycliffe Hall, Oxford
February 2023

Introduction

The British comedian Peter Cook was once asked to host a chat show. Before the first episode, he was nervous, and wanted to prepare thoroughly. So he had a host of questions written down that he could ask his first celebrity guest. He even wrote down the opening pleasantry, 'How are you?' So nervous was he, however, that it came out as '*Who* are you?', which wasn't a good start!

But it is one of the most important questions anyone can be asked. 'Who are we?' is one of the questions that every worldview, every philosophy, every religion – and every individual – has to answer. The Bible has a succinct and supersaturated statement about who we are, on its very first page – that we bear the image of God (Genesis 1:26, 37). This multi-meaninged phrase lies at the root of Jewish and Christian understandings of what it is to be human. We are self-portraits of God, and, just as one of the purposes of a portrait is to let others know what someone is like, so one of the purposes of human beings is to reflect the nature of God to one another and to the rest of creation.

Unfortunately – and all too obviously – we are not doing a very good job of that. What has gone wrong? That is another of the questions that every worldview has to answer. The answer

that Christian theologians have seen in the Genesis story is that
we have cut ourselves off from the God whose image we bear.
We have worshipped other gods – and therefore have become
like those other gods, because it is a fundamental principle that
you become like what you worship (Psalm 135:18). Thus the
image has become obscured. We are meant to be a window onto
God, but that window has become enmired with grime, and
opaque. We were created to be self-portraits of God – God's
'masterpieces' (Ephesians 2:10, NLT) – but our varnish is
cracking, our paint is flaking and we are in urgent need of
restoration.

Restoration is about returning things to how they were
originally created and intended to be. It is a familiar term in
the world of art, and also one of the great themes in the
biblical story of salvation. God restores individuals, families, and nations, and ultimately, he will restore the whole
created order. He enacts his great story of restoration on the
canvas of history and cosmology, and also on the smaller
canvas of each of our lives, so that we can enjoy his presence
more fully, live more freely and reflect his image more
closely.

This book explores the theology and practice of personal
restoration. Many of the subjects it considers have traditionally been associated with 'inner healing'. However, the term
'restoration' is used here to emphasise that the healing of the
person concerns how we relate to others, our physical habits
and our outlook, as well as our feelings and emotions. This
kind of holistic restoration is basic to Christian growth
because it affects the way we relate to God, to others and to
ourselves. The more we allow God to restore us, the more we
shall enjoy his loving presence in our own lives, and the more
freely and healthily we shall be able to relate to others. Further,

as God's image in us is restored, the more we shall reflect God as he is to others (rather than a distorted version of who he is), and therefore the easier it will be for others to be drawn to him, including our friends, families, churches, and those who give churches a wide berth. In short, the goal of restoration is God's glory rather than our comfort. Understood in this way, restoration is not only 'emergency care' for the deeply wounded but a crucial part of our Christian walk. It is about following Jesus and becoming more like him, and is a process which, as Christians, we need to be involved in for the whole of our lives.

The Story of the Book

This book is inspired by the work of our close friend, Ruth Miller, who died in 2013. Ruth was not widely known, but her ministry of pastoral counselling helped bring God's restoration to hundreds of people, including both of us. She experienced God's restoration in her own life continually, and exercised a significant ministry, counselling around 300 clients in her own home, ministering in healing prayer teams under the leadership of Leanne Payne and Lin Button, and speaking in a variety of settings on issues relating to restoration.

Many people, including ourselves, encouraged Ruth to capture her insights and experiences in a book, but a diagnosis of secondary cancer in June 2011 made this seem impossible. However, because we had benefitted so much from Ruth's approach to restoration and discipleship, we were keen to share her insights with a wider audience and, as it turns out, God had already begun speaking to Ruth about just this. Ruth recalled how the journey of writing this book began:

In December 2011 some friends visited us. Very quietly, one of my friends, Jackie, said: 'I think God may be saying there is some writing for you to do, but you are not to feel under pressure – it might be that someone else will be involved.'

I filed this away in my heart and got on with my Christmas preparations. We then spent an evening with our prayer partners, Rachel and Phil, celebrating the birth of their second baby and mourning my terminal illness. There was much laughter and many tears.

Two weeks later my phone rang. It was Rachel. 'Phil and I have been praying and we think your teaching material needs to be made into a book. How would you feel about me doing that for you?' I remembered what Jackie had said, and as I shared this with Rachel we sensed that God was behind the idea.

The rest is history, and the book you are now holding, while written by us, is very much a fruit of Ruth's ministry and reflects many of her ideas and practices as a pastoral counsellor. Part 1 is by Michael and sets out a biblical and theological framework for restoration; Parts 2, 3 and 4 are by Rachel and offer more practical and pastoral guidance which draws extensively on Ruth's own material. We suspect you will notice a change of style and tone – and sometimes even a difference of content – between our contributions, but we passionately believe that they belong together, because good practice must have firm theological foundations, and equally, good theological thinking finds its fulfilment in practice. If you find the theology of Part 1 hard going, then feel free to skip it and go straight to the more practical Parts 2 to 4 – but we would urge you then to give the theology another try, so that you understand more about what your practice is based on. Conversely, if you love the theology of Part 1, but are less comfortable with the more practical material of Parts 2 to 4, we would encourage you to persevere, so that your head knowledge becomes lived experience. Human beings flourish when their heads and hearts are fully engaged, and it may be that the style you find more difficult is the one you most need to engage with.

Within the book there are numerous testimonies, mainly from Ruth's clients, which are anonymised and used with permission. These have been strategically placed to illustrate particular points, and help give an insight into the approach to discipleship we discuss throughout the book. Because we want to give you an opportunity to hear Ruth's voice, we also quote her directly from time to time, where she can more fully explain, illustrate and apply ideas. These contributions are all placed in grey boxes. Sometimes the speaker is introduced, but where this is not the case, you are reading Ruth's own words.

How to Use this Book

This book is designed as a toolkit for Christian discipleship. It is not a comprehensive or systematic guide to healing and restoration, nor does it seek to address mental health issues, for which we recommend seeking professional help. Rather, it provides a theological understanding of restoration, and some tools to apply this theology in practical terms. It draws on the work of other Christians in healing ministry, and we hope that it will be one among many resources that can be used to bring restoration to God's people.

A key aim is to provide believers with some important theological and practical foundations for growth into mature disciples of Christ. If ideas resonate with you or shed new light on your thinking, it might be worth stopping to write these down, so that you can prayerfully reflect on them later. Do consider purchasing a designated prayer journal to jot down any notes or reflections as you read – anything you think God might be saying to you. More on using this journal will be discussed later in the book. Additionally, you may need to refer back to earlier chapters as you progress through the material. Given that the process of restoration is intensely practical, throughout this book you are invited to pause and reflect more deeply on how the ideas being presented apply to you. Each chapter concludes with a simple, practical exercise intended to facilitate your own journey of restoration.

If you are a leader of a small group, youth group or church, and wish to begin introducing these ideas to those in your pastoral care, the exercises at the end of each chapter can easily be adapted for use with individuals or groups among whom you minister. However, as restoration cannot simply be learned about and taught but, being an aspect of discipleship, must be experienced, lived and modelled, our greatest hope is that you will wholeheartedly pursue God's continuing restoration in your own life. From this place, you will be empowered to facilitate God's restoration in the people you pastor, and with this in mind, there are two appendices specifically addressing leaders who wish to minister restoration to others.

Our passion, which was also Ruth's passion, is for the Church to become increasingly healthy and whole. Our hope and prayer is that God will use this book to restore you into the incredible masterpiece that he created you to be in the first place.

Dr Rachel Atkinson
St Mark's Church, Coventry
February 2023

Revd Dr Michael Lloyd
Wycliffe Hall, Oxford
February 2023

PART 1
The Theology of Restoration

If we are image bearers, and if that image has become distorted and warped to the point of being barely recognisable in places, and if we want that image to be restored to its original glory, then we need to know as much as we can about what it is an image *of* and what the artist intended it to look like. So we begin this book by exploring what the image of God *is* – what it is to be human, and what human beings are intended to be and to do. The aim is to provide a biblical and theological framework for the rest of the book.

1

The Image of God – Created

The first thing that the Bible says about human beings is that we are made in the *image* of God: 'Then God said, "Let us make humankind in our image, according to our likeness"' (Genesis 1:26, NRSVA). The image of God is an important biblical concept on which much has been written, but there are actually very few references to this concept in the Bible. It is vital that we understand what is meant by the image of God, in order that we may know what it is to be human, what God's blueprint for human beings looks like – and therefore how we should live. In this chapter, we shall look at some of the passages that refer to the image of God, and we shall try to glean some wisdom from commentators and theologians about what the phrase means and what its implications are.

Light can be refracted into its colours – violet, indigo, blue and green, yellow, orange and red. Similarly, the concept of the image of God can be refracted into a number of related elements. Let us focus on seven of them.

1 Value

An artist drops into a gallery where her paintings are being exhibited, and casually asks the gallery owner if there has been

much interest in her work. 'Well,' says the gallery owner, 'I
have good news and bad news. The good news is that someone
came in and asked if I thought your paintings would appreciate
in value after your death. And when I said that I thought they
would, he bought all fifteen of them.' 'Wow!' says the artist:
'That's fantastic! What's the bad news?' To which the gallery
owner replies, 'He's your doctor!'

The image of God is about *value*. One of the biblical references to the image of God is Genesis 9:6:

'Whoever sheds the blood of a human,
by a human shall that person's blood be shed;
for in his own image
God made humankind.' (NRSVA)

The reason why murder is wrong is because human beings are
made in the image of God and are therefore *intrinsically valuable*. The fact that human beings were created to reflect something of the nature, character and beauty of God makes it inappropriate to take a human life, to put an end to that particular
reflection. Murder deprives the world of a unique source of
knowledge about God. Our image-bearing capacity gives us a
worth that commands respect. The fact that we were created by
God with a particular task to perform – to reflect his glory into
his world – means that no human being is there to serve the
needs or the whims of any other. We are made in the image of
God and have been given a task by him: we are therefore orientated *primarily* towards him, not primarily towards anyone else.
As we shall see, we get very warped and distorted when we
orientate ourselves primarily towards anyone or anything else.
(Ruth used to talk about being 'bent in on' someone else, as a
way of describing an unhealthy relational neediness and

dependency.[1]) Each of us has an intrinsic value, and we are called to recognise and respect this in every other person – and to treat them accordingly.

Nor is it solely the drastic crime of murder that contravenes this calling. James 3:9 widens it out: 'With the tongue we praise our Lord and Father, and with it we curse human beings, who have been made in God's likeness . . . My brothers and sisters, this should not be.'

Why is it wrong to curse or belittle another human being? Because they are made in the likeness of God and are therefore creatures of inestimable value.[2] They have something of God about them. They ought, therefore, to be treated with the utmost respect and reverence. The Greek word for 'praise' in James 3:9 means, literally, 'to say good words about'. The doctrine of the image of God means that it is utterly contradictory to speak good words of God and to speak bad words of someone who is in the image of God. Because of the immense value inherent in all human beings, it is inappropriate to 'dis' others verbally or to treat them shoddily. The value of every person is to shape how we treat them.

This seems to me to be part of the gospel. The value of every human being is the first principle of both ethics and pastoral psychology. One of the privileges of the Christian counsellor is that they know the person in front of them has value – absolute, unshakeable, unlosable value. And they know the *basis* of that value. They know the *origin* of that value. They know who they are valued *by*.

When you think about it, it becomes clear that value is a personal quality. Only a person can value you. You can't be valued by an impersonal force, such as electricity or gravity. So, if one has an ultimately impersonal view of the universe – that there is no one who brought it into being and no one behind it – then it becomes very difficult to ground the value that we all instinctively know human beings to have. But if one has a personal view of the universe – that there is a Person who created it, who is behind it, who can be met within it, who loves it, and who loves us – then there are objective grounds for this value.

I suggest that there are four advantages to grounding our value in God. If we ground human value in God, then it is:

Unearned

Many of us spend much of our lives trying to earn our value, trying to get people to like us, trying to rack up accomplishments. Mostly, this activity is counterproductive. It places too much strain on relationships that weren't intended to bear such weight. In one episode of *Ally McBeal*, there was a poignant exchange between Ally (one of the lawyers) and Elaine (a legal secretary). Ally asks Elaine why she didn't give her a birthday present. Elaine reminds Ally that she dedicated a song to her at the karaoke session in the bar, the night before. Ally retorts angrily that that was all about Elaine; it was all about her getting noticed, and asks when she is going to stop doing everything in order to get noticed. There is a slight pause, and then Elaine replies that she will stop doing everything in order to get noticed – when she is noticed. The desire to be noticed, to be liked, to accomplish something, to *be* someone – the attempt to earn our value – usually distorts who we are.

But if our value is grounded in God, then it is just given. It is just *there*. We don't need to earn it or achieve it. It is simply a fact. It is what we work securely *from* – not what we have to work neurotically *to*. This should help to save us from workaholism and desperately seeking relationships and all other self-destructive attempts to work up some value for ourselves.

Unlosable

Many people would say, 'Yes, of course value is a personal quality – I am valuable because my family and friends value me. I don't need to bring God into it.' The problem, of course, is, what happens if one of them stops loving me? Do I suddenly become less valuable? Did I become less valuable when my parents died? Are we less valuable after the break-up of a relationship? If our value is grounded in the love of our family and friends, it seems to me that the answer to those questions would have to be yes.

But if our value is grounded in the evaluation – the love – of God, then the answer is (joyfully) no. God's not going to stop loving us – he *is* love. And he's not going to die – he's eternal. We need not fear losing our value if that value is grounded in God.

Universal

If our value depended upon other people valuing us, then it would appear to follow that popular people would be more valuable than unpopular ones, and yet that is a conclusion from which we rightly shrink. Clergy take funeral services every week at which there is no one present except for the vicar and the funeral director. Does that mean that the person was not valuable, simply because they seem to have had no family or friends who valued them enough to be there? Again, on an impersonal view of the universe, I think one would have to say yes.

But on a personal view of the universe, there is a Person who created us all, and who values each one of us equally. That is why Jesus gravitated towards those for whom no one else had much time, because he knew their infinite value in the eyes of his Father.

Unlimited

Our need to be valued is infinite, and if we don't know ourselves to be infinitely valued, independent of what we do, the lack of that knowledge warps our actions and motivations, and can ultimately damage our whole experience of life. The lack becomes a black hole within us.

However, if God is our valuer, then we are grounding ourselves on the fact that his love for us is never-ending and boundless. We can encounter more and more of it as we journey in our relationship with him. We can turn ourselves outward to others and to the world, secure in the knowledge of our eternal lovedness.

2 Rule

In the Ancient Near East, kings would set up statues of themselves in conquered territories, in order to indicate their claim to ownership, and to make a public declaration of their dominion over this territory. The image was the embodiment of the king's rule. Where you saw that image, you would know whose territory you were in. The Old Testament scholar, Gerhard von Rad, put it this way:

> Just as powerful earthly kings . . . erect images of themselves in the provinces of their empire where they do not personally appear, so man is placed upon earth in God's image as God's sovereign emblem. He is really only God's representative, summoned to maintain and enforce God's claim to dominion over the earth.[3]

This is supported by the context of the very first reference to the image of God in the Bible:

Then God said, 'Let us make human beings in our image, in our likeness, and let them rule over the fish of the sea and the birds of the air, over the livestock, over all the earth, and over all the creatures that move along the ground.'

Genesis 1:26, author's paraphrase

Human beings are called to rule creation. And, as we are called to reflect the rule of *God*, this means that the sort of dominion we are to exercise over creation is to be the sort that God exercises over us: servant dominion, self-sacrificial dominion, liberating dominion. God rules us in the way that is best for us, not in the way that is necessarily best for him – the cross shows that. So we are to rule creation in such a way that it flourishes, rather than always and only for our benefit.

In other words, we are to care for creation. We are supposed to rule creation in such a way that it is obvious that the ultimate ruler is someone who loves his creation profoundly, and, where necessary, sacrificially.

3 Equality

The concept of the image of God was well known in the Ancient Near Eastern world. However, this was confined solely to the king. The name of the Egyptian king Tutankhamun, for instance, can be translated as 'the living image of Amon'. And a Babylonian text sees the king as the image of the Babylonian god Bel: 'The father of the king, my lord, was the very image of Bel, and the king, my lord, is likewise the very image of Bel.'[4] Genesis, conversely, has democratised the concept, so that *every* human being is made in the image of God, and therefore every human being is royal.

'We hold these truths to be self-evident, that all men are created equal, that they are endowed by their Creator with

certain unalienable Rights, that among these are Life, Liberty
and the pursuit of Happiness', says the American Declaration
of Independence, memorably. Sadly, however, the equality of
all human beings does not seem to be self-evident. It has not
seemed self-evident to defenders and advocates of apartheid,
slavery or the feudal system, who have denied the claims of
equality in confident and cavalier fashion throughout human
history. It does not seem self-evident to sexists or racists today.

Human beings differ enormously – not just culturally and
physiologically, but also in terms of their ability, longevity,
popularity and power. Human equality, therefore, cannot
simply be inferred from human society. Nor can it be inferred
from the natural world, in which the battle for survival is so
much of a preoccupation that the concept of recognising the
worth of another does not appear to get much further than the
protection of one's own offspring.[5] As Michael Jensen suggests,
'Equality is an idea that reaches desperately for foundations'.[6]
Where, then, may it be grounded?

Equality cannot be grounded anthropologically or cosmo-
logically; it can only be grounded theologically, in our equal
status as image bearers, and in the equal and infinite love of the
same heavenly Father. In other words, if human equality is to
be grounded, it will have to be grounded in God's view of us
– not in our view of each other, nor in our view of ourselves.
Just as, deep down, we know that every human being is valuable
(and to be treated accordingly) but do not know where that
value comes from, so we know, deep down, that every human
being is *equally* valuable but do not know where that equality
can be grounded. In both cases, the doctrine of the image of
God undergirds all that is humane and sane about our self-
understanding and moral reflection.

4 Creativity

One Calvin and Hobbes cartoon has Calvin playing in the sand pit. Hobbes approaches and asks, 'Do you have an idea for your project yet?' Calvin replies, 'No, I'm waiting for inspiration. You can't turn on creativity like a faucet. You have to be in the right mood.' 'What mood is that?' Hobbes asks; to which Calvin replies, 'Last-minute panic.'

However much some of us rely on last-minute panic to get it out of us, human beings are intrinsically creative. Creativity is simply part of what it means to be human. If we are made in the image of God, and God is the Creator, it is hardly surprising that we are creative. When we write a poem, or sing a song, or decorate a house, or use a metaphor, we demonstrate that we are more than vehicles for self-replicating DNA: we demonstrate that creativity is part of who we are. We demonstrate that we need beauty as well as air, if we are to live fully. And we reflect something of the beauty, creativity and richness of God.

It is staggering how pervasive this creativity is. It percolates through every human activity. Almost everything that human beings make or do transcends the functional. When we build houses, we don't aim simply at keeping out the wind and the rain: we like them to have a sense of proportion, we add decoration, we think about how they will look in their contexts, we make sure that the building has a good view – not only for defensive purposes (so that we have advance warning of any approaching threat) but also for aesthetic purposes.[7] When we make clothes, we are not solely concerned with keeping ourselves warm: we are interested in colour, patterns and cuts, we want to look elegant, we may want to cheer things up by wearing bright colours, or to express our sympathy by wearing black.[8] When we grow things, we don't just practise agriculture, we practise horticulture, showing that we are not just interested in the edible but in the beautiful. When we eat, we are not just concerned with nutrition but with presentation.

The Christian art historian Hans Rookmaaker argued that 'Art needs no justification.'[9] As Christians, we do not need to justify a career in art by reference to its evangelistic opportunities within the artistic community; creativity is simply part of what we are created to be and part of the human calling. However ambiguously, it points to the creativity and beauty of God.

Knowing that I have been through such a period myself, people sometimes come and see me to talk through their own experience of depression. On one occasion, I was talking to someone who was in the grip of it, and I was having difficulty working out what the cause of their depression might be. In the end, we basically gave up, and were just chatting. I asked them what they intended to do after their degree programme ended, and they said, 'Well, what I would like to do is an art course, but of course I couldn't justify that.' 'What do you mean, you couldn't justify that?' I asked. 'Well, it doesn't advance the kingdom, does it?' they replied. 'Ah,' I said, 'I think we might just have found the root of your depression.' Our creativity is part of who God made us to be. If we repress it – especially if we repress it in his name – it will skew us inside.

We will never know true fulfilment if we repress or ignore or exclude our creativity. We are to enrich others with our creativity, whatever form that takes, and we are to be enriched by the creativity of others.

5 Relationality

One of the great spiritual classics of our day is *My Ministry Manual* by Revd Gerald Ambulance, minister of St Ursula's High Pentecostal-Reformed Church in Lewisham. The Revd Gerald Ambulance is a spoof figure, created by Stephen Tomkins, who encapsulates the foibles of Catholic, charismatic and evangelical clergy, all rolled into one person. Revd Gerald gives us the benefit of his years of ministerial experience when he shares with us 'the twelve most popular questions I've come across in pastoral ministry, and the right answers'. Here is one of them:

> *Problem*: I'm confused about the Trinity. How can God and Jesus and the Holy Spirit all be God, if there's only one God?
>
> *Answer*: Look at it like this: Once upon a time there were three little bunnies called Flopsy, Mopsy and Cottontail. One day a nasty man caught them and put them in a rabbit pie. They were still three rabbits, but only one pie. (Although the pie got cut up into lots of pieces, admittedly.) To put it in plain language that even a complete dur-brain could understand, the three persons of the triune Godhead are one in substance, but in three hypostases. If you have any further questions, don't hesitate to ask . . . someone else.[10]

When the Church was forced to articulate the doctrine of the Trinity, it came to the realisation that God is not just personal, he is a relationship.[11] He is a relationship of love between the Father, the Son and the Spirit. God is not just *loving*, he is Love. There is a receiving as well as a giving of love within the being of God. When the first disciples witnessed the baptism of Jesus, they witnessed the three persons of the Trinity, communicating with one another, expressing their love for one another. And the Church came to the conclusion that that is what they have been doing for all eternity.

If we are made in the image of God, and if, as the Church claims, God is Trinity, then we are made in the image of the Trinity. We are made in the image of a relationship; therefore, we are intrinsically relational. As God constitutes a relationship, so are we made for relationship.

This meshes with our experience: more often than not, the most valuable and significant things in our lives are our relationships. (That is not to say that they are easy and straightforward; in fact, they are sometimes so fraught that people attempt to live without them. But there is always a cost to that.) A Macmillan nurse once said that, in her experience, when people are dying, they are interested in three things: the people they love, the people who love them, and the people they've hurt. If those are the things that matter most when we are facing death, then they are probably the things that simply matter most.

It is not an exaggeration to say that the health of our psyches and the happiness of our lives depend largely upon the quality of our relationships; Mother Teresa used to say that loneliness is the greatest cause of suffering in the Western world. If we wish to live lives of full humanity, then our attitudes and our diaries need to reflect that priority. Lives of relational richness point (inadequately but truly) to the richness of the relational God who made us in his image. Matt Jenson sums it up thus: 'to image God is to find one's being in relation to and encounter with another'.[12]

6 Sexuality

So God created humankind in his image,
in the image of God he created them;
male and female he created them.

Genesis 1:27, NRSVA

Genesis 1:27 seems to imply some sort of link between the idea of human beings being made in the image of God and the fact that we are created male and female. It seems to imply that male and female are both required for God to be fully imaged. Every individual human being is made in the image of God, but, if one only ever encountered human beings of one particular gender, something would be lost, something would be missing. Our understanding of God would be impoverished.

Notice the clear implication of the equality of the sexes. *Both* are made in the image of God. Earlier, we saw how Ancient Near Eastern cultures tended to see the king alone as being in the image of the god, whereas Genesis sees every human being as being in the image of God – there is a ruler/ruled democratisation. Here, it is underlined that male and female are equally in the image of God – there is a male/female democratisation. As so many societies globally remain largely patriarchal, this is a necessary underlining. It is really a particular restatement of the third refraction of the image of God we looked at – equality.

However, it is also related to the fifth refraction – relationality. Henri Blocher, in his reflections on the opening chapters of Genesis, suggests that human sexuality is 'a summons to community'. Because of our sexuality, he says, 'every human individual, being either masculine or feminine, must abandon the illusion of being alone'.[13] Sexual attraction draws us out of ourselves. Our sex drive is an impetus to engagement and relationship.

As Sister Margaret Magdalen (quoting Richard Holloway) writes:

> Sexuality is a large umbrella term and subsumes our need for relationship, connectedness, unity and wholeness which stems from our being made in the image of God. The same yearning for and fulfilment of that longing for unity which characterises the Trinity . . . lies deep within each of us. We feel it is not good for us to be alone. 'We feel mysteriously incomplete, so all our life is a searching for a remembered unity we have never yet known. Sexuality is one of the modes of our search . . .'[14]

Sometimes people minimise the quality of that relationship to which our sexuality drives us by keeping their sexual encounters casual, and thereby setting up painful tensions within themselves by saying something with their body ('I want our lives to be as entwined as this') that they are not prepared to say with their lives. Sometimes people choose not to follow the urges of that drive and to be single or celibate, for a variety of reasons to do with preference or a sense of their individual calling. Sometimes people genuinely experience little in the way of a sex drive. And sometimes people long to be married, but marriage just doesn't happen for them, for whatever reason, and they seek to be faithful to Christian teaching in that painful situation. But the very existence of any human being depends upon the coming together of male and female in what is an intrinsically intimate act.[15] Each one of us comes from relationship, and experiences in some form the 'summons to community' that is our sexuality.

7 Uniqueness

Question: How many politically correct people does it take to change a lightbulb?

Answer: None. Why should we impose our values on the lightbulb? If it wishes to be a lightbulb of no light, we should respect its uniqueness and individuality.

I don't know how unique and individual a lightbulb is. They all look very much alike to me; but I suppose that is the case with everything until you take the time and the trouble to get to know it better! I do know that every human being is unique. We are each of us in the image of God, yet each of us is unique. Each of us, therefore, reflects a different aspect of the nature of God.

This chapter began by saying that we are God's self-portraits. It is like a life class, where the model sits in the middle, and all the artists sit around the model and draw him or her. If they are good artists, then their drawings will all be good likenesses of the model, but they will all be different from each other because they are all drawn from a different angle.

So it is with us. We are all likenesses of God, but from different angles. Our differences are to be celebrated as God-given reflections of different aspects of God – not ironed out of us.[16] It is a lifelong task to develop the courage to be different. It is a lifelong task to cultivate those good and God-given parts of ourselves that we fear would not be acceptable to others, and that the world might ridicule or try to shut down. It is also a lifelong task to allow others to be themselves. God is the only person who draws out of us all that is good – however quirky (or threatening) others might find it. The more we allow others to be themselves, the more we shall reflect to others the quickening affirmation of God and help them be the people they were created to be.

Exercise: Gratitude

This exercise encourages us to thank God in prayer each day for who he has made us to be, by praying in the different aspects of what it is to be human. These prayers can be used either exactly as below or just as a starting point for your own personal thanksgiving. There is a prayer for every day of the week.

DAY 1: VALUE

Lord God, thank you that I am fearfully and wonderfully made. Thank you for making me in your image. Thank you that I am the work of your hands and the apple of your eye.

Thank you for the value you have placed upon me. Help me to know this value more securely so that it is at the heart of my being, and I can live freely from the truth of it. May I know myself to be equal with everyone, neither the inferior nor the superior of any.

Thank you for the value you have placed upon us. Help us to know that value more surely, more securely, more liberatingly. When others treat us like dirt, help us to remember that we are dirt into which you have breathed the breath of life, dirt you have kissed into being with your lips, dirt you have made to reflect your glory, dirt you have made to be porous to your presence and to radiate your love.

When rejected or bereaved, do not let me sink into the lie of limited lovedness, but keep me close to you, my eternal lover. As I am the recipient of your love, make me a channel of it to others.

I ask this through him whose eternal love led him to die for us – Jesus Christ our Lord. Amen.

DAY 2: RULE

Lord, when I look at your creation, I am astonished by its beauty, by its complexity and by its vastness. I marvel at its teeming diversity. Thank you for all that science has revealed to us, and that photographers and camera crews have laboured to share with us, of the otherwise hidden wonders of your world.

I am humbled that you call us to rule your creation on your behalf.

Give me a love like yours for all the creatures that share our world. Give me a passion to preserve our world's beauty and diversity. Give wisdom to our political and business leaders, and give resources to all conservationists and environmentalists, that the world may sustain us and we may cherish it.

I ask this through him whose rule is gentle and healing and self-sacrificial – Jesus Christ our Lord. Amen.

DAY 3: EQUALITY

Heavenly Father, I thank you for the comfort and challenge of true equality. I thank you for being the puncturer of pride and the reverser of abasement.

When I set myself above others, bring me down. When I set others above me, or when others set themselves above me, lift me up. Give me the wisdom and patience to give all people a knowledge of their equal value. Forgive and take away my prejudices, I pray, and open me up to the riches to be found in all those who are made in your image.

I ask this through him who taught us to pray to the same heavenly Father – Jesus Christ our Lord. Amen.

DAY 4: CREATIVITY

Creator God, I thank you for making me creative, like you. I thank you for the creative geniuses who have so enriched and deepened human life. Thank you for performers who give new life to music and drama, and for teachers who draw out and equip the creativity of others.

I thank you for my creativity, and pray that you would foster it and use it to beautify the lives of many.

I pray that you would raise up more Christian artists, writers, composers and choreographers who will capture the imaginations of our generation for you.

I ask this through him through whom all things were created – Jesus Christ our Lord. Amen.

DAY 5: RELATIONALITY

Triune Lord, I thank you for the joy of love, for the warmth, purpose, hope and sense of belonging that it brings.

I thank you for those whose love for me has opened me up to enjoy the potential, and to face the challenges, of life. I thank you for your love, which is the thread of my life.

Give me a love like yours – a love whose tenacity brings healing, and whose affirmation brings joy.

I ask this through him who taught us that love is the fulfilling of the law – Jesus Christ our Lord. Amen.

DAY 6: SEXUALITY

Triune God, I thank you for the mystery of our sexuality. Thank you that we need one another to know and reflect you more fully. Thank you for the mutually enriching difference of being

male and female. May it lead not to stereotyping, nor to
straightjacketing, nor to belittling, exploitation or competition
– but to community.

Help me to listen my way through difference, and to love my
way through incomprehension. Give me a unity and integration between what I say with my body and what I say with my
life. May I never misuse the power I have over others, nor allow
others to squeeze me out of the shape you have given me.

I ask this through him whose love brought self-acceptance to
women and men – Jesus Christ our Lord. Amen.

DAY 7: UNIQUENESS

Lord, I thank you that you delight in difference. I thank you for
endowing me with aspects of your nature that you have given to
no one else.

May I faithfully reflect to the world what I alone can reveal.
Give me the courage to resist comparison or conformity.
Remove from me only that which is inconsistent with your
character or incompatible with what you've called me to be.
Give me the freedom and flexibility of heart and mind to
welcome the uniqueness of others.

I ask this through him in whom every person finds their true
self and true place – Jesus Christ our Lord. Amen.

Further Resources

On the concept of the image of God generally

Middleton, Richard, *The Liberating Image* (Ada: Brazos, 2005). I don't agree with everything here, but it is a fine exploration of the concept of the image of God, and its radical ethical implications.

Wenham, Gordon, *Genesis 1–15* (Grand Rapids: Zondervan, 2014). This is a very clear and helpful exposition of the references to the image of God in Genesis.

On value

Keyes, Dick, *Beyond Identity* (Eugene: Wipf & Stock, 2003).

On rule

Harris, Peter, *Under the Bright Wings* (Vancouver: Regent College Publishing, 2000). The inspiring story of how one couple tried to live out the human calling to care for creation and set up a worldwide Christian conservation movement.

On equality

O'Donovan, Oliver, *The Ways of Judgment* (Grand Rapids: Eerdmans, 2008). Those with some theological (and preferably philosophical) background will find this a profound reflection on justice – including the vital role of the concept of equality within it.

On creativity

Schaeffer, Edith, *Hidden Art* (Carol Stream: Tyndale House, 1972), republished as *The Hidden Art of Homemaking* (1985). An inspiring and very practical guide to the expression of our God-given creativity.

On relationality

Cloud, Henry, *The Power of the Other* (New York: Harper Collins, 2016).

Grenz, Stanley, *The Social God and the Relational Self* (Louisville: Westminster John Knox, 2001). This is a work of academic theology, and those without theological training may find it hard going, but it is clearly written and unpacks much further what it means to be made in the image of the Trinity.

Smail, Tom, *Like Father, Like Son* (Grand Rapids: Eerdmans, 2006). Smail provides a really helpful checklist to ensure that we are reflecting all three persons of the Trinity in our humanity.

On sexuality

Angel, Andy, *Intimate Jesus: The Sexuality of God Incarnate* (London: SPCK, 2017).

Dominian, Jack, *One Like Us* (London: Darton, Longman & Todd, 1998). See especially Chapter 22 on 'Sexuality'.

Magdalen, Margaret, *The Hidden Face of Jesus* (London: Darton, Longman & Todd, 1994). This is an extraordinary book, which I recommend highly. See especially the section on 'Embracing his Sexuality' in Chapter 4.

On uniqueness

Benner, David, *The Gift of Being Yourself* (Westmont: InterVarsity Press, 2015).

Frost, Michael, *Keep Christianity Weird* (Carol Stream: NavPress, 2018).

2

The Image of God – Broken

A quick look at the internet comes up with the following suggestions as to the correct collective noun for theologians: a 'fury of theologians; an 'unbelief of theologians' (slightly unfair, that one); an 'apology of theologians' (people have often accused me of being an apology for a theologian, but that's slightly different). What no one has suggested as a collective noun is an '*agreement* of theologians'. So it is a rather revealing surprise to read Claus Westermann's assertion that 'One point on which scholars are agreed is that according to the Old Testament the person's "likeness-to-God" was not lost with the "fall", but remained part of humanity.'[1] And it is not surprising that there is such unanimity, because all the relevant passages in both the Old and the New Testament speak with one voice. As T. C. Vriezen pointed out, 'Gen. 9:6 speaks as much about God's image in man as does Gen 1.'[2] The same is true of James 3:9: 'With the tongue we praise our Lord and Father, and with it we curse human beings, who have been made in God's likeness . . . My brothers and sisters, this should not be.'

James assumes that the cursing of human beings is wrong *because* it remains true that those who are cursed have been made in God's likeness. This – together with the lovedness that it implies – remains the fundamental fact about us. It remains the case that we are orientated primarily towards God and not primarily towards anyone else. It remains the case that God has made us for himself, and our hearts are restless until they find their rest in him.[3]

The tragic disintegration of human beings, and the horrendous unravelling of their relationships which their rebellion against God brought upon them, has not destroyed the primary truth about them. Their primary identity has withstood the internal and external avalanche of brokenness that Genesis 3 and its subsequent chapters depict for us.[4] Who we essentially *are* holds under that self-inflicted onslaught, because God holds us and maintains us in his love, his plan and his purpose. Our identity is not unmade, because ultimately our identity is in God, who is Maker and not Unmaker. And it is in the space created by that fact that the Christian counsellor operates.

But that rebellion is at appalling cost. We retain our God-given, God-held identity, but every aspect of the outworking of that identity is now angular, fraught and complicated. The image remains, but is now obscured, both to others and to ourselves. So engrimed is the glass of our being (through which the light of God is meant to flood) that we can now see through it only darkly. Our world is deprived of much of the light in which it alone makes sense. It no longer looks like the sort of world a good and loving God would have made, because he didn't make it like this. It is no longer clear what the purpose of everything is, because we cut ourselves off from the One who has those purposes. The meaning of life is not universally manifest, because we have set ourselves at a distance from the One in whom alone that meaning can be found.

In this chapter, we shall trace how the fall – that opening up of a chasm between how we are and how we were meant to be – works itself out in the seven dimensions of the image of God that we explored in the first chapter.

1 Value

As Genesis 9:6 and James 3:9 – and the cross – make clear, we retain that value which we always had, as bearers of God's image and as objects of his love. Nothing has changed, in terms of our objective worth, and we are no less loved than we always were.

What has changed is our awareness of that worth. Having put distance between ourselves and the One who values us, we find it more difficult to believe in that value. We saw in the previous chapter that value is a personal quality. The more distant one is from the Person, therefore, the more dimly one is going to perceive the value. And that is both frustratingly painful as we are unable to know our own worth, and fearfully convenient as we are freer to doubt the worth of others when that suits us.

Because of our fallenness, we forget that our value is:

Unearned

We spend much of our lives attempting to earn the value that we already possess – driving ourselves, exhausting ourselves (and others) and beating ourselves up in the process. The attempt to earn our value takes two major forms: the drive to achieve and the drive to be liked and loved.

We think that if we can achieve something significant we will *be* someone significant. If we make a stack-load of money, if we turn this failing company around, if we play this sport for our country, if we grow this struggling church, if we complete this doctoral thesis, if we write a bestselling book, if we get this promotion, if we become respected in our profession – *then* we shall have earned our value. And the problem with this mentality (which is now the default setting in each one of us) is that it is unnecessary, it doesn't work, and it is counterproductive.

Such a mindset is unnecessary because we are already someone, as bearers of the image of God. We are already infinitely valuable, as objects of the love of God – valuable enough for him to be prepared to die, to win us back to himself. Trying to earn our value doesn't work, because no achievement seems to be substantial enough to satisfy the black hole of our neediness, as Andrew (Ruth's husband) found: 'For many years I tried hard to get people's attention and to be noticed by them, springing from a deep sense of inferiority. This remained crippling even after gaining a scholarship to Oxford, and later achieving two doctorates from there.'[5]

This mentality doesn't work because we are made to be infinitely valued, whereas our career achievements can only be finite. And it is counterproductive because it can keep us so focused on the future that we fail to enjoy the present.[6] We work for the next exam slightly harder than is healthy, so that we get the grade we need to go to the more prestigious university. When we get there, we have to work slightly harder than is compatible with a balanced life, in order to get the degree that will deliver the job we want. When we get that job, we have to work so hard at it (in order to keep up and have a chance of that promotion) that we neglect other aspects of who we are. When we get that promotion, we have to work even harder at it (because of the extra responsibilities it brings), with the result that our marriage and our friendships suffer. Always, we are sacrificing present enjoyment and relational richness on the altar of future achievement and acknowledgement (not least by ourselves). We are sacrificing other dimensions of who we are on the altar of earned value. Like all idols, it demands sacrifices and breaks its promises: it promises that if we make these sacrifices we shall *be* someone, but, actually, the sacrifices sometimes stop us from being the fulfilled people we could be, if we would only accept that our value is given and innate.

There is, of course, nothing wrong with attempting to achieve something significant. It is good to want to find a cure for some crippling medical condition. It is good to be determined to compose a symphony. It is good to be committed to developing and marketing a quality product. It is good, in William Carey's words, to 'attempt great things for God'.[7] These are all good things, but they should be done because of their intrinsic worth, not in order to try to establish ours. They should be done for their own sake, and for the sake of others, and for God's sake, not in order to try to fill the voracious void within us. Let them be ends in themselves, and not means to our own self-validation. For what could be more validating than to be called to reflect a unique refraction of the glory of God?

The second way in which we seek to earn our own value takes the form of trying to be liked and loved. This strategy makes two mistakes. First, it tends to leave God out of the equation, and tries to glean such lovedness as it can from human sources alone.[8] Second, it makes the mistake of *trying* to be loved, as if love is something that people can be blagged, bragged or bribed into doing. Again, this strategy a) is unnecessary, b) doesn't work and c) is counterproductive. It is unnecessary because we are already infinitely loved. We don't need to struggle towards lovedness: we simply need to soak in it. It doesn't work because it involves presenting others with a sanitised, airbrushed version of who we are. Obviously, we major on (a.k.a. boast about) our good points, and hide the things we think will spoil our image: equally obviously, even if the other person does come to like or love us, it will not really be us that they are liking or loving – not us as we truly are. In a famous exchange with the long-suffering Ernie Wise, Eric Morecambe is trying to present an image of himself as a tough guy, and claims to chew nails. Ernie enquires as to whether these are iron or steel nails. Eric admits that they are finger nails. Behind most such projected images lies vulnerability. And this strategy is counterproductive because we need more love than any human being or set of human beings can give us. So our neediness places a demand on the other(s) that they are not in a position to meet, and a pressure on the relationship(s) that they cannot bear – at least, not without significant cost.

It is therefore a lifelong – and liberating – lesson that our value does not need to be earned. It is simply a given. One of the great gains and glories of godliness is that it frees us to be ourselves.

Unlosable

There is a story of a mathematician who gave his life to compiling sine and cosine tables to a greater degree of accuracy than had previously been done. After spending a lifetime working on the project, he was on the point of publishing his life's work when someone else published a set of trigonometric tables that were several decimal points more accurate than his – and on which the second mathematician had been working for only two or three years, because they had worked out a formula. The first mathematician committed suicide. It is not easy to find the source of this story but, true or not, it demonstrates the bankruptcy of grounding one's worth on one's achievements. For, if one's achievements fail – as fail they well might in a world of chance and not necessarily of justice, let alone of compassion – then one's value fails with them.

Similarly, if we ground our value on the love of family and friends, then what happens when those who love us either die or stop loving us? If they are the source of our lovedness and our value, then we become less loved and less valuable than we were.

It is, of course, the case that failure or redundancy or bereavement or divorce or unrequited love can make us *feel* less valuable and less loved. If, however, our value is grounded in the love of God and the fact that we are made in his image, then that value remains intact, whatever befalls us.

Universal

Fallen human beings have a tendency to try and wriggle out from the moral demands implied in the universality of human value. We tend to try to diminish the defined group of people to whom we owe compassion. In the first century, the Romans created (or, rather, adopted from the Greeks, and adapted) the convenient concept of a great divide between Roman and barbarian. The Jewish people repaid the compliment by digging a conceptual ditch between Jew and Gentile. Nearly all the civilisations at the time – and for far too many centuries later – were based on a whole subclass which was not afforded the same rights and protections as were enjoyed by the 'higher' classes. We have already noticed that women were not afforded the same status under the law as men, in first-century Israel, and, to differing degrees, in other contemporary societies. When the apostle Paul wrote that, in Christ, 'There is neither Jew nor Gentile, neither slave nor free, nor is there male and female' (Galatians 3:28), he was not shadow boxing; there were whole tranches of humanity who were considered and treated as less equal than others.

We have made important strides in the past century or so in restoring the equality between men and women, though there is much more to be done. But what we have given with one hand, we have, as a society, begun to take away with the other. We are currently witnessing a growing nationalism across the world. Separatist movements are gaining currency. Much of our popular press is campaigning for our overseas aid budget either to be used as an instrument of our national interest, or to be redirected towards our own National Health Service, or to be cut altogether. All this suggests that we are seeing a contraction in the set of people about whom we actively care, a re-erection of barriers and a redigging of ditches between whole groups of people.[9] That is simply what we fallen people do, in different ways and to different extents at different times.

Unlimited
If we will not give a sense of value to others, then we will not be able to receive it from God.[10] And if we do not receive it from God, we are left to feed off the scraps of value thrown to us by family, friends and admirers, none of whom is free from the infection of selfishness. The amount of value we can glean from one another is inevitably finite and conditional; therefore, to depend on others for our self-worth can lead to feelings of dissatisfaction and insecurity, along with a need for constant reassurance. We, who are created by and for an infinite love, struggle for the air of value and the breath of love.

As we shall see in the next chapter, our lifetime's task is to turn the objective fact of our infinite value into *subjective* knowledge, letting our unlimited lovedness seep down into the deep places of our anxiety and insecurity.

2 Rule

Fizhugh Tuoti is quoted as saying, 'Give a man a fish, and he can eat for a day. But teach a man how to fish, and he'll be dead of mercury poisoning inside of three years.'[11] Called upon to care for creation, we have exploited and despoiled it. There are many reasons for this, but the root of the problem is that we have separated the concept of dominion from the concept of the image of God. Originally, they were held tightly together, as we saw earlier in Genesis 1:26.

In that verse, the meaning of the word 'rule' is governed by the word 'God'. We are in the image of God, and therefore the rule we are called to exercise is the same sort of rule that he exercises over us. As we saw in the previous chapter, that means the sort of servant rule we see in Jesus – rule that is exercised for the sake of the ruled, not of the ruler.

But remove God from the equation and rule takes on a very different character. Cut off from the God who sacrifices himself for his creation, rule easily becomes self-serving. Cut off from the love of God, rule easily becomes exploitative. Cut off from the wisdom of God, rule easily becomes short-sighted. Cut off from the heavenly Father who loves and values his children equally, the fruits of creation easily get distributed unequally. Cut off from the God of peace, the fruits of creation easily get fought over – be it for land, gold, oil, fish or water.

Cutting ourselves off from God is always self-destructive, like a puppet cutting its own strings. Not only are we meta-phorically cutting off our own source of life, but we are literally poisoning the air we breathe.

3 Equality

We are fortunate to live at a time, and in a culture, where, in theory at least, everyone has equality before the law, and (almost) every adult has an equal vote – thanks to courageous barons, archbishops,[12] chartists, suffragists and suffragettes and other campaigners. However, as fallen human beings, we constantly fall short of that equality which we have in the sight and love of God.

We fall short of that equality *personally*. All too easily, we see ourselves as better or worse than others. We compare ourselves to others to make ourselves feel better or to beat ourselves up. It is good for us – and for our relationships – to see ourselves as being the equal of everyone and the superior or inferior of no one.

In the famous class sketch,[13] John Cleese, Ronnie Barker and Ronnie Corbett are lined up in order of height, with John Cleese (the tallest) representing the upper class, Ronnie Barker the middle class, and Ronnie Corbett (the shortest) represent-ing the working class. They explain that John Cleese looks down at both the others, Ronnie Barker looks up to John Cleese but looks down on Ronnie Corbett, and Ronnie Corbett looks up to both the others. What do they get out of this arrange-ment? John Cleese says he gets a sense of superiority. Ronnie Barker says he gets a feeling of inferiority from John Cleese and a feeling of superiority over Ronnie Corbett. Ronnie Corbett says he gets a crick in the neck!

Thus, we fall short of equality *socially*, too. A question to be asked of every society, every institution, every company, every congregation, every family is, 'Who is being excluded?' There is usually someone. We pay lip service to the truth that all are equal, but in practice some are more equal than others, and, usually, someone is being treated as less equal than others. If so, then that is not only unjust, it is also dysfunctional, because we need one another. We need one another's contribution. Not to allow, or not to receive, or not to value everyone else's contribution is like lopping off bits of the body.

When we find ourselves looking down on others or assuming that it is more important that they should listen to us than that we should listen to them, we need to remind ourselves that they are made in the image of God every bit as much as we are; that they are therefore utterly equal to us, and have as much potential as a source of knowledge about God as we have. Where people are not being treated as equal before the law, we may have to stand up for them to be treated as fully human (as Jesus did for women, who were not treated as equal before the law in his day).[14] Where people are being excluded, we may need to make a point of including them and welcoming them (as Jesus did for children, who often seem to have been quite marginalised in his day).[15]

When we find that we are comparing ourselves to others or doubting our own relative worth, we need to remind ourselves that we are made in the image of God every bit as much as everyone else is. We are the equal of all: equally valued, equally loved, equally desired and equally longed for, with an equal right to be.

As we saw in the previous chapter, the equality of all humankind is not a truth one can simply infer from the world by observation. It is an article of faith for atheist and theist alike – in fact, more so for the atheist, because the world does not treat people equally. We all tend to give more time to attractive, articulate and entertaining people. All of us – teachers and even parents included – tend to like some people more than others.

Up to a point, there is nothing wrong with that. There is nothing wrong with choosing as one's friends people with whom one gets on best. Even Jesus had three disciples (Peter, James and John) with whom he seems to have spent more time, and one ('the disciple whom Jesus loved') to whom he was particularly close. The problem comes when a close friendship becomes an exclusive clique, and when personal preference gets turned into unequal treatment. When that happens, people get squashed and hurt, and relationships become resentful.[16]

In contrast to us, God has no favourites – a fact that is an important strand in St Paul's teaching.[17] Our common reflection of the image of God gives us an objective equality. As a result, it is our calling to treat all others as equal, and to campaign against the ways in which inequality oppresses those whom it seeks to belittle, and impoverishes those who perpetuate it.

4 Creativity

Just as our value, calling and equality remain intact this side of the fall, so we remain essentially creative. This is despite the fact that, having cut ourselves off from the Beauty that created us, our creativity is in some ways warped and used for selfish and divisive purposes rather than carried out purely for its own sake (and for the sake of the enrichment of others and the glory of God). So although we are fallen our creativity remains – and it remains a pointer to the nature of the Creator.

It is now, however, an ambiguous pointer. It still reflects God's rich revelling in diversity and his imaginative inventiveness. It now reflects, also, our own competitive self-promotion and febrile tendency to control, springing from a neurotic fearfulness about our own worth relative to others.

Sometimes we produce great art for a bad reason. Much great architecture is commissioned as a kind of 'Look at me!' exercise. Apparently, the most imposing Great Hall complexes in the Anglo-Saxon period were often located not in the middle of the king's territory where they could be more easily defended, but on a border with the neighbouring kingdom, put up not only with the intention of being enjoyed as a place of community, celebration and culture but also with the intention of impressing and intimidating others.[18] They were erected to display the wealth and power of the king rather than being built for the simple love of beauty.

Similarly, as fallen men and women, we dress not just out of delight for the creativity of pattern, cut and colour, but as a competitive 'Look at me!' manoeuvre. Sometimes, we dress more to conform to the uniformity of fashion than as an expression of our own uniqueness and individuality. (It is an extraordinary accomplishment of advertisers to persuade teenagers, for instance, to express their rebelliousness and individuality by dressing entirely alike, at the behest of fashion houses!) Our fear of standing out, which is a fear of not being accepted, leads us to stifle our creativity and settle for conformity.

Sometimes we produce bad art for a bad reason. The creativity of the photographer (or painter or novelist), for instance, can be used in the service of pornography – that is, to give the viewer or reader an image that is malleable to their desires and fantasies rather than to confront them with the reality of the other. Pornography gives us a mental object that we may control without obvious consequence: art gives us an uncontrollable subject with which we have to engage. Pornography lets us think that the object is there for our gratification: art requires us to accept that the subject is who they are, regardless of our response. Christian morality seeks to wean us from the sterile unreality and impersonality of the former to the enriching reality and personality of the latter. And, because pornography can be so addictive (to us who carry the wounds and worries of forgotten self-worth), that weaning process sometimes needs the help of the counsellor.

Sometimes we seek to suppress that creativity entirely, thus producing no art, for a bad reason. It can be a repressive form of rationalism that seeks to drum the imaginative out of us. Dickens' great character Mr Gradgrind, in *Hard Times*, seeks to instil in his pupils the love of hard facts, and the abjuration of anything artistic or creative. In one passage, an official visiting the school asks the students: 'Suppose you were going to carpet a room. Would you use a carpet having a representation of flowers upon it?' One of the pupils, Sissy Jupe, replies that she would: 'If you please, sir, I am very fond of flowers,' to which the official responds: 'And that is why you would put tables and chairs upon them, and have people walking over them with heavy boots?' 'It wouldn't hurt them, sir', returns Sissy. 'They wouldn't crush and wither if you please, sir. They would be the pictures of what was very pretty and pleasant, and I would fancy . . .' This riles the official:

> 'Ay, ay, ay! But you mustn't fancy,' cried the gentleman, quite elated by coming so happily to his point. 'That's it! You are never to fancy.'
>
> 'You are not, Cecilia Jupe,' Thomas Gradgrind solemnly repeated, 'to do anything of that kind.'
>
> 'Fact, fact, fact!' said the gentleman. And 'Fact, fact, fact!' repeated Thomas Gradgrind.[19]

Dickens is here satirising the Utilitarians, and one leading Utilitarian, Jeremy Bentham, who helped found University

College, persuaded the new college not to teach either theology or music – a telling combination.[20] However, it is not only rationalism that has been opposed to creativity. Branches of (or movements within) the Christian Church have also been negative about our creativity: partly out of an admirable but a misdirected desire to be faithful to the second commandment;[21] partly out of a stolid inability to see how fiction can be truthful; partly out of an unbiblical mistrust of anything physical. And the twentieth-century totalitarian regimes so sought to shape the creativity of their subjects that much great art was destroyed, and many great artists were persecuted or had their creative freedom horrendously constricted and compromised.[22]

Our creativity, however, is innate; like grass that is concreted over, it will find a way through. And, as it does so, it points – ambiguously but significantly – to the God whose image we cannot erase.

5 Relationality

We are made in the image of the Trinity, and therefore we are made for relationship. We may have rebelled against the relationship by which we were made and thus have ruptured our relationships with one another,[23] but relationship is still what we are *for* and what we are called to.[24] As a result of our brokenness, this calling now encompasses hurt, loss and grief, and requires patience, forgiveness and sheer slog, as well as delight, love and lovedness.

At the baptism of Jesus, we encounter the three persons of the Trinity relating to one another: the Son being obedient to the Father, the Father expressing love for the Son, and the Spirit marking out the Son as the object of divine love and empowering him for the messianic mission to restore a broken

world. It is a set of relationships characterised by mutual glorification, and delight in the other. That mutual glorification is
the template for all healthy relationship.

But all too often, that is no longer what characterises our
relationships. We don't delight in the other: we delight in
ourselves, and in what the other can do for us. We don't glorify
one another: we put each other down, on the mistaken assumption that, the more people who are beneath us, the higher we
are in the pecking order. (Actually, of course, putting others
down drags us down.)

We are made for relationship, but our relationships are
broken. Therein lies much of the pain and frustration of human
existence. Nor is it just our relationships with one another that
are broken. We were made for the presence of God, and, much
of the time, experience only too keenly the distance between
God and us. (C. S. Lewis, in the dark days of bereavement after
the death of his wife Joy, calls God 'so very absent a help in
time of trouble'[25] – a bitter parody of Psalm 46:1.) We were
created for the vision of God, and actually see only 'through a
glass darkly'.[26] We were designed to 'drink freely of love',[27] and
actually our souls and bodies thirst for him as 'in a barren and
dry land where no water is'.[28] We have cut ourselves off from
the springs of joy, and therefore may often experience God
more as an ache than as satisfaction.

Maybe because of the brokenness of our relationships, we
often forget how central they are to our purpose and our flourishing. All too easily, we become so absorbed with the attempt
to achieve our value through accomplishment that we neglect
our marriages, families and friendships. Starved of our time,
those relationships become more difficult, and we retreat
further into the refuge of our work, thus perpetuating a down-
ward spiral into relational poverty. We know, and it is often

remarked on, that not many people say on their deathbed, 'I wish I had spent more time in the office!' – but our diaries remain fuller than is compatible with thriving relationships.

6 Sexuality

For the Judaeo-Christian tradition, our sexuality is God-given, good and has a purpose. The purpose of sexuality is, as we saw in the previous chapter, to summon us to community. Of course, people often try to evade that summons, by keeping their sexual encounters casual or uncommitted. But the Judaeo-Christian tradition has always regarded this as unwise, for the simple reason that it believes that people flourish when they are committed to one another. It has always, therefore, believed that love is only safely expressed sexually in the mutually committed context of marriage. People thrive when they do not have to *earn* love. Children should not have to earn their parents' love, and a married person should not have to earn their spouse's love. We recognise this principle with regard to children, but fail to recognise that it applies equally to adults, thereby depriving ourselves of the security we crave. People thrive when they are loved unconditionally, when their lovedness is a given.[29]

Now this is counter-intuitive. You might have thought that people would only perform if *required* to perform, that people wouldn't behave well unless there were a hint of threat hanging over them – that you keep them on their mettle by making your love conditional. (After all, it has been wisely said that politicians are like nappies: you should change them frequently – and for the same reason! At least the threat of changing them keeps them vaguely attentive to the views of the electorate.) But actually, people behave best not when they are required to, but when they know themselves to be loved. What generally brings out the best in someone is not insecurity but security – when they are safe in your love.

In *Four Weddings and a Funeral*, Charles says in his best man speech that he is in awe of those who can commit themselves to one another in the way that Angus and Laura have just done in the wedding service. He says that he couldn't do it himself, but thinks it wonderful that they can. That honest but sad admission reveals the ultimately selfish nature of an uncommitted approach to sexual relationships. Actively to avoid a marriage commitment seems to say: 'I want you – but only as long as it works for me. I want to be able to get out if you no longer meet my needs. I want to be free to leave if the thunderbolt strikes again with someone else. While it benefits me, I'll be there for you. When it doesn't, I'll be off.'

Whereas, in marriage, each person says to the other: 'I love you. I am committed to you, whether it works for me or not. You are not an instrument of my happiness. Come happiness or unhappiness, we'll face it together. You're not there to meet my needs and make me happy: you are there to be yourself for your fulfilment and for my enrichment. You won't be out if you don't perform. You won't be rejected if you don't please. Just be yourself – that will be my greatest enrichment.' It is, in other words, for better for worse, for richer for poorer, in sickness and in health. In the security of that unconditional commitment, human beings tend to thrive. And in the security of that unconditional commitment, sex finds its proper meaning, for people are saying with their bodies what they are also saying with the rest of their lives.

Our sexuality is an impetus towards relationship, and sex is only safely, meaningfully and uninhibitedly enjoyed within the security of an unconditional, exclusive and permanent relationship.

7 Uniqueness

It is people's differences that enrich us. If everyone were the same, we would not need each other. Where someone else is most like me, I have least to learn from them. I already know within myself what there is to be learned from our *likenesses*; it is our *differences* that can most expand my understanding of God.[30]

The fall and our alienation from God, however, has made us fearful of difference. Gender is no longer a joyful complementarity, but a competitive perplexity. Differing giftings and callings are differently valued and thus crystallise into classes with competing interests; the boundaries between those classes become increasingly impermeable, and people on both sides find derogatory names for those on the other side. Different races and cultures, though increasingly close to one another in our globalised world, are increasingly the trigger for mutual suspicion and fear – and we seek to fortify the boundaries between us. Thus, we cut ourselves off from potential enrichment, growth and expansion of our understanding and knowledge of God.

One would have hoped that the Church, believing that in Christ there is neither Jew nor Gentile, slave nor free, male nor female,[31] would have encouraged each person in their own uniqueness and, at its best, it does. But the Church is made up of fallen men and women, too, and sometimes we also try to force people into a mould of our own making, rather than let them be people of God's own making. Someone who taught pastoral studies at a seminary that overlooked a Heinz factory once told his students: 'We are doing exactly the same thing as that factory – churning out identical products on a conveyor belt: priest, priest, priest . . .' Thankfully, one of the students pointed out that at least Heinz has fifty-seven varieties! There are at least 7.442 billion different varieties of human being alive today, 7.442 billion portraits of God, each from a different angle and each, therefore, with something different to teach us about God, if we will but attend to them.

'We all, like sheep, have gone astray.'[32] It is sin that leads to sheep-like uniformity and suppresses our God-given uniqueness. We are afraid of what people will think of our different interests, quirks, taste, dress sense, preferences, and so we rein them in at best, and repress them at worst. We are afraid to be ourselves, and afraid to let others be themselves. And thus we rob the world of the vivid colours of God's self-portraits.

Thankfully, the Artist is committed to his self-portraits, and, therefore, to the careful, loving work of restoration.

Exercise: Self-Examination

For this exercise in self-examination, may I suggest that you use these seven aspects of what it is to be made in the image of God as a checklist for your human flourishing? There is a reflection and challenge for each day for a week.

DAY 1: VALUE

Reflection: Ask yourself, 'From where do I get my value? How dependent am I on the opinion and evaluation of others? Do I really know myself to be loved by God, or do I find that hard to believe?'

Challenge: Ask God to reveal where you have been seeking your value – from what you achieve or from others. Ask God to show you the extent of his love for you. You may like to read an account of the crucifixion in one of the Gospels to aid your understanding. And when you next go to Communion and take the bread and wine into yourself, try and internalise the value that God sets upon you to have thus given himself for you.

DAY 2: RULE

Reflection: Ask yourself, 'Are there things I could do to minimise my negative impact on the natural world, and to maximise my positive impact?'

Challenge: Review your recycling and your giving, your car usage, your investments and your energy supplier. If you have a garden, are there plants you could plant that would attract and feed birds, butterflies and bees – and increase your enjoyment of creation? Make one positive change this week.

DAY 3: EQUALITY

Reflection: Think about how you perceive other people. Ask yourself, 'Who do I look up to? Who do I look down on?'

Challenge: When you notice that you are comparing yourself with someone else, consciously remind yourself that both you and they are made in God's image and that you are of equal worth before God – neither of you is superior nor inferior to the other.

DAY 4: CREATIVITY

Reflection: Ask yourself what place beauty has in your life. How often do you take time to listen to music or look at art or read great literature? Did you used to play an instrument or draw, write poetry or ballroom dance, but no longer do? When was the last time you cooked a special meal and took time over the presentation?

Challenge: Schedule in some time in the coming weeks when you can intentionally appreciate beauty (visiting an art gallery, listening to music, taking a scenic walk) or actively indulge your own creativity (cooking, writing, painting, etc). If you need inspiration, Edith Schaeffer's book, *Hidden Art* (Carol Stream: Tyndale House, 1972), republished as *The Hidden Art of Homemaking* (1985), is full of practical suggestions for expressing creativity, creating beauty and using both to affirm and inspire others.

DAY 5: RELATIONALITY

Reflection: Ask yourself, 'How much of my time is given to work and functional activity? How much of it is given to family and friends?'

Challenge: Review your diary. Ask God to bring to your mind any friend or family member who needs to hear from you in some way. Plan in a phone call or some quality time with them.

DAY 6: SEXUALITY

Reflection: If you are married, ask yourself, 'How much am I expecting my spouse to meet my needs and make me happy, and how much am I wanting them to be themselves and to let that be my enrichment?' If you are single, ask yourself, 'Am I saying with my body only what I am prepared to say with my life?'

Challenge: Ask God to show you any ways in which you are using people for your own satisfaction.

DAY 7: UNIQUENESS

Reflection: Ask yourself, 'How much do I want to be like someone else? How much do I let myself be squeezed out of my true shape by the expectations of others, and by the fear of their displeasure or rejection?'

Challenge: Ask God to give you the wisdom to know who you are, and the courage to be it.

Further Resources

Very little has been written recently on the subject of the fall. This is partly because of the perceived difficulty of maintaining belief in a historic fall since the Darwinian discovery that there was pain and killing and disease in creation long before human beings ever evolved. I have argued in recent publications that it is possible to believe in human evolution and in a historic fall – in fact, in some ways, the former logically requires the latter. This may be found in:

Lloyd, Michael, 'Theodicy, fall and Adam' in *Finding Ourselves after Darwin* (Grand Rapids: Baker, 2018), Chapter 16.
Lloyd, Michael, *Café Theology* (London: Hodder & Stoughton, 2020). See especially Chapter 2 on 'Fall'.

The Image of God – Restored

A man phoned the technical support department of the shop where he had bought his printer. He explained that it was printing very faintly – and he had only recently put in a new ink cartridge. The assistant in the technical support department said that it probably only needed a clean, but that, if he brought it in, they would have to charge him the minimum fee of £50, so he might prefer to read the manual and clean it himself. Very impressed with this unexpected honesty, the man said, 'Does your boss know that you are turning down business?' 'Oh yes,' said the assistant. 'In fact, it's her idea. We usually make more money on repairs if we let people try and fix them first!'

In the previous chapter, we looked at the ways in which the image of God got defaced and obscured when human beings cut themselves off from the love from which they sprang. We saw how the seven refractions of the image of God were distorted and diminished, and we traced the outline of how that soured human experience and made the world seem a highly ambiguous place, rather than being clearly the creation of a loving and good God.

But we saw, too, that this broken and ambiguous world, and we broken and ambiguous bearers of a rather battered image, are just as valued and loved as we always were. So valuable and so loved, in fact, that the Artist was not content to acquiesce in our damagedness and distance, but determined to restore us to the purity, perfection and intimacy which was always his purpose for us.

In this chapter, we will focus on how this great process of restoration occurs in Jesus, on the cross and in the Church.[1]

1 Value

Value and Jesus

First, Jesus was someone who knew (and taught and practised) the value of every human being:

> Therefore I tell you, do not worry about your life . . . Is not life more than food, and the body more than clothes? Look at the birds of the air; they do not sow or reap or store away in barns, and yet your heavenly Father feeds them. *Are you not much more valuable than they?*[2]

> Matthew 6:25–6

He takes it that we all know, deep down, that a reductionist view of human beings is damagingly superficial. Animals may live to eat and reproduce, but there is more to human beings than that. Jesus has a high view of the complexity, the multi-vocationality and therefore the value of human beings. But deeper, even, than this grounding of human value in complexity is Jesus' theological grounding of human value in the love of a heavenly Father.

We are the object of his knowledge, care and provision,[3] and, just as children who know that their parents value them (and think constantly about them, care for them and look out for them) grow up with a greater sense of their innate value, so those who know themselves the object of their heavenly Father's love and attention grow in the knowledge of their infinite value.[4]

Second, Jesus knew himself to be loved by his heavenly Father. What John's Gospel records as his words on the night before he died is particularly telling (my emphasis in italics):

- 'As the *Father has loved me*, so have I loved you' (John 15:9).
- 'May they be brought to complete unity to let the world know that you sent me and have loved them *even as you have loved me*' (John 17:23).
- 'Father, I want those you have given me to be with me where I am, and to see my glory, the glory you have given me *because you loved me* before the creation of the world' (John 17:24).

Third, as Jesus knew himself to be eternally loved by God, he was unshackled by the tendency to seek value through others. And because Jesus receives the affirmation and value and love that God offers, he is able to tell the truth to each person in every situation, undistorted and unfiltered by the need to impress and be liked. He told others what they needed to hear – not what he thought they *wanted* to hear if they were to like him. Even his opponents noticed this (perhaps through hard experience!): 'Teacher, we know that you are a man of integrity. You aren't swayed by others, because you pay no attention to who they are' (Mark 12:14).

Value and the cross

Many of us will remember being told by maths teachers to 'show your working'. The cross is where we see God 'show his working'.

As we have already argued, our value as image bearers was not lost at the fall, but our *sense* of that value was. Nowhere do we see that value more clearly placarded than on the cross. The length to which someone is prepared to go to rescue something shows how much that thing matters to them. The length that God went to, to rescue us, betokens the immensity of our value in his sight: 'Greater love has no one than this: to lay down one's life for one's friends.'[5] When seeking, therefore, to restore a proper sense of our own value, it is to the cross pre-eminently that we must go.

Value and the Church

Tony Campolo tells the story of a night when he was in Hawaii and went into a greasy spoon diner, about the only place that was still open at 3.30 a.m. He ordered coffee and a doughnut when suddenly, eight or nine prostitutes came in:

> Their talk was loud and crude. I felt completely out of place and was just about to make my getaway when I overheard the woman beside me say, 'Tomorrow's my birthday. I'm going to be 39.'
>
> Her 'friend' responded in a nasty tone, 'So what do you want from me? A birthday party? . . . Ya want me to get you a cake and sing "Happy Birthday"?'
>
> 'Come on,' said the woman sitting next to me. 'Why do you have to be so mean? I was just telling you, that's all. Why do you have to put me down? . . . I don't want anything from you. I mean, why should you give me a birthday party? I've never had a birthday party in my whole life. Why should I have one now?'[6]

Campolo decided right then and there to throw a birthday party for her. And the next day, when Agnes and the other prostitutes came into the diner, it was bedecked with crepe paper decorations and cardboard signs saying, 'Happy Birthday,

Agnes!' The staff of the diner had baked a birthday cake. Campolo recalls:

> Never have I seen a person so flabbergasted so stunned so shaken. Her mouth fell open. Her legs seemed to buckle a bit. Her friend grabbed her arm to steady her. As she was led to sit on one of the stools along the counter, we all sang 'Happy Birthday' to her. As we came to the end of our singing with 'happy birthday dear Agnes, happy birthday to you,' her eyes moistened. Then, when the birthday cake with all the candles on it was carried out, she lost it and just openly cried.[7]

A church that throws parties for prostitutes at 3.30 in the morning is a church that is reflecting to people the value they have in the eyes of God. Everything we do as a church should be reflecting the infinite value that members and non-members have in the heart of their Maker. The best advice I was ever given about preaching was this: 'When you preach, never try to make people feel guilty. You don't need to – they feel guilty anyway. The trick is to make them feel loved.' The Church is there to help people know their own worth as bearers of the image of God.

Through preaching the God of love we meet in Jesus, through persistently teaching people to pray to the God of love we meet in Jesus (thus receiving love from him), and through continued actions that embody the love of that God, the liberating truth of our value in the eyes – and heart – of the God we meet in Jesus will gradually irrigate the love-parched soil of our hearts.

2 Rule

Rule and Jesus

We saw in Chapter 1 that human beings are called to 'rule over the fish of the sea and the birds in the sky, over the livestock and all the wild animals, and over all the creatures that move along the ground' (Genesis 1:26), and that the kind of rule we are called to exercise is one that reflects *God's* rule – the kind of rule that is more for the sake of the ruled than of the ruler. In the person of Jesus, creation at last receives that selfless restorative rule that God always intended it to receive from human beings.

First, Jesus clearly observed the natural world carefully. As Sister Margaret Magdalen notes: 'Judging by the number of references to wildlife (the foxes, wolves, dogs, birds and fish) as well as the not-so-wild (ewes, lambs, swine), animals must have fascinated him, and perhaps he them, for holiness produces a strange affinity with animals.' [8]

Second, Jesus clearly contemplated creation, and found it a way into a deeper understanding of the Creator. He found – and expected his disciples to find – flowers of the field, grass and sparrows 'to be the icons through which the disciples would penetrate the mystery of God's providence and protection, and discover hidden wisdom and truth about God's relationship with his creation'.[9]

Third, Jesus healed creation. Being in perfect relationship with his Father, he is able to restore harmony to the world around him. He is able to mediate his Father's rule into a broken and hazardous environment. In the face of violent storms on the Sea of Galilee, he has peace within himself, and is able to bring that peace to the very elements, to the relief and astonishment of his disciples.[10] In the face of crippling disease, where a disordered nature is in conflict with human welfare, Jesus is able to restore the healthy order and integrity that was always God's intention for his creatures. In the face of death, he not only weeps[11] – thus demonstrating the wrongness and should-not-be-ness of death in his view, and in the purposes of God – but he is able to undo the life-snuffing, grief-generating, uncreating, God-defying work of death.[12]

Here at last is a human being doing what human beings were always called to do: ruling creation under God and subduing the fallen world[13] so as to unveil how it was always intended to be in the creative purposes of God, and how it will one day be, when God is all in all.[14]

Rule and the cross

That subduing of the chaos of creation to which human beings were called, and which he exhibits around him in his nature miracles, Jesus completes for the whole cosmos on his cross. Just as all things were created by him, so all things were reconciled to God through him, 'by making peace through his blood, shed on the cross'.[15] As Gregory of Nyssa put it: 'the creation, in the world and above the world, that once was at variance with itself, is knit together in friendship: and we . . . are made to join in the angels' song, offering the worship of their praise to God.'[16]

So much has our generation focused upon Jesus dying *for me* that we have tended to forget that he died for all things, for the whole creation. So focused have we been on the personal dimension of the cross that we have often neglected the cosmic. But that imbalance has had negative consequences for the natural world because we have focused on *our* value, to the detriment of the value of creation. Indeed, we have tended to assume that we are so valuable to God that we can do what we like with the natural world. And that has accentuated the already broken relationship between ourselves and our environment, and led to the virtual abandonment of our calling to care for creation. The cross calls us to see *all things* as fellow beneficiaries of the cross, equally reconciled to God – and therefore to see ourselves as called to live as harmoniously as possible with all that God has made.[17]

Rule and the Church

If the Church claims to love the Creator, it needs to be seen to love the creation. How we treat God's creation needs to reflect God's loving rule of us, if what we say about God is to have any consistency and credibility.

Most churches own a building and, possibly, a bit of land. Are we heating that building in a way that causes minimal pollution of the atmosphere?[18] Are we managing that land in a way that maximises its benefit to wildlife? Most Christians rent or own a home and maybe a garden, so the same questions could be asked of us. Most Christians purchase cleaning products, so will be having an impact on the environment that way. Most Christians vote, and could be asking questions of those who solicit that vote, about how seriously they take the protection and sustaining of our world.

Some Christians will be called to give their working lives to the care of God's creation, be it through scientific research, through fundraising, through administration, through education or through hands-on fieldwork. All human beings are called to be living representations of the God who made, sustains and loves his world; who died for its reintegration; and who will one day heal it, remake it and flood it with his glorious presence.

3 Equality

Equality and Jesus

One of the most notable features of Jesus' life is the breadth of company that he kept, along with the cavalier disregard for convention that he frequently demonstrated in keeping that company.

Conversation between men and women in public places was forbidden by the rabbis,[19] yet Jesus unashamedly initiates a conversation when he is alone with a woman in a public place[20] – so manifestly brazen and risky a manoeuvre in first-century Palestinian culture that, when his disciples discover him in conversation with her, they ask him, 'What are you after?'[21] As Andy Angel comments, 'They suspect him of being up to no good.'[22]

Jesus enjoys the company of women,[23] he is supported by female benefactors,[24] he defends women against carping criticism,[25] he praises a woman for sitting at his feet like a trainee rabbi,[26] and the first reports of his resurrection are carried by a woman,[27] whose testimony would not have been acceptable in a Jewish court of law at the time.

Equally, Jesus overrules his disciples when they assume that he is too busy to give mere children his time.[28] Not enough work has been done on the place of children in the Jewish society of Jesus' day, but Don Carson's summary is perhaps fair: 'Although children in Judaism of the time were deeply cherished, they were thought in some ways to be negligible members of society: their place was to learn, to be respectful, to listen.'[29] (It is perhaps not insignificant that, as Larry Hurtado points out, 'the term "child" in Aramaic and Greek can also mean "servant"'.[30]) Jesus seems to be unhappy with this marginalisation, and insists on their equal access to him, to his time, and to his blessing.[31]

Jesus also gives much of his time to those who are morally compromised and therefore at the fringes of society. His non-judgemental welcome of prostitutes and collaborators is striking. Again, it went against the mores of the day, and he was criticised for it.[32] In the story of the woman caught in adultery, he manages to protect the woman from a baying mob; to extricate her from the lethal reproach of the law, rewriting that law for his people in the process; to expose the hypocrisy of her accusers and convict them of their own sinfulness – all without giving the minutest suggestion that sin is anything other than a force for the destruction of all that is good and supportive and hopeful.

Jesus welcomes all who come to him, regardless of gender, age, moral standing or, lastly, of nationality. In the previous chapter, I argued that one of the consequences of the fall is that we tend to try to diminish the defined group of people to whom we owe compassion. Jesus' healing of the Samaritan leper targets that tendency, and seeks to widen out again the set of those deserving of our proactive compassion.[33]

As Bernard O'Connor helpfully summarises, Jesus:

> mixed freely and easily with people of all sorts, the rich as well as the poor . . . He mixed with sinners and thought nothing of it. For him it was a matter of indifference who they were or where they stood on the social ladder or in popular esteem. They were all equally children of the one Father, his own brothers and sisters.[34]

In the equal embrace of Jesus himself, our equality is recognised and reflected back to us, and we are challenged to go and do likewise.

Equality and the cross

Jesus' calling of twelve disciples (mirroring the twelve tribes of Israel) shows that he thought of himself as re-constituting, re-shaping and re-forming Israel. The way he ate with those who were beyond the confines of what was acceptable shows that he was seeking to gather back into Israel all who had been excluded – or had excluded them-selves – from it. Who one eats with is a potent political issue. Adam Gopnik comments:

> Nothing is more fundamental to human relations than decid-ing who has a place at the table – and nothing is more essential to our idea of humanism than expanding that table, symboli-cally and actually, adding extra chairs and places and settings as we can.[35]

But there was more expansion to come. In his ministry, Jesus had largely limited himself to gathering in 'the lost sheep of Israel'.[36] He was, however, aware that 'I have other sheep that are not of this sheepfold. I must bring them also.'[37] And the precise context of that saying is Jesus speaking of his imminent death: 'I lay down my life for the sheep.'[38]

On the cross, that process of expansion was completed. Those of other sheepfolds (i.e. Gentiles) were brought into the one sheepfold of the renewed and enlarged Israel. Those who were far off were brought near.[39] Those who were at enmity were reconciled to one another as they were reconciled to God. Distinctions and identity markers were relativised and rendered irrelevant in comparison with the identity marker of common baptism into Christ[40] – circumcision, brand marks, chromo-somes and language were all divested of any right to divide. The criteria that marginalise were themselves marginalised.

Dividing lines and signs dreamt up by diseased human minds dwindled into insignificance. The cross extended the table to the point at which every human being who ever existed could sit down at it.

Equality and the Church

Jesus' work in abolishing class and nationality and gender as identity markers for the kingdom was recognised and continued (imperfectly and incompletely, to be sure) by the early Church. Sociologist Rodney Stark adjudges that 'Women in early Christian communities were considerably better off than their pagan and even Jewish counterparts'[41] – due to their enjoying an older average age for marriage and childbirth, a greater say in whom they married, symmetrical expectations of chastity, equal criteria for divorce, an abjuring of abortion (which was highly dangerous to the mother and usually decided upon by the father) and infanticide (which was predominantly of female babies and decided upon by the father), a greater involvement in the life and leadership of the religious community and near equality in commemoration after death. Indeed, Stark suggests that one reason why Christianity was particularly attractive to women in the early Church was 'because it offered them a life that was so greatly superior to the life they otherwise would have led'.

Likewise, Jesus' attitude towards children seems to have influenced the early Church to give them a more valued and central place in the life of the community than would have been the case for children of pagan families. Not only were they usually free from the threat of abortion or exposure, they were also not hindered from having a significant presence in Christian worship. Douglas Hare comes to the same conclusion with regard to children as Rodney Stark came to with regard to women: 'from a sociological point of view, this may have been one of the reasons why Christianity spread so rapidly in the Roman world . . . Christianity offered a *family* religion in which both sexes and all ages could participate together.'[42] O. M. Bakke argues that early Christianity is the point in time when children became people.[43]

A sorry past moral history was not a barrier to church membership or leadership – when the gospel was taken to predominately pagan cities such as Corinth and Ephesus, it was expected. Race ceased (in the end) to be a relevant consideration in the early Church – that was the battle St Paul fought and won. And slaves were to be regarded as dear brothers and sisters in the Lord.[44] Oliver O'Donovan goes so far as to assert: 'It is wrong to think of the church as simply tolerating slavery because it could not abolish it. It believed that Christ had abolished it.'[45]

Given that, it is striking and sad that so few of the Church Fathers spoke out clearly against slavery. Gregory of Nyssa saw very clearly the incompatibility of slavery with the belief that human beings are made in the image of God:

> 'I got me slave-girls and slaves.' For what price, tell me? What did you find in existence worth as much as this human nature? . . . God said, 'Let us make man in our own image and likeness.' If he is in the likeness of God and rules the whole earth, and has been granted authority over everything on earth from God, who is his buyer, tell me? Who is his seller? To God alone belongs this power; or, rather, not even to God himself. For his gracious gifts, it says, are irrevocable. God would not therefore reduce the human race to slavery, since he himself, when we had been enslaved to sin, spontaneously recalled us to

freedom. But if God does not enslave what is free, who is he that sets his own power above God's?[46]

If it took a shamefully long time for Christian societies to abolish slavery and the slave trade in their horrific reality – and it did – then at least it is fair to say that the doctrine of the image of God was one of the drivers. Abolitionist leader Frederick Douglass employed the doctrine to excoriate the institution and practice of slavery: 'The slave is a man, "the image of God", but "a little lower than the angels".'[47]

Wherever the Church today comes across people who are overlooked, undervalued or silenced, wherever a modern form of slavery denies the dignity of God's self-portraits, she is called to defend that dignity with every fibre of her being. The Church must summon all to acknowledge in word and deed the essential truth that when we put down another we do not thereby exalt ourselves – instead we put down, demean and tarnish ourselves and brick up the beauty we were created to radiate.

4 Creativity

Creativity and Jesus

Creativity is not something we often associate with Jesus, but it is there to be gleaned from the Gospels.

Jesus is someone who contemplated the natural world and noticed its beauty: 'Even Solomon in all his glory was not arrayed like one of these.'[48] He also had a non-functional view of food; meals, for him, were an opportunity for fellowship, for welcome of the otherwise unaccepted and for celebration of the kingdom. He had a similarly non-functional view of drink – the provision of wine at the wedding feast in Cana was about saving the family from social embarrassment; it was about community celebration, and revelation of the glory of God.[49] He also appreciated music: visits to the temple and ordinary life would have been infused with singing and making melody. And these early musical experiences come out in his imagery: 'To what can I compare this generation? They are like children sitting in the market-places and calling out to others: "We played the pipe for you, and you did not dance; we sang a dirge, and you did not mourn"' (Matthew 11:16-17). The last thing Jesus did before going to face his betrayer on the Mount of Olives was to sing a hymn.[50]

However, it is in Jesus' use of language that his creativity was most evident. His storytelling drew and held crowds. His teaching was metaphor-rich: 'You are the salt of the earth', 'You are the light of the world', 'They come to you in sheep's clothing, but inwardly they are ferocious wolves'. His language was likewise rich in similes: 'The kingdom of heaven is like . . .'. He used the rhetorical device of repetition: 'Blessed are the . . . for they will . . .'. He used rhetorical questions: 'Which is easier: to say, "Your sins are forgiven," or to say, "Get up and walk"?'[51] He used the rhetorical device of aposiopesis (when you deliberately don't finish your sentence): 'But so that you may know that the Son of Man has authority on earth to forgive sins . . .'.[52] He used the rhetorical device of hyperbole. As Mark Forsyth suggests:

For top-grade hyperbole we need to go back and consult the Son of God:
'And why do you look at the speck in your brother's eye, but do not consider the plank in your own eye? Or how can you say to your brother, "Let me remove the speck from your eye"; and look, a plank is in your own eye? Hypocrite! First remove the

plank from your own eye, and then you will see clearly to remove the speck from your brother's eye.' All things are, of course, possible with Jesus, but having a large plank of wood in your eye and not noticing is an extreme example. It's almost as silly as trying to get a whole camel through the eye of a needle, which is an impossibility, or, to put it technically, an adynaton. . . . Before an adynaton will work, pigs will fly, hell will freeze over and the devil will go skiing. You might as well try getting blood out of a stone.[53]

It is unlikely that Jesus was trained in rhetoric, or that he had read Cicero on oratory.[54] But he was a natural orator, who used words and phrases and parts of speech naturally and to memorable effect. Unlike some of his followers (who, as C. S. Lewis remarked, were so literal-minded that, if you pulled their leg, it would fall off!), Jesus used language that was not literalistic or functional or flat, but rich, striking, imaginative, humorous and unforgettable.

Creativity and the cross
The cross is the descent of the God of beauty into ugliness, at the hands of creatures who are called to reflect that beauty:

He had no beauty or majesty to attract us to him,
nothing in his appearance that we should desire him.[55]

As St Bonaventure comments: 'Who would look for beauty of form now in such a roughly handled body?' Paradoxically, however:

along with the outward formlessness, inwardly beauty was preserved. . . . Men saw the most beautiful of the sons of men on the cross, and since they look only at what is external they saw him as one who possessed neither beauty nor form, for his face was despised and his posture out of joint; yet it was from this formlessness of our Saviour that the price paid for our beauty streamed forth . . . But who may find words for his inner beauty, since the entire fullness of the divinity dwells in him?[56]

As Christ was made sin for us, that we might become the right-eousness of God,[57] so he became ugliness for us, that we (and all creatures) might become the beauty of God. That is the paradox – and the reversal – of the cross.

Nothing is more beautiful than this descent into ugliness.
Nothing is more creative than this descent into nothingness.
Nothing is more vital than this descent into death.
Nothing is more fruitful than this descent into fruitlessness.
Nothing is more sanctifying than this descent into sin.
Nothing is more inspiring than this expiring.

That paradox helps explain the fact that more beautiful repre-sentations have been made of the ugliness of Jesus' death than of any incident of his life. No wonder it is a scene that has appealed to artists throughout the last two millennia.

Creativity and the Church

The Church has always seen it as part of its mission to be a patron of the arts, because creativity is part of what it means to be human. Creativity is part of what it means to be in the image of God, and the mission of the Church is to restore women and men in that image. If the vision of humanity that we offer to the world is to have anything like the richness that it ought to have (and without which it will not attract the world), then it needs to have an honoured place for the arts.

Not only are the arts a sign that human beings are made in the image of the Creator and are therefore intrinsically creative, but Christian artists and writers and composers help make a Christian vision of the world believable. That's because they address the imagination, and what people can imagine shapes what they can believe. As another Catholic writer, Flannery O'Connor, put it, 'the Christian novelist lives in a larger universe'.[58]

Each local church, therefore, needs to make its building, worship and music as beautiful as possible, whatever their style, culture or flavour. As we have seen, it needs to preach in such a way that no one is left with the impression that they cannot justify doing an art course because that doesn't advance the kingdom. It needs to encourage every member of its community in their innate creativity. If we have any professional actors or dancers in the congregation, we could pray for them (and not just for ministers and missionaries) in the regular intercessions – that would send a strong signal that the Church values and supports her artists.

Even if we do not have anyone in our congregation who is able to make a major contribution to the arts themselves, we can foster an environment in which art is valued, and artists are encouraged. We could let a local orchestra or dance group use the church to practise and perform in – for free. We could run a poetry competition in the local community – anything to foster a creative environment and allow the Michelangelos and the J. S. Bachs, and the C. S. Lewises and the Dorothy Sayerses, and the Marilynne Robinsons and the George Herberts of the future to emerge and to enrich the life of the Church and of the world, and to shape the climate of opinion and imagination so that it is more amenable to the Christian vision.

We need to adorn the life and worship of the Christian community with all forms of creativity 'for beauty', just as

Solomon adorned the temple with precious stones, carvings and embroidery.[59] Then people may experience God in beauty and as beauty, and reflect that beauty in their own creating and their own living.

5 Relationality

Relationality and Jesus

Genesis 3's diagnosis of the human condition is that the theological division between people and God is the root cause of the sociological divisions between people and people. In the person of Jesus, that fundamental division between people and God was overcome.

From very early on, Jesus had an unusually close awareness of, and relationship with, God. Jesus' early sense of God as his Father – 'Didn't you know I had to be in my Father's house?'[60] – continued to grow in a natural way which Jesus came to realise was unique. The Aramaic word for Father (Abba) became his favoured way of addressing God. His prayer life was so noticeable and attractive that his disciples wanted him to teach them how to have something similar.[61] It was both disciplined and extravagant. He would turn naturally to prayer in moments of particular need and distress.[62] Time with his Father was something he cherished but found difficult to protect, given the demands upon his time and energy.[63]

This unblocked relationship with God made for an internal harmony of the different elements of his psyche, for a striking harmony with the physical world around him, and – what concerns us here – an ability (through forgiveness, non-retaliation and the relentless proffering of love) to live in maximal harmony with others. St Paul urges us, realistically: 'If it is possible, as far as it depends on you, live at peace with everyone'[64] – that is what Jesus was able to do.[65] One person walked away from relationship with him – but the last look he had of Jesus was a look of love.[66] Another betrayed him – but went about his sad business fuelled by the unleavened favour of Jesus.[67] Others nailed him to a cross – but heard him pray for their forgiveness.[68]

Not only did he himself live in maximal harmony with others, but (to an extent naturally limited by their fallenness) he inspired others to do the same. His disciples

> loved him even when they were bewildered by him. He commanded their loyalty, respect and support, even though by responding to his call they found themselves in daily proximity to men who, in the normal course of their life's work, they would never have encountered let alone chosen as companions. He, as the unifying power amongst them, was able to hold together the Zealot and the quisling . . . the cautious quiet introvert with the impetuous, blustering extrovert, the intellectual with the unschooled, the town dweller with the country born.[69]

We noted previously that, all too often, we are so taken up with the pursuit of value through accomplishment that we fail to give our friendships, relationships and marriages the time they need. Jesus was careful to carve out time for the relationships that mattered to him. He sought to protect time with his disciples (and remember that he called them 'friends'[70]) from the needs and demands of ministry.[71] He sought to protect time with his friends, Mary and Martha, from the encroachment of domestic chores.[72] He recognised that the giving of love necessarily included within it the giving (and receiving) of time.

Relationality and the cross

The betrayal of Jesus is the beginning of his descent into relationlessness. He asks his three closest friends to stay with him in his agony – and they fall asleep. His disciples all desert him. One recovers himself and follows Jesus into the house of the High Priest, and then denies knowing him. A small group, including Jesus' mother and the beloved disciple, are there at the cross – and presence is never nothing – but it is *he* who has the resources and reserves to care for *them*.[73] And even as his relationality dwindles, and the supports and comforts are cut away, he continues to restore relationality to others – Pilate to Herod, and the thief to his Maker.[74]

And then, rather like an eclipse of the sun – where the light gets darker and darker, and then it is as if someone switches off the light altogether – Jesus is plunged into the utter darkness of being cut off from his Father. 'Whoever follows me,' said Jesus, 'will never walk in darkness' – but that's because *he did*.[75] That intimacy with the Father which Jesus had always enjoyed, which he could not deny,[76] whence came his value and his security and his ability to say what needed to be heard, which had been the source of his identity, authority and joy – not only is it gone but, worse than that, there is a sense of being walked out on, let down: 'My God, my God, why did you abandon me?'[77] Psalm 27 contains the confident assertion that 'Even if my father and mother abandon me, the Lord will hold me close.'[78] The irony, of course, is that his earthly mother was present at his death (John 19:25): his heavenly Father was palpably absent.

The wilderness experience has returned to Jesus with a vengeance. He hears the same voice on the desert wind, questioning his sonship, his identity, his lovedness, his vocation.[79] On the Day of Atonement, two goats would be chosen by lot:

one would be offered as a sin offering, and the other would be driven out into the barren and exilic wasteland, devoid of company or comfort. On his Day of Atonement – on *the* Day of Atonement – Jesus, as he was crucified outside the camp, embodied both.

John Saward approaches the heart of it, as he riffs on the reflections of Hans Urs von Balthasar:

> The Son's obedient embracing of Godforsakenness is a work of substitution. He endures desolation for us, as our Head and in our place. He enters into solidarity with all who feel abandoned and forgotten by God. In what the Greek Fathers boldly called his 'foolish' love of mankind, God wants to experience the absence of God . . . There are no uncharted territories. Even in the most hellish deserts of this life, no man need despair. Godforsakenness, too, can be a holy place, for it has been hallowed and made hopeful by the person and presence of God incarnate himself.[80]

Betrayal, desertion, abandonment, estrangement, and bleak and utter loneliness have been taken into the relational God. And therefore, paradoxically, contact has been made between the depths and the heights. A causeway has been built back to that relationality for which we were made – a road to reconciled relationships.

Relationality and the Church

Jesus descended into relationlessness that he might restore us to the full richness of relationality for which we were created. The Church therefore needs to be a community of relational celebration and enjoyment. It needs to enjoy its relationship with God, and to train people in the generally unglamorous disciplines of prayer.

Its leadership needs to be relational leadership, which recognises that it is 'together with all the saints' that we explore and experience all the dimensions of the love of God. Church leaders need to recognise that good leadership is not about getting one's own way or imposing one's own vision: good leadership makes sure that everyone is listened to and heard – critically, because we are all fallen, but also lovingly, especially in regard to the less confident and articulate. The local church needs to be a place which is different because of the presence of each member, where everyone is able to make their individual contribution to how the community worships and does its mission. We need to get to the situation in which every member is not saying, 'This is how *I* like to worship and I'll go elsewhere if it departs too much from that', but rather, 'What will enable that newcomer to feel at home, to worship naturally and to make their own unique contribution, and what can I do to facilitate that?'

A church that celebrates our God-reflecting relationality joyfully will sometimes put aside time for the community to be together without any particular agenda – no service to be planned, or music to be rehearsed, or talk to be listened to, or outreach to be organised, or task to be accomplished. I remember one church holiday when we decided to organise virtually nothing for the whole long weekend (except one daily act of worship), and we saw God work in ways that was not usually the case when we filled every unforgiving day with sixteen hours' worth of 'distance run'.

There is a balance to be struck here. On the one hand, we need, as I say, to create space for community to happen and for relationships to deepen. On the other hand, we need to do that in a way that gives space to those who want to keep their distance, to explore from the edge, to maintain their own safe

space. Paradoxically but importantly, creating space for relationality involves not imposing that expectation on those who
would experience it as an intrusion.

Furthermore, although there is a deep need and hunger for
community that the Church must provide space for, the Church
must not take up so much of its members' time as to prevent
them from enjoying and fermenting community elsewhere. We
must not take up so much of their time as to place a strain on
marriages, families and friendships. We must not demand so
much of their time that their children feel God to be a threat to
their lovedness. We must not demand so much of their time
that they don't know many people outside of the Christian
community and so fail to have much of an impact on our society. We need to be a community, but we must avoid being a
ghetto. We need to revel in our relationality, not promote it
with one hand and deter it with the other.

6 Sexuality

Sexuality and Jesus

As with creativity, sexuality is not something we often associate
with Jesus, but it, too, is there to be gleaned from the Gospels.
The story of the woman with the ointment, exemplifying Jesus'
ease with touch (even sensuous touch), together with his warm
relationships with women, his deep (and quite physical[81])
friendship with men, his non-judgemental attitude towards
those whose sexuality was particularly broken – all these evince
someone who was at ease with his own sexuality.

As we have already observed, when his disciples returned
from the shops with food to find Jesus talking alone with a
woman, they thought that he was up to no good – hence their
(unvoiced) question, 'What are you after?'[82] They were wrong

to think that, as it turns out, but the point for our purposes is that they assumed that he was capable of being attracted to this woman. As Andy Angel comments:

> Within and through this narrative John communicates with his audience that the people who met Jesus, including those who spent the most time with him, experienced him as being like any other man. He was a man with all the sexual desires, drives and motivations that are part and parcel of masculinity. Without this assumption, the narrative would make no sense . . . If the disciples had thought otherwise, their silent questions would never have entered their heads.[83]

To quote Andy Angel again, Jesus 'practises self-control over his bodily appetites (including his sex drive) in order to serve God faithfully.'[84] He seems to have felt it right to deprive himself permanently of that exclusive commitment to one partner in which alone sexual expression makes its fullest sense. We do not know why, but Sister Margaret Magdalen hazards a guess. He had come to bring – and to embody – the kingdom:

> Love within the kingdom would lift those who were made to feel little more than the flotsam and jetsam of society – dispensable and disposable – to a new level of dignity, a new sense of personal worth, a new hope of acceptance, a new halting belief that they might after all be lovable.
>
> The embodying of this vision could only take place through an immeasurable energy of love. This is where Jesus directed the sheer power of his sexuality. I really question whether or not any one human being could have coped with being on the receiving end of such power in an exclusive partnership. Would he or she not always have felt disadvantaged by the paucity of

his or her love in comparison? The scope of his love was such that it *had* to take in the whole world.[85]

This is, of course, just speculation. But such little evidence as we have suggests that Jesus always exercised respectful restraint in his sexuality. It is noticeable that, though the disciples are embarrassed to discover him alone with a woman, he is unembarrassed to be so discovered – so free of embarrassment that he is able to talk, in that very context, of his obedience to the Father.[86] Thus, Christian belief in the sinlessness of Jesus extends to this area of his life, as well as to every other.

The way he managed his sexuality was revelatory and therapeutic. While the woman at the well is initially reticent to talk about her sexual past and immediately changes the subject,[87] within a few verses she is speaking about it excitedly to all around:[88]

> Jesus' unselfish love has a healing effect on the woman. Her relationship history is central to her identity and she experiences shame around it. Something about the way Jesus speaks or comes across to her leaves her affirmed and accepted. Her actions demonstrate this. She shows no shame in telling her fellow townsfolk that Jesus has told her all about her relationship history, and this witness brings them to faith. Her sex life has become the locus of salvation and the vehicle of witness.[89]

His self-restraint, self-control and self-sacrifice have restored her sense of self: despite 'having the same sexual desires as the next man . . . Jesus preferred to bring healing to the sexual life of another person rather than seeking pleasure for himself in fulfilment of his own desires'.[90] At the beginning of his Gospel, John tells us that 'we have seen his glory, the glory of the One and Only, who came from the Father, full of grace and truth'.[91] That glory shines through every aspect of his humanity, including his sexuality: 'John . . . develops his picture of Jesus the man in whose sexual desires and behaviour he and others have seen the glory of God.'[92] May our sexual desires and behaviour be similarly porous to the glory of God – and therefore similarly healing.

Sexuality and the cross

We just saw that Jesus' disciples were shocked to find him associating with a woman alone by the well at Sychar, but it was hardly out of character for Jesus to mix with those traditionally regarded as beyond the margins. On the banks of the Jordan, he lined up with the complacent, the uncompassionate, the callous, the corrupt, the coercive and the complaining – a veritable brood of vipers, in fact![93] Throughout his ministry, he was to be found (and was attacked for) partying with tax collectors, prostitutes and other sinners. As he died, he was 'numbered with the transgressors', and, as a corpse, he 'was assigned a grave with the wicked'.[94] He made a bit of a habit of 'mixing with the wrong people'.

And that habit is the gospel. The fact that Jesus reveals God as One who comes after the morally messed up (as a shepherd comes after a lost sheep or a father after his prodigal), rather than withdrawing himself from us, is the unexpected good news of the Christian understanding of God. It is the gospel. In our fear-filled projections, God would have stood on his privilege and purity, and, at best, waited for us to change. But, from the start, he proactively associates with humanity at its worst. And, from the start, that included those for whom sexuality was the arena in which their inner warpedness was most evidently displayed.

This was true of Jesus' birth. Examine, as Herbert McCabe does, the family into which he was born, and we find the gospel in genealogical form: 'One aim of Matthew is to show that Jesus really was tied into the squalid realities of human life and sex and politics.' To concentrate here mostly on the sexual highlights – or, rather, lowlights – of his genealogy:

Jacob [was] an unscrupulous but entertaining character who won *his* position in the line that leads to Christ by lying and cheating his old blind father.

He was cheated himself, however, slept with the wrong girl by mistake and became the father of Judah.

Judah slept, again by mistake, with his own daughter-in-law Tamar: she had cheated him by disguising herself and dressing up as a prostitute . . . Anyway when Judah heard that his daughter-in-law had prostituted herself and become pregnant, he ordered her to be burnt alive. He was disconcerted when he discovered that he himself had been the client and that the child, Perez, was his.

Boaz didn't exactly sleep with Ruth by mistake but he was surprised in the middle of the night to find her sleeping at his feet. (Though unconventional behaviour by women ought not to have surprised Boaz, for according to Matthew his mother was Rahab, and commentators seem to assume that he must have meant Rahab the prostitute in Jericho) . . .

David fell in love with a girl he chanced to see bathing naked one evening; he arranged for her husband to be murdered, slept with her and became the father of Solomon, the next in the line of succession towards Christ our saviour.[95]

Jesus might have been justified to ask what kind of family he was being born into. But he is not ashamed to own deeply sinful people as members of his own family.[96]

The same was true of his death, as Martin Luther noted:

> Our most merciful Father . . . sent his only Son into the world and laid upon him all the sins of all men, saying: Be thou Peter that denier; Paul that persecutor, blasphemer and cruel oppressor; *David that adulterer*; that sinner which did eat the apple in Paradise; that thief which hanged upon the cross; and briefly, be thou the person which hath committed the sins of all men; see therefore that thou pay and satisfy for them.[97]

We have already seen how John, in his Gospel, presents Jesus as tempted in all respects as we are, including sexually – yet without sin. Nevertheless, by becoming sin for us, Jesus voluntarily takes on all our sexual sins – and all the other sins of history.

Sexuality and the Church

We have seen that Jesus seems to have been someone who was at ease with his own sexuality, and experienced as safe by others in theirs. The Church needs to reflect that ease and that safeness. It needs to be able to talk about sexuality naturally, both in its preaching and its pastoral care, neither giving undue attention to it, nor ignoring an area of life in which people struggle. It should neither pretend that sexual sins cannot be horrendously damaging, nor treat them as more sinful than other sins – and it should never forget that sexual sins, like all other sins, have been taken dissolvingly into the person of Christ on the cross.

Sexual sin *isn't* any more sinful than other sin, but it is an area in which the Church has failed in a particularly shameful manner in recent years. The way in which some Christian leaders have abused and exploited those over whom they have power, and the way in which others have attempted to cover up that guilt, is one of the main reasons why the Church is currently held in low esteem and denied a respectful hearing by our contemporaries. We need to regard safeguarding not as a bureaucratic chore, but as an essential element in our pastoral care and a vital investment in our missional integrity. We desperately need Christians to reflect their Lord in his sexual safeness.

We noted earlier how healing such safeness can be. So it was for one student at my college. As she left Wycliffe, she told me that, for all the richness of what she learned academically, the greatest benefit was being in a community where she felt 'valued, loved and respected all through the year . . . For me, the greatest lesson has been that good men exist who are faithful to their wives, respect women and love Jesus.'[98] This had not previously been her experience.

The Church needs to be at ease talking about sexuality and safe in its practice of it. It also needs to bring the guilt-dissolving, sin-challenging, hurt-healing, character-reforming power of the cross to bear on people's struggles in this area.

7 Uniqueness

Uniqueness and Jesus

In Monty Python's *Life of Brian*, Brian is mistaken for the Messiah and, getting fed up with people following him, remonstrates with the crowd and tells them that they shouldn't be following him or anyone else. They need to think for themselves. They are all individuals. In unison, they chant their agreement that Yes, they are all individuals! Brian tries again, and tells them that they are all different. Again, in unison, they chant their agreement that Yes, they are all different – except for one man in the crowd who claims that he isn't! Predictably, the crowd tells him to shut up.

The person who *was* the Messiah was similarly comfortable standing out from the crowd. As a boy, he literally stood out from the crowd when he stayed behind in Jerusalem to ask questions of the teachers of the law. Luke does not mention that any of his peer group were with him. And when his parents eventually found him, his response to their upbraiding revealed a growing sense of his unique relationship with his Father and of his unique calling[99]– an embryonic sense that he was the Messiah (and not 'a very naughty boy', to quote the Python sketch further).

Once that embryonic sense of his unique calling had been tested and developed in the wilderness, Jesus embraced the cultural, social and theological differentness of that vocation. We have already seen how it wasn't 'done' to hold prolonged conversations with members of the opposite sex in public – but he did. It was highly unusual to remain single into your thirties – but he did. It wasn't 'done' to touch lepers, or those who had haemorrhages, or the dead, as these would make you ritually unclean – but he did. It wasn't 'done' to mix with the racially and religiously impure such as the Samaritans – but he did. It wasn't 'done' to mix with the sexually immoral, or with those who collaborated with the occupying Roman forces (either directly or by working for Herod) – but he did.

So eccentric was his behaviour that mental derangement was a category that his contemporaries seriously entertained to explain it. He thought he was 'opening the kingdom of heaven to all believers',[100] regardless of their social, moral or cultic standing: some of his contemporaries (including, at first, his family) thought he was plain mad.[101] They simply had no categories in which to place his behaviour (perhaps we should say 'his policy', for it was thought through and theologically cogent), or at least, they had no *positive* categories.[102]

Those put off by the seemingly constrictive similarity of contemporary Christians may take encouragement from the (literally) extraordinary behaviour of Jesus. He was redefining Israel, and redefining God, reshaping expectations, expanding categories and increasing options through his own coura- geously different living.[103]

In all these seven refractions of the image of God, Jesus reveals to us what it is to be human, and invites us to 'go and do likewise'.

Uniqueness and the cross
Towards the end of C. S. Lewis's science fiction novel *Perelandra*, humans, gods and angels take turns to speak of the Great Dance that has been going on 'from before always':

> 'There was no time when we did not rejoice before his face as now. The dance which we dance is at the centre and for the dance all things were made. Blessed be He! . . .'

> 'Never did he make two things the same; never did he utter one word twice . . .'

> 'Each grain, if it spoke, would say, I am at the centre; for me all things were made . . .'

> 'Each grain is at the centre. The Dust is at the centre. The Worlds are at the centre. The beasts are at the centre . . .'

> 'Where Maleldil [God] is, there is the centre. He is in every place. Not some of him in one place and some in another, but in each place the whole Maleldil . . .'

'Each thing was made for Him. He is the centre. Because we are with Him, each of us is at the centre. It is not as in a city of the Darkened World where they say that each must live for all. In His city all things were made for each. When He died in the Wounded World He died . . . for each man. If each man had been the only man made, He would have done no less.' [104]

As the good shepherd left the ninety-nine sheep in the wilderness and came looking for the one that was lost, so the good shepherd would have laid down his life for just one sheep.[105] The love of God is not just general ('God so loved the world'), it is also particular: this particular sheep, this particular person, this particular particle is at the centre of his concern, and is the object of his self-sacrificing love.

On the cross, Jesus is Peter that denier, Paul that persecutor, David that adulterer, me with my unique angle on the nature of God and my particular sins, you with your unique reflection of God's glory and your particular blockings of that glory. On the cross, every person and every particle is reconciled to God, and reconciled to every other person and every other particle. But to reconcile is not to homogenise. It is sin that homogenises; holiness particularises. The cross therefore frees every person and every particle to be the unique being it was created to be: 'Never did he make two things the same.'

Uniqueness and the Church

Annabel Rivkin and Emilie McMeekan launched the 'midult' in order to rebrand middle age.[106] In their column in the *Telegraph Magazine*, they give us 'The Midults' Guide to . . . People we think are odd: those who don't wear earphones in the gym':

Not the ones who have clearly forgotten their earphones and
are practically weeping from boredom and demotivation on the
cross trainer, ready to abandon all hope. But the people power-
ing through, deliberately . . . doing what? Listening to their
laboured breathing? Listening to our laboured breathing?
Doing the most boring thing on the planet with no uplifting or
distracting anthem? Not normal.[107]

Part of what is so well observed here is our overwhelming
tendency to label all difference as deviance. Some practices are
deviant, but most are just different. As Roger Ruston puts it,
'To see the image of God in people not like us should expand
our comprehension of the God-like, rather than reduce everyone to the same model of the human.'[108]

Churches, therefore, need to be oases of difference and of
acceptance – places where people feel refreshingly able to be
themselves, and not feel they have to conform to societal norms
which squeeze them out of shape. Where behaviour is not actually sinful, or unwise, or significantly unhelpful to others, we
need to learn to accommodate it without the heat of friction.
After all, the triune God is one who models difference within
unity. (The Father is not the Son, the Son is not the Spirit, the
Spirit is not the Father.) The Spirit is the Spirit of holiness and
unity, but not of uniformity.

I remember talking to one young Christian who had been
taught that if you want your church to grow, it needs to be
socio-economically monochrome. You should have a mental
picture of the sort of person you are trying to attract to your
church – what sort of clothes they wear, what sort of music they
listen to, what sort of mobile phone they have, etc. This suggestion reminds me of the famous put-down in *Pride and Prejudice*.
Miss Bingley was pouring cold water on her brother's idea of

holding a ball at Netherfield: 'I should like balls infinitely better . . . if they were carried on in a different manner . . . It would surely be much more rational if conversation instead of dancing made the order of the day.' To which her brother replied, 'Much more rational, my dear Caroline, I dare say but it would not be near so much like a ball.'[109] Similarly, churches might grow more quickly if they were socially monochrome, I dare say, but they would not be near so much like Church. Of course, some evangelistic initiatives are legitimately focused on particular sectors of the population – so, for example, one might get a Christian classical musician to come and talk about their faith, which would clearly attract those who love classical music. My point is that the Church qua Church should never so restrict its embrace.

The whole point of the cross was to unite people of difference and dividedness to one another by reconciling them all to God, and the whole point of the Church is to live out in our relationships what God did on the cross. The cross encompasses the eradication of sin, the reconciliation of the divided, and the celebration of unsinful difference.

Reflecting the Glory of God

Isaiah 40:18 asks:

> With whom, then, will you compare God?
> To what image will you liken him?

The answer would be to a translucent human being, who reflects the glory of God, and through whom the beauty of God shines.[110] That is the only divinely authorised image. Unfortunately, there is only one utterly translucent human

being – that is why the New Testament calls Jesus *the* image of
the invisible God.[111] By taking Jesus as our model, by letting his
cross redeem, heal and shape our whole being, and by taking
our place as a unique member of his body, we become more and
more reflective (and receptive) of that glory – and therefore
more and more fully ourselves.

Exercise: Prayers of Request

This is an exercise in supplication. Having thanked God that we are fearfully and wonderfully made in his image, and having faced some of the ways in which we block and obscure that image, we now ask him to restore his self-portrait, and to renew our thinking so that we reflect more fully the glory of our Creator.

DAY 1: VALUE

Lord Jesus Christ, we thank you for the value that you placed on everyone you met, be they socially despised, morally messed-up or habitually unregarded. We crave for ourselves that confidence in the Father's esteem, love and pleasure which gave you such stability and poise in yourself, and such disconcerting freedom from distorting dependence on the opinion and good regard of others. Give us that same closeness to the Father which cannot fail to induce in us an ever-deepening knowledge of our lovedness and worth.

As we contemplate your cross, as we enter into it at every Communion service and as it enters into us, may we absorb all the dimensions of your love for us, and our worth in your eyes.

And as we grow in knowledge of the depth of our lovedness, make us, we pray, less and less threatened by, and more and more respectful of, the dignity and value of others. May your Church be a place where people see their worth reflected back to them in ways they have never known elsewhere. Make us, we pray, a community where you are venerated, so all are venerated, and all creation is cherished. Amen.

DAY 2: RULE

Teach me, my God and King,
In all things Thee to see . . .

A man that looks on glass,
On it may stay his eye;
Or if he pleaseth, through it pass,
And then the heaven espy.

George Herbert[112]

Lord Jesus Christ, through whom and for whom all things were made, help us, we pray, to see your world as you see it, to meet the Creator in the creation, to meet the Giver in his gift. Thank you for your evident love for the world you made, the world you entered, the world for which you died, the world you will one day restore and make completely porous to your glory.

Help us to see all things as fellow recipients of your love and fellow beneficiaries of your death. As your rule was expressed in sacrificial love for the world, so may we be prepared to restrict our lifestyles and our luxuries, that your world may survive and thrive.

And may we, your Church, be known as observers, explorers, lovers, defenders, exegetes and minstrels of this beautiful and fragile world which you created, that you might indwell it, and which you have placed into our care. Amen.

DAY 3: EQUALITY

Lord Jesus Christ, you defied (in your life) and destroyed (by your death) the divisions that we erect out of fear, out of inherent fractiousness, out of a desire to dominate, out of moral laziness, out of convenient forgetfulness that we are children of the same heavenly Father.

We thank you that, in reconciling us to the Father, you reconciled us to each other; in breaking down the dividing wall of hostility between us and the Father, you shattered all the dividing walls of hostility that tear apart the human family.

May we, your family, live in defiance of the inequalities that isolate, belittle and embitter. May we be agents of your exaltation of the disregarded, and your liberation of the enslaved. And may we be a community that so internalises your evaluation of us that we are freed from the need to put down, and impelled by the desire to build up. May we know, and may others know through us, that your infinite love so embraces all, that there is room for no rank or degree. Amen.

DAY 4: CREATIVITY

Lord Jesus Christ, we thank you that the imagery you used in your teaching was of such piercing beauty that, even when translated into myriad languages and transposed into vastly different cultures, it retains the freshness and force to shock us into new ways of seeing, being and doing.

We thank you that you paid the price for our beauty.

Make us beautiful, we pray. Make us appreciators of beauty, promoters of beauty and radiators of beauty. As you restore us in the image of our Creator, rekindle and purify our creativity, that we may adorn our walls, our homes, our worship and our world with refractions of your beauty and glory. Amen.

DAY 5: RELATIONALITY

Lord Jesus Christ, eternally rooted in a relationship of love, you knew the Father with an infectious intimacy; you protected time with him, time with your disciples and with your friends.

You took utter estrangement into yourself, that we might be reconnected with the loves we spoil and struggle to maintain, the loves from which we choose to turn, and the Love from which we sprang.

May we revel in those restored relationships. Make us disciplined and natural pray-ers. Make us joyful givers of time to family, friends and those you send our way. And make our churches places of such welcome and warmth that it is easy to believe in the triune relationality of God. Amen.

DAY 6: SEXUALITY

Lord Jesus Christ, we thank you for the unembarrassed ease and purity of your sexuality. We thank you for the therapeutic effect such faithfulness and respect had on others. We thank you for your shame-dispelling acceptance of those who fell short.

We thank you that, in death as well as in life, you associated with the 'wrong types', and that, thereby, you absorbed our shame and gave us your unsulliedness.

Make your Church a place of safety and respect, where there is integration between what people say with their bodies and what they say with the rest of their lives; where something of your holiness is practised and where something of your healing is therefore experienced. Amen.

DAY 7: UNIQUENESS

Lord Jesus Christ, we thank you for your willingness to be yourself, even where that meant standing out from the crowd, risking misunderstanding, suspicion and condemnation.

I thank you that you died for me, particularly – that you took upon yourself my particular sins, to make me the particular person you made me to be. May I increasingly become that person.

And may your Church be an oasis of joyfully accepted difference, where people feel able to be themselves, and the glorious diversity of how you have made us is accommodated and celebrated. Amen.

Further Resources

On Jesus

Magdalen, Sister Margaret, *Jesus – Man of Prayer* (London: Hodder & Stoughton, 1991).

Magdalen, Sister Margaret, *The Hidden Face of Jesus* (London: Darton, Longman & Todd, 1993).

Angel, Andy, *Intimate Jesus: The Sexuality of God Incarnate* (London: SPCK, 2017).

Wright, N. T., *The Challenge of Jesus* (London: SPCK, 2000).

On the cross

Wright, Tom, *The Day the Revolution Began* (London: SPCK, 2017).

On the Church

Wright, Tom, 'Undermining Racism: Reflections on the "black lives matter" crisis', at: (https://ntwrightpage. com/2020/06/14/undermining-racism-complete-text/), accessed 4 January 2022.

PART 2

Spiritual Practices
for Restoration

Having presented a biblical and theological vision for restoration in Part 1 of this book, over the next four chapters we will consider four spiritual practices for restoration: listening to God, rediscovering 'heart knowing', confessing and forgiving. Occasionally, short testimonies from Ruth's clients are included to ground these points, and each chapter closes with some simple, practical exercises or prayers. These are tools intended to help you encounter God and experience his restoration in your life, and you may need to return to them over and over again as you pursue more of God's healing and restoration.

4

Listening to God

Listening to God is an important starting place on our journey of restoration, for two reasons. First, as we listen to the Father's voice, we discover our true identity as his unique sons and daughters. In order to have a secure sense of identity we need to know that we are loved and wanted, that we are valued and chosen, and that we have a destiny and a future. Sadly, these foundations are not always laid in childhood as God intended, and false ideas and images of who we are flood into the void. We begin to believe that we are unlovely, insignificant, worthless or hopeless. It is as we learn to tune out these lies and instead tune in to the voice of our Creator that we discover who we truly are: as the foundations of our identity are re-established, we can learn to live securely as God's precious children. This may happen on particular occasions and in significant ways, but it is something we need to seek on an ongoing basis, by regularly asking God how he sees us and what he thinks about us.

Second, listening to God restores us as we gain God's perspective on our life story. Each of us can tell the story of our life so far, but God has his own perspective. He sees not only the events of our lives, but how those events have affected us, and he wants to show us where he was at key moments in our story. If we do not listen, we'll never know how he felt about or saw our circumstances, or how he wishes to heal our trauma and restore us in his image. Listening to God's perspective on our story may highlight areas that need healing, or may itself bring healing as we glimpse God's view on our life experiences.

Listening Prayer

Listening prayer is, very simply, about having a two-way conversation with God – rather than just believing in him, we can live, grow and minister in relationship with him. In the same way that listening is a key part of all relationships, listening prayer is a fundamental part of our relationship with God, which the Bible describes in terms of a parent–child relationship. Just as good fathers want a close relationship with their children, so God longs to restore the intimacy that we lost at the fall, where Adam and Eve walked and talked with him.

A child growing up in a loving, healthy family expects their parents to communicate with them. Similarly, we can expect God, our loving heavenly Father, to speak to us and get involved in our world. In response, we can cultivate attentiveness to him by listening actively. This is rare in our culture; so often we are storing up our next contribution to the conversation, interrupting with a funny story or even checking our phone. We might be hearing, but we're not really listening. In order to grow in our relationship with God, we need to learn the art of active listening. In practical terms, this means not only speaking to God, but listening for his response. It means not always starting with our agenda, but asking God to show us what he wants to do in a certain situation and praying into that. And above all, it means developing an attitude of active listening and asking questions like 'Father, how do you see me?', 'How do you see this situation?', 'What do you want me to feed on today?', or 'Who do you want me to minister to?' In this way, we begin to gain God's perspective on ourselves and our circumstances as well as on people and situations around us.

This kind of listening prayer is a simple yet effective way to open up the lines of communication in our own relationship with God, and should be distinguished from prophecy where God's word is mediated through others so that it brings strength, encouragement and comfort (see 1 Corinthians 14:3). Prophecy can certainly have an important role to play in our restoration, but when we hear God for ourselves, what we know in our heads begins to penetrate our hearts and therefore our whole being. This is what leads to real transformation. A mother may tell her daughter that her daddy loves her, but when her father says directly 'I love you!' this has more impact, because the truth she knows becomes an experience.

Obedient Listening

Listening to God is also important because it enables us to follow him more closely. The root meaning of the verb 'to obey' is 'to listen' – so obedience begins with listening, and true listening leads to obedience. Obedience is important, because through it we remain connected to Christ. Jesus draws out this link when he says: 'If you keep my commands, you'll remain intimately at home in my love' (John 15:9–10, MSG).

When we listen to God in order to obey him, we are maturing in Christ. In the parable of the sower, Jesus teaches that fruitfulness depends not only on hearing, but on accepting and responding to the word of God, and immediately after this parable he says, 'Consider carefully what you hear . . . With the measure you use, it will be measured to you – and even more.

Whoever has will be given more. Whoever does not have, even what they have will be taken from them' (Mark 4:24–5). This suggests that when we listen to God's word and obey it, we receive more wisdom and insight. But if we do not listen in order to appropriate the truth we have received, we lose the little we already have. New Christians often grow very quickly because they are hungry to obey and their hearts are focused on God. On the other hand, a person who has been in the Church a long time and perhaps even had theological training may know a lot about God and the Bible, but if they have not listened in order to *obey*, they can be in danger of losing the knowledge they think they have.

A great place to begin practising obedient listening is seeking to obey the commands of Christ in scripture. Every choice we make to obey God's word is a sign of our commitment to walk with him and grow up in him, and as we obey, we receive more understanding of his ways and grow in our love for Jesus. As we choose to obey God in the area of financial giving, for instance, we start to understand, through experience, more about his provision.

Coming to a place of mature obedience is a journey, and may be likened to stages of human development – infant obedience, adolescent obedience and adult obedience, the latter being the goal. These stages of obedience do not necessarily correlate to actual infancy, adolescence or adulthood, because it is quite possible for a child to exercise a mature obedience of love and trust, or for an adult to be stuck in infant obedience. It is also possible to move backwards and forwards between these different stages, or to be in different stages on different issues in our lives. We will usually have a predominant stance, and it is worth considering what stage of obedience most fully describes the way we relate to God.

Infant obedience

Infants obey to avoid punishment. If we are stuck in this stage in our relationship with God, we may well be frightened of him, seeing him as stern, unpredictable, or even as someone whose prevailing mood is one of anger. We can also find ourselves going to extraordinary lengths to avoid owning up to sin, because we don't want to get punished.

Adolescent obedience

This is an immature obedience where we obey compliantly rather than comprehendingly. It's rather like obeying the school rules, which we probably thought were ridiculous, but which we obeyed anyway because we didn't want to get caught! The Pharisees were like this – they kept rules for rules' sake, without understanding that relationship with God is at the heart of the law. So when Jesus healed a man on the Sabbath, they were outraged; they failed to grasp that the law is not an end in itself, but provides boundaries within which relationship with God can grow and flourish. Getting stuck at this stage means we will have a legalistic approach to life and faith – we keep the rules religiously, without understanding that they are there to nurture our relationship with God and others.

Adult obedience

In the mature, adult stage of obedience, we obey because we love and trust God. By this stage we have recognised that God is a good Father – not a punisher or law enforcer – and that he is a lot wiser than we are. We can obey him because we are learning to trust his character, even if what we asks of us does not always seem to make sense. This means that we can relinquish control over our own lives and start to become partners with God, being adventurously expectant and greeting God with a childlike (not childish) attitude, saying, 'What next, Father? I want to follow you.'

This kind of obedience is the goal, for, as Paul explains in Galatians, while the law has a purpose, the ultimate destination is to become mature in our relationship with God:

> Until the time when we were mature enough to respond freely in faith to the living God, we were carefully surrounded and protected by the Mosaic law. The law was like those Greek tutors, with which you are familiar, who escort children to school and protect them from danger or distraction, making sure the children will really get to the place they set out for. But now you have arrived at your destination: By faith in Christ you are in direct relationship with God.
>
> Galatians 3:23–7, MSG

How Does God Speak?

As we learn to live with our ears inclined to God, it helps to recognise and be open to the many different ways in which he might speak to us. Scripture is the primary way, and it provides the fullest revelation of who God is and how he works. We can most effectively listen to God by regularly reading the Bible, meditating on it, memorising it and hearing it explained.

As we read the Bible, we also see other ways God speaks. God spoke to Moses 'face to face, as one speaks to a friend' (Exodus 33:11). In the New Testament, Jesus describes his disciples as 'friends' (John 15:14), so it is not surprising that God would speak to us in ordinary, direct ways, as one would speak with a friend. His voice can sometimes be audible (although this is rare), but much more commonly comes in the form of quiet, gentle impressions and thoughts, either in the context of prayer or simply through the experiences of daily life. This is the 'still, small voice' or 'gentle whisper' of God (1 Kings 19:12) which can easily be ignored or dismissed if we are not expecting God to speak to us and are not tuned in to him.

Another way God speaks to us is through our imagination. This may come by way of 'pictures' (impressions which form in our minds), dreams, or waking visions. We can also cultivate imaginative prayer in the form of visualisation exercises, meditating on scripture or simply envisioning ourselves in conversation with Jesus – more on this will be discussed later in the chapter.

God speaks to us through his creation (Psalm 19:2; Romans 1:19–20). The intimate connection between Creator God and the created world has been celebrated by figures such as the Celtic saints, St Francis of Assisi[1] and St John of the Cross.[2] Noticing and meditating on creation has sometimes been called the 'discovery of God in his creatures'[3] – mountain ranges may open our eyes to God's majesty, a thunderstorm may remind us of his power, while birds feeding in the garden can invite us to depend on God for our daily needs.

God may also speak to us through symbols, sacraments, liturgy, art and music (Ephesians 5:19), as well as through the spiritual gifts he gives to build up the Church (1 Corinthians 12:7–11). These include prophecy, tongues and their interpretation, and words of knowledge, where the Holy Spirit reveals particular things about a person or situation that unlock his work in their lives.[4] Some of these things will be familiar to us, and some less so, but as we grow in our relationship with God we can ask and expect him to open us up to new routes for us to hear his voice.

Discerning Our Father's Voice

As we listen to God, there is always going to be a significant margin for error (as indeed there is in interpreting scripture), and we need to ask whether we are listening to the voice of:

- God the Father;
- the world and our culture;
- ourselves, with all our experiences and unhealed wounds;
- Satan (who even used scripture against Jesus – see Matthew 4:6).

The best way to discern God's voice is to soak ourselves in scripture. As we familiarise ourselves with God's truth, we become like sheep who not only recognise their shepherd's voice (John 10:27), but also can distinguish it from other, deceiving voices. People trained to spot forged bank notes study genuine notes for at least a year. During this time they don't look at any counterfeit notes, so when they do see the counterfeits they spot them quickly and easily because they know the genuine article so well. As we become familiar with the genuine voice of God by soaking ourselves in biblical truth, we will be able more easily to distinguish God's voice from the voice of our culture, ourselves or Satan.

Discerning our Father's voice takes time and requires practice. Even Jesus 'grew in wisdom' (Luke 2:52). As a boy, he did not come fully furnished with all knowledge and wisdom, but had to grow in these things, just as his body had to grow up. We might speculate that Jesus also grew in his capacity to listen to God, as wisdom is always the fruit of listening.

The discipline of listening to God needs to be practised with discernment, humility, and always and only under the authority of the Christian scriptures. It also needs to be practised in the context of the Christian community. It is important to discuss with others what we think God is saying, presenting our thoughts with humility, and giving others permission graciously to challenge us. The dogmatic assertion that 'God has told me to . . .' effectively excludes the counsel of other Christians and can lead us to make unwise choices which harm ourselves or others. So we need to learn how to test our listening, recognising that we all have blind spots. This approach provides the permission and safety to have a go and to learn in the context of a loving family. We will certainly make mistakes along the way, but God is a good and patient Father, so rather than being discouraged when we get it wrong, we encourage one another to keep on practising.

How Can We Actively Listen to God?

It is worth setting time aside to engage regularly with some of the exercises outlined below, so that rather than passively waiting to hear God, we begin actively listening to him. As we do so, we will grow in our ability to hear and recognise his voice, and begin to develop a lifestyle of listening. Some people like to spend five minutes a day in listening prayer, while others prefer to set aside an extended time each week. There is no prescribed way, and over time we will settle into a rhythm that works for us and reflects our unique personalities.

As we grow in listening to God, it can be really helpful to keep a prayer journal. Many Christians are familiar with the idea of recording their spiritual journey in a diary, by noting down helpful scriptures, teaching, significant events or moments of progress. However, it is also extremely useful to record our 'God conversation', where we lay out our thoughts and feelings before God, as well as noting down what we think he is saying to us. This is not a journal of self-pitying intro-spection, where we look inwards on ourselves, but rather one of looking upwards to God and choosing to listen to what he says.

Below are some suggestions of what you might include in your prayer journal, but not all these exercises will suit every-one. If you are struggling to engage with something on this list, simply try one of the other ideas.

Note what you think God is saying

Start by writing down what you think God is saying to you – it doesn't matter if it is not totally clear at first. When children start to draw, they begin with scribbles. They might insist that they have drawn Mummy, Daddy and the cat, but often none of it is recognisable. When we start listening to God we are often at the 'scribble stage' – we will not get it all right, and cannot expect to be able to do what someone more experi-enced can do. However, God delights in our scribbles, and as we keep on practising, we will hear God's voice more and more accurately.

Have imaginative conversations with Jesus

One way to listen actively to Jesus is to imagine yourself in conversation with him in a particular situation or place. Sometimes it is helpful to bring particular memories to Jesus, asking him where he was in these things, how he feels about them, and how he sees you. As you bring a memory of some-thing that has happened into your mind's eye, look for Jesus in the picture and start a conversation with him. Speak to Jesus from your heart and wait for his answers, which may come in the form of his actions or words in your mind.

People often find that what they see and hear from Jesus surprises them and opens up new insights and perspectives, and it can be particularly helpful when we don't understand a situation or cannot discern where God was in it. The revelation we receive obviously does not change what has happened in the past, but it allows Jesus (who is outside time) to come into the past and show us the truth about how he feels about us.

If we are aware that we are processing painful or traumatic situations, it is advisable to do this exercise with the help and guidance of a Christian counsellor. If you are doing it alone and find yourself becoming distressed through reliving a traumatic event, we recommend that you slowly stop the meditation and seek support from a professional. In the moment, you can manage your breathing and focus on your surroundings. Playing a worship song or reading a Bible passage may help you to feel more grounded.

Hold on to God's promises
The Bible is full of promises which God makes to his people – find the ones that are particularly relevant to your situation and note them down. It can be helpful to personalise these promises by inserting your own name or using personal pronouns (e.g. 'God will never leave me or forsake me', based on Deuteronomy 31:6).[5] Whatever our feelings or circumstances seem to be saying, these are the deep truths we can hold on to and by regularly reading these promises, and perhaps declaring them aloud, our mind can be 'renewed' (Romans 12:2) – a process that happens by replacing negative thinking or defeatist attitudes with God's truth. In this way, our pattern of thinking is restored to be in alignment with what God says, rather than what other voices might say.

Meditate on scripture

We can use our imagination to meditate on the Bible, and this offers a good place to begin in listening prayer because it ensures that our imagination is firmly rooted in scripture. In the ancient practice of Lectio Divina (Divine Reading),[6] we read and meditate imaginatively on a simple phrase like 'The Lord is my Shepherd' (Psalm 23:1), in order to experience God's care for us more deeply. Alternatively, we can meditate on a longer passage, and engage all our senses to indwell the story. This approach was developed by St Ignatius of Loyola, who encouraged imaginative meditation on scripture as a springboard for talking with and listening to Jesus. An Ignatian meditation is included at the end of this chapter for you to try.

Record answered prayers

In scripture, God's people often remind themselves of how he has intervened to deliver them from situations, such as being enslaved in Egypt. Writing down times when God has answered prayers helps to develop this discipline of 'holy memory' by reminding us what God has done for us. Our testimonies of God's past goodness build hope and faith that he will continue to answer our prayers.

Jot down fragments of insight

Record any fragments of insight you have from God. These insights may be provoked by a very simple situation, but something starts to connect for us, and we get more understanding and wisdom. At a wedding, for instance, we might get more insight into Jesus' longing for his bride, and can note that down in our journals as a springboard for meditation and prayer.

Engage with dreams

Note down any dreams that you sense are important even if you don't understand them. These are usually the sort that stay with you vividly the next day. Often dreams show us what is really going on in our hearts, what we are uneasy about, and what needs healing. We naturally want to push difficult emotions away, but when dreams bring them to our attention, it is a good opportunity to ask God for healing in these areas. If we are confused about the meaning of a dream, we can ask God to reveal this to us. Often we have our own symbolic system which we need to learn to discern, perhaps with the help of a wise counsellor.

List any questions, doubts or fears

Write out your questions, your doubts and your fears. One of the best ways to do that is in the form of a letter to God. You might write something like this, and return to it as God brings revelation:

> Dear God, I don't understand . . . and have a question. I am really scared of . . . I am confused about . . . and I don't know what to do about it. Please could you make these things clear?

Acknowledge the desires of your heart

Use your prayer journal to name the desires of your heart. These are the things that you long for – your requests, dreams and hopes. They can include physical and emotional desires, because God is interested in the whole of us and not just the bit we regard as 'spiritual'. Often, your introspective mind will say, 'I can't write that down, because I shouldn't really want it or I can't work out how it could ever happen.' But we can present the desires of our hearts to Father God and leave them with him, because he loves to hear and fulfil what will be good for us, although this is not always the same as what we want.

Process brokenness and healing

It can be very helpful to note down any problematic patterns you notice in your own behaviour, such as disproportionate anger, drivenness, unhealthy perfectionism, or a tendency to withdraw from people. It can be wise to ask God to reveal the roots of these behaviours to you. If you become aware of any connections between wounds from your past and your current behaviour, make a note of them and ask God for his perspective and truth, then note that down too.

As part of this journey, you may need to confess wrong behaviour patterns, or extend forgiveness to people who have hurt you. It is worth recording these things in your journal as a 'marker in the sand' – a reminder that you have confessed this sin or forgiven that person, or at least begun the process.

Overcoming Blocks to Hearing God

The most effective way to grow in our ability to listen to God is to practise. We need to learn to wait on God and not to give up or get discouraged if we don't hear anything immediately, and we will also want to work at tuning out the many distractions that fill our minds and prevent us from hearing God clearly. Rather than trying to push these distracting thoughts away, it can be helpful to 'park' them by simply writing them down to be dealt with later. However, there are various things that can act as blockages to us hearing God, and these need to be recognised and dealt with in order for our spiritual ears to be opened.

Our experience of communication in our own families can impact and limit our ability to communicate with God, as we tend to project these patterns onto him. Good communication involves time, talking (including being honest about our feelings), listening and being listened to, eye contact, and appropriate touch. It is worth asking God to highlight any ways in which the communication we experienced in our family is affecting our relationship with him. We can note these things in our listening prayer journal and ask God to help us form new patterns of communication with him.

Introspection also affects our ability to listen clearly to God. This is 'the hell of self and self-consciousness',[7] where we are constantly putting ourselves under a microscope, endlessly analysing ourselves, replaying conversations, second-guessing situations, comparing ourselves with others, and trying to work out future scenarios. Introspection is characterised by painful circular thinking, an obsession with how I'm doing and how I'm feeling, and is motivated by shame, insecurity about our own identity, and a fundamental dislike of ourselves. Because introspection causes us to be *self*-centred, not *God*-centred, it affects our ability to listen to God – we listen to our fallen self and think that is truth, rather than listening to and receiving the healing words of Christ. We also find ourselves constantly asking whether this is God speaking or whether we have made it up, rather than choosing to trust in God's desire to speak to us, and accepting that it is okay to get it wrong, as long as we hold what we think we are hearing lightly. There are no 'magic prayers' to free us from introspection. The remedy is to choose to live in the present, where Jesus is (rather than replaying the past or worrying about the future), and to see things from his perspective. When we are deeply affected by introspection this can be incredibly difficult and we may only be able to manage minutes at first, but over time we can learn to practise the presence of Jesus rather than to practise the presence of ourselves.

Listening to God is fundamental to our restoration as image bearers, and it opens the door for the abundant life for which we were created. Ruth described how, for her, the practice of listening to God began with small steps, but immediately impacted her life:

At age thirty-three, I noticed that everybody at my church seemed to be hearing from God and I wasn't. I came across a book called *God Tells the Man Who Cares* by A. W. Tozer,[8] where he wrote: 'Today we must listen until our inner ears hear the words of God.' As I read those words, I had a strong impression that I should read Deuteronomy. I started reading, all the while trying very, very hard to waggle these 'inner ears' that I previously didn't know existed, so I could hear what God might be saying. I kept reading until I got to Chapter 4, where it says: 'But if . . . you seek the Lord your God, you will find him if you seek him with all your heart and with all your soul . . . For the Lord your God is a merciful God; he will not abandon or destroy you or forget the covenant with your ancestors, which he confirmed to them by oath.'

I began to cry. All my life I have been afraid of being abandoned and destroyed by God – that was my biggest fear really – and, as I cried, I heard a whisper – 'I love you.' It got a bit louder – 'Ruth, I love you.' And finally – 'I don't just love you, I like you and I like your company.' It was the still, small voice of the Father speaking directly to me through scripture, meeting my deepest need for love and restoring my true identity.

Exercise: Ignatian Meditation

Ignatius of Loyola (1491–1556) founded the Jesuit order. He discovered the power of imagination and visualisation in prayer, and taught others to use their imaginations to bring the scriptures alive. He encouraged people to imagine themselves into the text, especially stories about Jesus, and to let that lead them into an imaginative conversation with Christ. In Ignatian meditation we do not read scripture with our heads, analysing it and asking what this meant to the original readers – important though that is. Instead, we read scripture devotionally, with our hearts, meditating on it with our imaginations and asking what Jesus wants to say to us today.

MEDITATION ON MARK 4:35–41

Prepare by making yourself comfortable and stilling yourself before God. Be aware of any tension in your body and relax those areas. Notice your breathing, and perhaps consciously slow it down. Acknowledge any distracting thoughts that are coming into your mind; instead of trying to push them away (which makes them more persistent) simply note them down to be dealt with later.

The passage (taken from the NLT) begins by the side of a lake. It is evening and Jesus is talking with his friends. Imagine the scene, paying attention to the light, the weather, the temperature, and the sights, sounds and smells around you. Now place yourself in the scene. Think about what you are doing, what you are wearing, how you feel and who else is there.

As you slowly read the story, imagine yourself as part of it, and allow yourself to experience the emotions it provokes. Try not to analyse or think too much, but allow yourself to feel. The

subsidiary questions under each portion of scripture may help
you enter the scene in your imagination.

*As evening came, Jesus said to his disciples, 'Let's cross to the
other side of the lake.' So they took Jesus in the boat and started
out, leaving the crowds behind (although other boats followed).*

- Imagine yourself getting into the boat with Jesus and the
  others. Where are you and what are you doing?
- What kind of boat is it? What colour is it? What does it smell
  like? Is it comfortable or not?
- How do you feel about being in this boat?
- Can you feel the movement of the waves?
- What can you see and hear?

*But soon a fierce storm came up. High waves were breaking into the
boat, and it began to fill with water.*

- Imagine the storm: see the waves. Feel the wind and rain on
  your face. Hear the roar of the wind.
- How are you feeling now?

*Jesus was sleeping at the back of the boat with his head on a cush-
ion. The disciples woke him up, shouting, 'Teacher, don't you care
that we're going to drown?'*

- Become aware of your thoughts and feelings.
- What are you doing? What do you want to do?

*When Jesus woke up, he rebuked the wind and said to the waves, 'Silence!
Be still!' Suddenly the wind stopped, and there was a great calm.*

- Enjoy that calm. In the stillness Jesus is looking at you.
  Notice his face. Is he smiling? Is he serious? Is there anything
  you want to say to him?
- Listen for his response. What is he saying to you?

*Then he asked them, 'Why are you afraid? Do you still have no
faith?' The disciples were absolutely terrified. 'Who is this man?'
they asked each other. 'Even the wind and waves obey him!'*

- What happens next? What is Jesus doing? What is he saying
  to you personally?
- Take a moment to finish your conversation with Jesus. Take
  time to be with Jesus and talk to him.

Further Resources

Bodishbaugh, Signa, *The Journey to Wholeness in Christ* (Grand Rapids: Baker, 1997).

Huggett, Joyce, *Listening to God* (London: Hodder & Stoughton, 1986).

Payne, Leanne, *Listening Prayer* (Grand Rapids: Baker, 1994).

Rediscovering Heart Knowing

The existence of two ways of knowing has long been recognised. In the seventeenth century, René Descartes, a mathematician-philosopher, famously declared, *Cogito, ergo sum* – 'I think, therefore I am'.[1] In his maxim, we see a reliance on the rational and scientific as our route to knowledge, an approach that came to dominate Western culture. In contrast, Blaise Pascal, a mathematician and scientist of the same era, and also a devout Christian, concluded: 'The heart has its reasons which reason knows nothing of . . . We know the truth not only by the reason, but by the heart.'[2] So Pascal affirms the existence and value of intuition and experience as a way of knowing.

Many people refer to rational knowing, or knowing about, versus experiential or relational knowing. The words 'head' and 'heart' effectively capture these two different approaches. Of course, the heart can refer to more than the emotions, and in the Bible it is used to mean the very core of a person, including their thoughts and will, as well as their feelings. So, although these terms certainly have limitations, for clarity we will use the word 'head' to refer to intellectual, rational knowing, and 'heart' to denote experiential, intuitive knowing – like that of a baby who knows she is loved before she understands the words 'I love you'.

Mature Christian faith involves the ongoing integration of thinking about and experiencing God, and so both of these ways of knowing have an important place. If we settle for only a head understanding or a heart experience of God, then our knowledge of God will be incomplete. In order to have a more whole relationship with God and to live life more fully, the rational and experiential aspects of our being need to work together in harmony. In some contexts and cultures, the heart experience of God needs anchoring more strongly to the head through deeper theological understanding. This is the case in some charismatic cultures, and arguably for some in the millennial generation. But for many Western evangelicals, the heart still lags behind the head, while for others, parts of the heart are shut down, or cut off from the head in some way.

Some of this stems from an overemphasis on head knowledge in Western culture and Christianity which came about as a result of the Enlightenment. During this period, there was a new emphasis on scientific knowledge and rational thinking, and knowing became firmly located in the head. This worldview profoundly affected the Church; an emphasis on knowing God experientially gradually gave way to an emphasis on intellectual and rational knowledge of God. Scripture began to be read less devotionally and more analytically and exegetically.

Today, many are living with the legacy of a rationalistic culture and Church, where feelings and emotions are given little value. This may have been modelled in our families, who might have been unable to provide us with the 'emotional language' needed to discuss our feelings. Experiences at school often taught us to value intellectual above emotional intelligence. The society around us has historically equated showing emotion with weakness, and the Church may have absorbed society's emphasis on rational knowledge, teaching us to engage with God and the scriptures primarily with our heads rather than our hearts. As a result, many of us have inherited an intellectual and analytical approach to life and faith where, to a greater or lesser extent, we have adopted an overemphasis on reason so that our heads are nourished, but our hearts are starved.[3] This can damage our emotional and spiritual health and lead to three heart problems: being wounded, disconnected or impoverished.

Wounded Hearts

When we value the head more highly than the heart we can fail to acknowledge damage that has been done to the heart, and may attempt to deal with the heart's pain by rationalising a situation. So, when very young children suffer traumatic events, such as divorce or the death of a parent, we may say, 'Oh, he'll never remember – he's too young. It's best to pretend it never happened.' There can be an assumption that children are not affected by events early in their lives because they lack mature rationality. But the heart knows and remembers, and, prior to language development, trauma is severe because there is no language to cushion the blow. Indeed, it is precisely because children are unable to understand deeply traumatic events in their heads, such as a mother's absence through death or illness, that their hearts are most damaged. Such events leave deep wounds in our hearts, but are often unrecognised or down-played, because our society can only speak in terms of the rational. This may be compounded if churches encourage us to suppress pain and disappointment by confusing this with being brave or victorious in the face of suffering, when in fact the pain in our hearts has not been healed.

If the pain of the heart is pushed under the surface by the mind, these unhealed wounds continue to fester. They infect the way we relate to God, ourselves and others, possibly without our even realising it. So, a person who has suffered childhood abandonment may find it difficult to trust others or to trust God in the present, even if they have no memory of being left alone, and their current situation is stable and happy. It is only when heart wounds are acknowledged and healed by Jesus that the person can begin to live in a different way.

Chloe, Ruth's daughter, shares how a childhood trauma wounded her heart and continued to affect her sense of safety until it was brought to Jesus in prayer:[4]

Just before my first birthday I was rushed to hospital with a serious breathing problem. I was placed in an oxygen tent for a few days, and although my parents could sit by my bed and I could see them, they couldn't touch me. I don't have any conscious memory of this but I used to have a lot of bad dreams, all of which revolved around being unsafe.

When I was around ten years old, I had a dream so vivid that I still remember it clearly to this day. I was standing in a house, looking out through glass panes in the front door. I couldn't get out of the house. As I looked out, I could see my mum at the end of the path trying to get to me, but she couldn't. I was crying out to her, but then my dad came along and said, 'She'll be fine, just leave her.' They both walked away, leaving me staring out of the window crying.

After this dream, a Christian counsellor prayed with me using holy water, and from that day the dreams stopped and never came back.

Disconnected Hearts

Another symptom of the divide between the head and the heart is that we become disconnected or 'cut off' from our own hearts. One way this manifests itself is that we can know a truth in our head, but be unable to really believe it in our heart. So, we might sincerely believe that God loves us, but we are unable to receive and experience that love, and live as if we have to earn his love by working harder or praying more. Or, we may fully assent to the theological truth that God is gracious, but, because our hearts have not experienced this grace, we are very hard on ourselves and others when we make mistakes.

Sometimes, we believe one thing in our heads but act in a totally contradictory way. When we are trapped in addictions to things like alcohol, sex or work, our addictive compulsions completely contradict what we believe to be right in our head and this can lead to deep shame, or a sense of failure because we are not living up to our own expectations. We recognise the predicament of Romans 7:15 only too well: 'I do not understand what I do. For what I want to do I do not do, but what I hate I do.' This conflict may be part of the ongoing battle between the desires of the flesh and the desires of the Spirit (Galatians 5:17), or a result of the fact that although we have been saved by Jesus, we are still in the process of being sanctified by him. However, these behaviours can also happen because, consciously or subconsciously, we are seeking to numb the pain in our hearts.[5] If we are living in a culture where the heart is divorced from the head, we may be told simply to 'try harder' in different ways, when the issue at hand cannot be resolved solely by 'trying harder' without first addressing our heart's wounds. In order to mature fully, and experience more and more freedom, we need to appreciate and accept our full humanity, rather than try to fix heart problems with head solutions.

The extent to which our heads and hearts are disconnected varies in degree. For some, it will affect virtually every area of life and faith, whereas for others it will be limited to particular areas, possibly where there has been previous damage to the heart that needs to be healed. Our awareness of this split also varies. Some people are able to acknowledge that, while they can believe something on one level, they cannot receive that truth on another level. Others are so 'stuck in their heads' that they do not even recognise there is a different, experiential form of knowing to be entered into. In order to be whole, the head and the heart need to be connected to one another, so that our head knowledge roots itself in our hearts and becomes an experiential reality. When this happens, we are able not only to grasp the objective truth that God loves us, but also to truly and deeply 'know this love that surpasses knowledge' (Ephesians 3:19) and be transformed by it.

Impoverished Hearts

A further consequence of valuing the head above the heart is that our heart knowledge of God is impoverished, because supernatural, experiential and intuitive experiences are margin-alised. In practice, this means, first, that we may be unwilling to trust our own hearts; because we do not know what to do with intuitions and feelings, we ignore them or disregard them as ways in which God could speak to us. Second, we might be suspicious of supernatural resources such as prophecy, dreams and visions, because we have not been taught how to interpret them, or have seen them misused. Third, we may read the Bible with only our head engaged; so while we are comfortable with

Bible study and exegesis, we feel less at home with the kind of imaginative engagement with scripture that aims to lead us into an experiential encounter with Jesus, as we discussed in the previous chapter.

If we relate to God primarily with our rational and cognitive faculties (heads), this has limitations, because only half our ways of knowing are involved. But as we learn to draw on the resources of the heart, our relationship with God will be enriched.

Uniting the Head and the Heart

The head and the heart are not separate ways of functioning which are in competition with each other, but are created to coexist and complement one another. David seeks this integration of what we might call the head and the heart in Psalm 86:11, when he prays: 'Put me together, one heart and mind; then, undivided, I'll worship in joyful fear' (MSG). We would do well to echo David's prayer for a united heart and mind, as this will enable us to live life more fully, and to love God more wholeheartedly.

Embracing our feelings

Where our hearts have been underemphasised, uniting the heart and mind means learning to acknowledge, express, listen to and value our feelings and emotions. If we have been using our heads to defend ourselves against feeling pain in our hearts, allowing ourselves to *feel* may be terrifying and will take great courage. However, letting our feelings surface, in a safe context, is the first step towards allowing Jesus to heal our pain, rather than constantly pushing it away or masking it. Beginning to operate with our hearts engaged enables us to start really living.

Jesus said: 'I have come that they may have life, and have it to the full' (John 10:10); he does not offer life in all its comfort but life in all its fullness. This means experiencing the full colour spectrum of life *with Christ*, knowing him in sadness as well as in happiness, in mourning as well as in celebrating.

Relating to God holistically

Uniting the head and the heart also involves opening the whole of who we are *to God*. When we allow the head to dominate our Christian lives, this severely limits our ability to experience and hear from God. Equally, when we allow the heart to dominate the head, we lay ourselves open to uncritical and fanciful interpretations of what God might be saying. Instead, Eugene Peterson insists that God gave us 'Imagination (the heart's language) and Explanation (the head's language), designed to work in tandem'.[6] In order to experience more depth and richness in our relationship with God, both our head and our heart must be activated and alive to him.

Learning the language of the heart

When we relate to God with our heads, we use words (the language of the head), but words are limited and cannot describe everything about God and what he is doing. So, as we begin to open our heart to God, we will need to learn its unique language, which is visual rather than verbal, involving imagery, symbol, story and feelings. In short, while words are the language of the head, pictures are the language of the heart.[7]

Scripture itself is rich with imagery that speaks to the heart. Take, for example, Isaiah, who not only speaks about the future inheritance of the people of God in words and concepts, but also uses poetic imagery, encouraging us to picture the restored people of God as a beautiful city with 'battlements of rubies', 'gates of sparkling jewels' and 'walls of precious stones' (Isaiah 54:11–12). Similarly in the New Testament, Jesus uses metaphors and images to communicate profound truths. In the parables, he draws on familiar domestic and agricultural images, like a woman losing a coin (Luke 15:8–10), or a farmer sowing seed (Luke 8:5–15), to connect with people's hearts, because the heart is a very fertile soil in which profound change can take root. Likewise, Paul uses analogies to help us visualise spiritual truths and understand unseen spiritual realities by, for instance, comparing redemption to adoption, and the Christian life to a race. Scripture certainly speaks to our rational minds, but it also engages our imagination, stirring our hearts to greater love of God and understanding of his ways.

Each one of us has been given an imagination by God – the place where mental pictures are formed, that can help us understand spiritual truths, as well as evoking powerful emotions.[8] As we rediscover the heart language of imagination, this provides a way of listening to what God is saying to our hearts, relating to him 'deep to deep' (Psalm 42:7), and opening ourselves to his restoration.

Exercising our Imagination

God often speaks directly to our imagination, through 'pictures', dreams or waking visions, and these gifts can offer insight into what is really in our own hearts, or help us to glimpse God's perspective on people and situations. Pictures may form in our minds, particularly in times of prayer, and are often more like a fleeting impression than a picture in a frame or on a film. However, these impressions can be developed as we ask Jesus questions about what we see: 'What is this?', 'What does it mean?' and 'Show me more', for example. This kind of imaginative revelation is an important tool for restoration, for two reasons. First, it acts as a window into the heart, and can pinpoint areas that need to be healed. Second, as God speaks his truth into our hearts, often in pictorial form, this replaces the untrue, negative images we have of ourselves. We can use any pictures, dreams or visions we receive as part of our prayer-ful conversation with God.

We can also more consciously exercise our imaginations as a tool for restoration. Sometimes we shy away from this, believing that images and pictures are only valid when they come in the form of supernatural revelation. But God has given each of us an imagination which we can proactively exercise to engage with him. Imaginative prayer is one way of doing this. This includes imaginative meditation on scripture, which provides a way of connecting with and encountering God, and prayer visualisation exercises (like those included at the end of this chapter), which can be used to ask God to show us what is in our hearts that needs healing, and to bring these issues to him. These kinds of *imaginative* encounters with God are not *imaginary* encounters with God; on the contrary, they can facilitate a real experience of God which is accessed through the heart language of imagination.

Another way we can use our imagination is to connect with the cross. We are often encouraged to 'lay our burdens at the foot of the cross' or to 'give it to Jesus on the cross', and these rather abstract concepts can be grounded as we picture ourselves giving certain situations, actions or memories to Jesus on the cross, then waiting and watching to see what he does with them. One idea is to imagine yourself standing at the foot of the hill of Calvary holding a box, inside which are hurts, pains and mess from your past. Then start climbing up a path towards the top of the hill and stop at the cross. Imagine yourself standing, sitting or kneeling there, then open your box and see what Jesus does with the contents. As we do this our imagination connects us with a spiritual reality, and we can receive God's perspective and healing.[9]

We can also use our imagination to help us 'practise the presence of God'.[10] This is about focusing on God in the present moment, and is particularly associated with the French Carmelite monk Brother Lawrence (1611–91), who encouraged attentiveness to God in every circumstance and action of the day. We can use the imagination to place ourselves with Christ, perhaps spending time with him in a 'special place' in our imagination. As we imagine Jesus with us, this provides us with an important tool to visualise and experience unseen, spiritual realities.

Dealing with overanalysis

In order to exercise our imagination and encourage the heart to listen to God, we may need to 'switch off' the analytical part of our brain for a few seconds, because it has a tendency to dominate, bully and discard as nonsense the workings of the heart, telling us that we have made it all up. We are often tempted to ignore or push away revelation we are receiving through our imagination, and so, to counteract this, it is helpful to write down what we feel God is saying and then test it against the Bible and see if it results in good fruit in our lives. Over time, we will learn to sift the contents of our hearts and minds and to discern what is from God and what is from ourselves.

Dealing with ungodly images

Many Christians fear using their imaginations because of the presence of ungodly images. These often cover up wounds that contain a lie, and this is precisely where God wants to apply his healing and truth. For example, a person who has suffered childhood abandonment (wound) may feel unloved (lie). Their longing to belong and be loved may well lead to unhealthy romantic or sexual fantasy, which comes in many forms, including pornography. The real issue is the wound in their heart, and when this is healed, the fantasy starts to die because it has nothing to feed on.

Ungodly images also come from the influences which surround us. Our imagination is rather like a blank screen onto which the heart projects images – either good or evil. The images that fill our imaginations depend on what we have experienced and seen. Jesus said, 'The eye is the lamp of the body. If your eyes are healthy, your whole body will be full of light. But if your eyes are unhealthy, your whole body will be full of darkness' (Matthew 6:22–3). Because of what we have been exposed to or have chosen to look at, we all have rubbish stored in our hearts, and at times this gets projected onto the screen of our imagination.

It is particularly disturbing that these ungodly images often come up when we try to get still and listen to God or worship him, which is one reason why some people find it painful to be alone with God. Similarly, they may pop up when we are in holy, loving relationships. Ashamed and embarrassed of our diseased desires and images, we shove them back into the depths of our hearts, slam the lid shut, and forget about them until next time. But God actually wants to bring these images up, not to taunt us, but so that we can give them to him and be free of them. He wants to cleanse our imaginations so that they can be used for holy purposes. Unholy images cannot just be 'done away with'; they need to be replaced by healthy ones. The best way to deal with them is not by trying to fight them, but by giving them to Jesus and allowing him to exchange them for life-giving pictures – things that are true, noble, right, pure, lovely, admirable, excellent and praiseworthy (Philippians 4:8). This is *how* we 'take captive every thought to make it obedient to Christ' (2 Corinthians 10:5). An exercise to help cleanse your imagination from any ungodly images is provided at the end of this chapter.

Many Christians distrust their own imagination, or regard any use of the imagination as dubious, perhaps associating it with New Age practices or popular psychology. Alternatively, our imaginations may be dormant through an excessive dependence on logic, or diseased through exposure to the degraded use of imagination which our culture promotes. Certainly, our imaginations can be used for evil (as can our rational thinking), but God does not want us to fear or ignore our imagination, or shut it down on this basis. To do so is rather like refusing to use the internet because it hosts harmful material. Instead, as we have seen in this chapter, we are invited to use our imagination as a means to encounter God, rather than for fantasy or wishful thinking. It is an essential tool for hearing from God, receiving his truth, and practising his presence. As our hearts begin to function in unity with our heads we become more whole, and a rich new world opens up to us, in which we can live life more fully, know God more richly, and therefore bear the image of God a little more closely.

One of Ruth's former clients details how a series of traumatic events revealed a deep division between her head and heart, and how imaginative encounters with Jesus facilitated her emotional healing.

Living almost entirely 'in my head' generally worked well until it was significantly challenged by a traumatic experience of loss over a two-year period. After the first loss, that of my grandmother's death, my response to the feelings of grief was to rationalise them away. My thinking was: 'she was very old; she had a good life; at least she's not suffering any more; she wouldn't want me to be sad; everyone must die sometime' and so on. Yes, of course I missed her, but I'd tell myself, 'that's normal; I must be positive and cheerful.' The pain of the loss was largely prevented from surfacing by these thoughts. The 'head' remained firmly in the position of filtering any feelings of grief.

Over the next two years I experienced more significant losses and the emotional pain became overwhelming. Rational understanding could no longer overcome it. I became sick with grief – broken, vulnerable and tearful.

My journey to recovery and healing was eventually found in Jesus by prayerful counselling facilitated by Ruth. On one occasion as we prayed, I saw a house with a smart front door with all the rooms on the left-hand side. As I exercised my imagination, I spent time in the sitting room with Jesus, listening to his version of my story. In that place I went through some forgiving, received some healing for my wounds, and soaked in his love. This felt reasonably comfortable. The rooms on the left-hand side of the house were familiar. Jesus was meeting me in them and was speaking to me gently in ways which helped my 'head' understand my situation. Although I was feeling difficult emotions and pain, Jesus spoke to me rationally and logically about my situation with loving concern.

Several months later, I felt Jesus encouraging me to go upstairs with him in my symbolic house. As I did, I was amazed to find that the house had a whole other side to it. There were rooms on the right-hand side, rooms I didn't know existed, let alone had ever been in before. The front door was now in the centre of the house and the house was much bigger than I had ever previously thought. Jesus began to show me parts of myself that I didn't even know existed before. These parts were my heart. I had a heart full of things I'd never acknowledged – imagination, feelings and meaningful experiences I'd had in my life. I started to realise these things of my heart were part of me too, and my identity was in both. The 'head' and the 'heart' were becoming united.

Following that revelation, I started to explore the rooms on the right-hand side of the house. On occasions this would take the form of me taking a period of time, twenty minutes or so, simply lying down on my bed doing nothing else except staying in a place of 'feeling' – whatever the current emotion was I let it surface and stay out in play. No censorship, no suppression with logical thought, no limitation.

I have subsequently lived with both head and heart better connected, working in greater unity. No longer does my 'head' have the final say. I've got quicker at letting feelings in a situation be expressed, and am more able to show empathy, understanding and love to others. My identity is truer, fuller, stronger and more alive. I'm experiencing exactly what Jesus has promised: life in its fullness.

Exercise: Prayer Visualisations

Prayer visualisations help us to use our imagination in prayer and listen to God. There is no right or wrong way to do them, and the following ideas are just guidelines. As you do these exercises, you may not 'see' anything in your imagination – don't worry and don't try to force it. Alternatively, you may not understand what you are seeing, so write down whatever comes to your mind and continue to ask God to show you what it means. When you have finished any of these exercises, don't forget to jot down the heart of your experiences in your prayer journal.

The first two exercises offer a way of connecting with our own heart, as well as listening to God with our imagination. Some people like The Garden of the Heart, while some find The House more helpful. Try both, or choose one and weave it into your times with God over the next few weeks, perhaps spending five minutes each day with him in the place you have chosen.

The third exercise is specifically intended to enable us to bring any unhelpful images to God, so that we can receive his cleansing, rather than trying to push them aside or fight them in our own strength.

THE GARDEN OF THE HEART

Jesus referred to his Father as 'the gardener' (John 15:1) who skilfully prunes and tends us so that we grow well. In the sixteenth century, Teresa of Ávila also used garden imagery to symbolise the soul.[11] In this visualisation exercise, taken from Bodishbaugh's *The Journey to Wholeness in Christ*, we ask God to show us our heart as a garden, and then invite him to show us what is there, point out any areas he wants to heal, and begin the process of restoration.

Prayerfully and quietly, not striving, allow Jesus to show you whatever is in your garden. Allow time to look around, noticing everything that is there. Then ask him to show you if any weeds of fear are growing in the garden, anything that does not belong. If you find any, pluck them up and name each one. Then hand them to Jesus and watch carefully to see what he does with them.

Some weeds may be as large as trees with deep roots. You will need Jesus' assistance in pulling these out of the ground. Some weeds may be disguised and you will need his assistance to see them. It is important to give him permission to show you anything he knows you are ready to discover. As you watch what Jesus does with your surrendered fears, you may see him transform them into something useful or beautiful. Some fears must be destroyed. All this imagery is symbolic of something important happening in your spiritual growth.[12]

THE HOUSE

In his farewell discourse, Jesus uses the powerful imagery of being 'at home' with God. In John 14:2, he assures his disciples that 'in my Father's house are many rooms'; then, in John 15:9–10, he encourages them to make themselves at home in his love. In this imaginative exercise, we visualise a room in God's house, and ask God to show us what he is doing and wants to do in us, and what he has got in the room he is preparing for us as we make ourselves at home in his love.

Begin by imagining yourself at the driveway up to God's mansion. It doesn't matter what state you are in – you may be muddy, cut and bruised, or in a bad mood. Come as a child, knowing that God is an excellent Father. As you approach the house, you come to a big fountain and the drive goes round it.

There may be other people there as well. When you are ready you can go up the steps to the front door of the mansion, and at the top of the steps there will be some servants waiting. At this point you have a choice. You can either have a look around the mansion to get your bearings before you go to your room, or you can go straight to your room.

Your room will have your name above the door and one of the servants will take you in. At some stage, if Jesus is not already in your room, invite him in so that you can begin to talk to each other. Look around and see what is in your particular room and what God has prepared for you. Talk to him about it. Learn to listen to him too. Is there anything he has to show you or to say about this room?

If you are really stuck, just talk to God the Father and tell him what you would like in your room (rather like a child telling a parent what they would like for their birthday or for Christmas).

An alternative way of doing this exercise is to imagine a whole house, which represents your whole life, with different rooms symbolising different parts of your life and heart. Imagine taking Jesus into your house and see which rooms he wants to explore. Ask him what he wants to show you in each of these rooms, then stay with the image and ask him what he wants to do about what he is showing you.

CLEANSING THE IMAGINATION

This exercise helps us to deal with ungodly images (perhaps sexual, violent or traumatic) and can be done as they pop into the mind or in a more proactive way, as described here. It can be done alone or with a group. If the latter, a safe place should be created by encouraging everyone to keep their eyes closed.

- Ask God to bring up all the unclean images. They may come into the conscious mind as snapshots, or more like reels of film, but, as they appear, you could put your hand on your forehead and imagine pulling them up and out, and handing them to Jesus. This is simply a physical gesture to symbolise a spiritual transaction.
- Watch to see what Jesus does with them.
- When you have finished, ask Jesus to give you new images and wait for them to appear.
- Pray that the Holy Spirit would cleanse, wash and renew your imaginative faculties, perhaps using holy water to symbolise this cleansing.

Further Resources

Lees, S., *Will the Real Me Please Stand Up* (London: Hodder & Stoughton, 1997).

On how Western thinking has marginalised and neglected the heart
Stern, Karl, *The Flight from Woman* (St Paul: Paragon, 1985).
Tournier, Paul, *The Gift of Feeling* (London: SCM, 1981).

On using the godly imagination
Payne, Leanne, *The Healing Presence* (Eastbourne: Kingsway, 2009), Part III, 'Imagery and Symbol'.
Peterson, Eugene, *Under The Unpredictable Plant* (Grand Rapids: Eerdmans, 1992), pp. 167–72.

6

Practising Confession

We have already seen that while we were created as God's image bearers, our sin has obscured that image in us. Sin diminishes us and damages our relationships with God and others. It is a universal problem – Paul says that 'all have sinned and fall short of the glory of God' (Romans 3:23). It is also a pervasive problem: the Anglican prayer of confession recognises that sin comes from our 'ignorance', our 'weakness' and 'our own deliberate fault'. Because of this, we must find a way to deal with our sin problem on an ongoing basis. God's solution is confession, which involves taking responsibility for our sins before God and saying sorry to him.

Confession is one of the most basic tools of restoration, because it fundamentally deals with the chasm between ourselves and God created by the fall, and reconnects us to our Creator. However, it takes courage to confess sin, and is often uncomfortable. Like swallowing medicine, which is often unpleasant but brings us back to health, God offers us the medicine of confession and forgiveness to heal and free us from the effect of sin in our lives. As a result, we begin to taste 'true love', because forgiveness enables us to know and experience God's abundant and unconditional love in our hearts.

Avoiding Confession

Confession is God's provision for dealing with sin, but several things can hold us back. First, the concept and language of sin is unpopular not only outside the Church, but often within it too. As a result, it may feel uncomfortable to acknowledge that we have been responsible for putting a barrier between ourselves and God. Or we may worry that we will not be able to let go of our sins and live differently. True confession leads to repentance (turning around), which is challenging, because we often don't know how to, or don't want to, change. Sinful patterns of behaviour become so familiar that they provide us with comfort and security, albeit a false comfort and security which falls far short of the true peace God intends for us. So we can end up being in prison with the door open, but too scared to leave; we settle for the security of the prison, when confession offers us a way out of it for good.

In addition, we are often reticent to confess our sins because we fear being punished, shamed, humiliated, rejected, disliked, exposed, judged or criticised. These fearful reactions may stem from past experiences when our confessions have been met with judgement rather than grace, perhaps leaving us feeling exposed and alone. Sadly, even within our families and churches, our confessions are not always received with grace and mercy. God, on the other hand, always meets our confession with unconditional love and acceptance (Romans 8:1). After committing adultery with Bathsheba, David prayed with humility and confidence: 'a broken and contrite heart, O God, you will not despise' (Psalm 51:17). Whatever our human experiences have been, we do not need to fear disgrace or rejection from God, but can trust in his unfailing love and mercy, and his promise and power to forgive.

Approaching God with Confidence

As we come to God to confess our sins, it is important to remember that we come as his beloved sons and daughters (John 1:12; Galatians 4:7). The fact that we have sinned does not change this core identity. God's overwhelming love for us is not conditional on our behaviour, and so it is not changed by our sin. As you confess wrongdoing, it may help to visualise yourself coming to God as a royal son or daughter. Alternatively, you might like to reflect on your identity (who you are) in Christ,[1] and remember this is not somehow wiped away by your sin. One way to do this is to read chapters 1 to 3 of Ephesians, inserting your own name into the verses, to help you appreciate some of the things Jesus has done for you and understand how he sees you. When we grasp who we are in Christ, we can approach God with confidence, hope and expectation, rather than grovelling our way into his presence, believing that we are fundamentally an awful person, unworthy of love.

Ruth described how she saw one client restore her relationship with God after a long period of alienation from him:

> I was praying with someone who had given up on God altogether and hadn't talked to him for a whole year. She just confessed that, and a few other things that went with it, and then she gasped: 'I can't believe it. I haven't got to start from scratch again – he has put me back exactly where I was. I haven't lost anything – I am still loved.'

The wonderful truth is that God doesn't want to punish us for our sinful behaviour, but instead welcomes us back to intimacy with open arms.

Making a Diagnosis

The process of confession begins with naming the problem. This means that we need to accept responsibility for our own sin, and be specific in describing it. In order to do this, we must understand two important distinctions.

Sins and wounds

One of the keys to naming our sin is to recognise the difference between our wounds (things which have been done to us) and our sins (things done by us). Take the example of a camellia bush. If it comes into bud very early because it is in a sheltered place, beautiful buds appear and start to open, but then if the frost comes, all the edges start to go brown, the flowers are spoilt and the beauty of the camellia is marred. The camellia, of course, is not responsible for the fact that it has been damaged – the frost is! We easily get confused about the source of damage in our own lives, and feel responsible for, or even guilty about, things that others have done to us. Of course, we may mourn over our wounds, but just as the camellia is not responsible for the damage done to it, we are not responsible for our wounds, and do not need to confess the damage caused by other people.

That said, when we have been wounded by others, we often sin in response. Our sinful reactions might include lashing out at the person who has hurt us, shutting them out, or gossiping about them. At a deeper level, we may believe the lies that have been spoken against us, or allow fear, resentment or self-hatred to take root within. Talking to God about our wounds can help us begin sifting through where we have been sinned against and where we have sinned as a result, so that we can deal with the damage appropriately. Confession is the prescription for our own sin; forgiveness is the prescription for the wounds caused to us by others. Knowing the difference between the two is an important starting place, and if we simply ask the Holy Spirit, he is more than willing to show us which is which.

True and false guilt

A second distinction we must make is between true and false guilt. False guilt is when we feel guilty about someone else's pain, even though it is not our fault. For instance, someone may feel sad when a romantic relationship ends, but choosing to end a relationship, in and of itself, is not a wrong action, and not one about which we should feel guilty. When we are seeking to discern the difference between true and false guilt, a helpful guide is to ask ourselves whether we are experiencing a sense of conviction or condemnation. To do this, we need to ask God the question, 'Have I sinned?' If we have, there will be a quick and specific answer from the Holy Spirit. This is conviction, which leads to confession and allows us to exchange our feelings of true guilt for peace in the knowledge that we've been forgiven. Condemnation, on the other hand, comes from the accuser,[2] and may manifest as persistent feelings of shame, regret, fear or unworthiness that won't go away. This is false guilt, and no amount of confession will lift it. In this case we need to simply recognise that this is not coming from God, to reject these thoughts, and to remind ourselves often of the truth that 'there is now no condemnation for those who are in Christ Jesus' (Romans 8:1). Often, we experience a mixture of true and false guilt, and need to be able to disentangle the two so that we can deal with each appropriately.

I was part of the ministry team at a conference, and found myself in conversation with a well-known Christian leader. I felt a bit intimidated at meeting somebody famous, and during our conversation I said something that was not quite true, in order to impress him.

Back home, I felt God say: 'Do you remember what you did when you were talking to that person?' So I decided to write to him and own up, but I was scared about what he might think of me. In my worst moments, I even thought, 'That's it. I will never be on that prayer team again and I will lose all those friends.' I was struggling partly with a sense of false guilt, but there was also some specific sin that needed to be confessed.

As I confessed, in my mind's eye I saw Jesus coming along, taking this cross off my back and carrying it himself. I began to get my perspective right by seeing what Jesus was doing: taking the burden and weight of my sin.

I then wrote to the person in question, confessing my specific sin. He replied, saying: 'Of course you are forgiven. This is no big deal. Having sorted that out, let's get on with the real business of living – when you and your husband come to the States, do come and visit us.' It was one of the most healing letters I had ever received! He knew the sinful thing that I had done, but he forgave it and still wanted to know me.

God's Prescription for Health: Confession

Having named and owned the specific ways in which we have sinned, rather than opting to beat ourselves up, sort ourselves out or hide from God, we must choose to give our sin to Jesus and let him deal with it.

Confession should always centre on the cross, otherwise what is prescribed will be 'less than', ineffective, or even harmful. Secular therapies, and even many forms of 'Christian counselling', help people to understand or diagnose their problems, but bypass the cross in the search for a solution. In contrast, the biblical prescription for our sin problem is confession at the cross of Christ. It is here that Jesus takes our sins, sorrows and wounds onto himself, and offers us forgiveness, freedom and reconciliation with God in exchange (Isaiah 53:4–6). Confession is ultimately an act of faith in this deep mystery of salvation: we confess our sins, simply trusting that Christ's death provides the means of forgiveness, cleansing and restoration.

When we become a Christian and accept Jesus as our Saviour, the big sin of our rebellion against God is forgiven and settled at the cross, and our broken relationship with God is restored. This is the kind of forgiveness Jesus referred to in John 3:16 when he said that 'Anyone who trusts in him is acquitted' (MSG). However, we also need to ask God to forgive us for specific sins, committed both in the past and in the present, and this requires the kind of ongoing confession that the apostle John encouraged us to practise in confident assurance of God's forgiveness: 'If we confess our sins – make a clean breast of them – he won't let us down; he'll be true to himself. He'll forgive our sins and purge us of all wrongdoing' (1 John 1:9, MSG).

Spring cleaning

When we first begin to follow Jesus we often have sin piled up from the past, and so our lives need a major spring clean. It is a good suggestion to review our past with Jesus, and confess anything we are reminded of. Leanne Payne, who was a prominent teacher in healing prayer ministry, recommended dividing our lives into portions – childhood, school years, college years, our twenties, thirties, and so on – and telling God about any way in which we remember sinning or reacting wrongly to someone sinning against us.[3] We then receive God's forgiveness for each occasion. Sometimes, this process will prompt us to write letters or speak to people face to face to confess sin, but much of it will be dealt with in private, perhaps with the help of another trusted person. Being systematic in this way helps us to give our lives a thorough spring clean.[4]

Reviewing our past may reveal hidden sins that need to be brought into the light of God's love. Many of us have a sort of 'log-jam' of secrets that we don't know what to do with. We can be tempted to hide them under the carpet and hope they will disappear, but Proverbs 28:13 reminds us: 'You can't white-wash your sins and get by with it; you find mercy by admitting and leaving them' (MSG).

Trying to ignore our sins and pretending we are good enough for God is a bit like stuffing all our sins in a cupboard and hoping they'll go away. We certainly hope that nobody else will open the door and see our 'messy cupboard'. In doing this, we are treating Jesus like a visitor, when instead, he wants to make himself at home within us and clean up our lives. Allowing Jesus to spring clean our lives involves opening up our 'messy cupboards' with him and looking inside together, instead of letting the mess stay hidden, where it will inevitably fester and be discovered later. This process can feel overwhelming, but the important thing is to be brave enough to open the cupboard and make a start somewhere. As we do so, God will work in us to bring more and more cleansing, restoration and freedom to our lives. John the Baptist describes God's 'spring cleaning service' like this:

[He] will ignite the kingdom life within you, a fire within you,
the Holy Spirit within you, changing you from the inside out.
He's going to clean house – make a clean sweep of your lives.
He'll place everything true in its proper place before God;
everything false he'll put out with the trash to be burned.

Matthew 3:11–12, MSG

Regular cleaning

As well as having a major spring clean, our lives also require
regular cleaning to deal with everyday mess. Jesus teaches us to
pray, 'Forgive us our sins, as we have forgiven those who sin
against us. And don't let us yield to temptation, but rescue us
from the evil one' (Matthew 6:12, NLT). He is offering us a
pattern of regularly asking for forgiveness from sins, forgiving
others, and seeking deliverance from temptation. Regular
cleaning means confessing the daily sins of omission (good
things we have failed to do) and commission (bad things we
have done) as soon as we become aware of them. It can be
tempting to say to ourselves, 'I will deal with that later, when I
have time to sit down and sort it out properly,' but the truth is
we could have confessed it in the time we have taken to think
about it.

As we get into the habit of regular confession, we will find
ourselves confessing some common, recurring sins. These
differ for each of us, but include things like self-reliance, lack
of trust in God, criticism, cynicism, self-hatred and material-
ism. Just as we clean our teeth daily, so regular, daily confession
of these and other sins keeps us clean and healthy and protects
our relationship with God.

A context for confession

Often, we will confess our sins directly to God, but there are times when we also need to confess our sins to other believers. The New Testament urges us to 'make this your common practice: confess your sins to each other and pray for each other so that you can live together whole and healed' (James 5:16, MSG). We confess our sins to God so that we may be forgiven, but sometimes it is necessary to confess our sins to somebody else so that we may be healed. Protestants have often neglected this aspect of confession, but there is great strength in it, because it punctures our pride and diminishes the power our sins have over us.

Confessing our sins to one another can only happen in a safe and confidential environment, whether with a prayer partner, a small group or a counsellor. It requires vulnerability, but is incredibly precious, because it leads us into a deeper experience of grace, ultimately from God, but also from one another and even from ourselves.[5] We are allowing ourselves to be fully known and still loved, first by Father God, second by a small group of trusted brothers or sisters in Christ, and third by ourselves, as we own our weaknesses before others in an attitude of self-acceptance.

God's Prescription for Health: Receiving Forgiveness

As we confess our sins, God's forgiveness is assured, but as with any gift, we need to actively receive it, and three habits can help us here.

Faith

In order to receive forgiveness, we must place our faith in God's character and his desire to forgive, and in the power of Jesus' death on the cross as the means of forgiveness.[6] We can develop this trust by memorising, and meditating and leaning on biblical promises about God's forgiveness, such as:

- 1 John 1:9: 'If we admit our sins – simply come clean about them – he won't let us down; he'll be true to himself. He'll forgive our sins and purge us of all wrongdoing' (MSG).
- Isaiah 1:18: '"Come now, let us settle the matter," says the Lord. "Though your sins are like scarlet, they shall be as white as snow; though they are red as crimson, they shall be like wool."'
- Psalm 32:5: 'Then I acknowledged my sin to you and did not cover up my iniquity. I said, "I will confess my transgressions to the LORD." And you forgave the guilt of my sin.'
- Psalm 66:18–20: 'If I had cherished sin in my heart, the Lord would not have listened; but God has surely listened and has heard my prayer. Praise be to God, who has not rejected my prayer or withheld his love from me!'

It can be tempting to think that some sins, such as adultery or murder, are too big to be forgiven and that we will never be free of the guilt and shame of them, but from God's perspective, sin is sin. When we think that it is impossible for us to be forgiven, this is really unbelief – it is based on a wrong view of God, which can often be a projection of the way our parents treated us. Satan also likes to deceive us into believing that we are trapped and that there is no way out. The truth is that God has provided a way out of sin and into life through Jesus' death, so while acknowledging our sin and guilt, we confess our sins focusing on and trusting in the hope of total cleansing that Jesus offers.

Humility

We receive God's gift of forgiveness by gratefully accepting it, and trusting his judgement above our own. If we say, 'I can never forgive myself,' this is actually pride, because we are saying that we are not going to accept the mercy and the kindness that Jesus is offering. Deep down, we consider ourselves a better judge than God, and decide to stay guilty, ultimately rejecting Jesus' death for us. Holding on to sin shows ingratitude and pride, whereas gratefully receiving forgiveness shows humility.

Choice

When we confess our sins, we often do not *feel* forgiven. Feelings swing all over the place, and the antidote to feelings that tell us we are not forgiven is to root our emotions in Christ and his truth, perhaps using the scriptures above. To receive God's forgiveness we need to choose to believe we are forgiven, even when we do not feel it.

Receiving God's forgiveness does not change our past, but it releases us from the effects of the past on the present. We come out from under God's judgement to receive his mercy, grace and redemptive love, so that our relationship with him is wholly restored, and we reflect his image a little more closely. Owning up to our sins and confessing them in the first place is difficult, and deeply counter-cultural. Instead of doing things the way the world does them (pushing our sin under the carpet and getting on with life) we are doing things God's way (walking in his light and in his healing power). This takes courage, but it enables us to find the true freedom and peace which Jesus promised: 'Peace I leave with you; my peace I give you. I do not give to you as the world gives. Do not let your hearts be troubled and do not be afraid' (John 14:27).

Exercise: Confession of Sin

Confession can take place with a Christian friend, prayer partner or small prayer group, or in a prayer ministry situation. The person hearing the confession does not necessarily need to be an ordained priest, because all believers are part of God's 'holy priesthood' (1 Peter 2:5–9), and in a well-functioning Christian community each of us will make and hear confessions at different times. Above all, the person must be trustworthy and faithful, and a safe environment should be created by honouring confidentiality.[7] The exercise below provides a basic framework for confession.

CONFESS SIN

Avoid rehearsing all the details and emotions of a situation at this point. Instead, pray a short prayer in which you confess specific sin and say sorry to God. If you are the person hearing the confession, encourage the other to be succinct and specific, and, most importantly of all, to actually say sorry.

HEAR CHRIST'S FORGIVENESS

Using the authority given by Jesus, your prayer partner can pronounce Jesus' forgiveness to you, perhaps using words like: 'In the name of Jesus, you are forgiven the sin of . . .'

The person pronouncing forgiveness is not doing the forgiving, but rather they announce, confirm and remind you that Jesus has forgiven you.

It is often helpful to picture releasing our sins to Jesus on the cross, and then to ask Jesus to show us what he is doing with them. This helps us to 'see' with the eyes of our heart the truth of what it means for God to 'cleanse us from all unrighteousness' (1 John 1:9, NRSVA). If you are hearing a confession, facilitate this by encouraging the person to imagine giving their sins to Jesus on the cross and asking them what he might be showing them. This can also be done in a group setting, with each individual engaging privately with God.

RECEIVE FORGIVENESS

Actively receive God's forgiveness by faith. If you are ministering to someone else, or to a group, encourage them to receive this forgiveness, perhaps by simply saying, 'Receive God's forgiveness.' Pray for them to be filled up with Jesus' love, and invite them to receive this love. It can be helpful to use physical elements such as oil[8] or holy water[9] to make the sign of the cross as a symbol of the cleansing they are receiving.

Further Resources

Bonhoeffer, Dietrich, *Life Together* (London: SCM, 1954).
Van der Hart, Will, and Waller, Rob, *The Guilt Book: A Path to Grace and Freedom* (London: InterVarsity Press, 2014).

Forgiving Others

Forgiving others is the natural counterpart to receiving the forgiveness of God for ourselves, and is another vital key to the restoration of God's image in us. In the Lord's Prayer, Jesus teaches us to pray, 'Our Father in heaven . . . Keep us forgiven with you and forgiving others' (Matthew 6:12, MSG). There is a clear connection between being forgiven and forgiving others – or to put it another way, forgiven people *forgive* people.

On one occasion, Peter asks Jesus, 'Lord, how many times shall I forgive my brother or sister who sins against me? Up to seven times?' The Jewish rabbis taught that you should forgive a person three times, so he must have thought he was the epitome of grace. But Jesus responds by saying, 'I tell you, not seven times, but seventy-seven times' (Matthew 18:21–22). He is effectively saying, 'Keep on forgiving, and stop keeping count.' Then, in the parable of the unmerciful servant which follows this exchange (Matthew 18:21–35), Jesus calls us to offer total and unlimited forgiveness to others, because this is how we have been treated by God. Jesus clearly teaches that as recipients of God's grace, the forgiven are under an obligation to forgive.

Moreover, when we begin to realise how much we have been forgiven by God, and how much this forgiveness cost him, it becomes easier to forgive others who have hurt us, and to recognise them as damaged human beings like ourselves. A growing appreciation and experience of God's mercy and kindness *towards* us calls forth mercy *within* us. So forgiving others is not about denying, forgetting, excusing or minimising their offences against us, but about offering them the same undeserved gift that we have received from God.

However, the amazing outcome is that forgiveness also sets us free! The New Testament uses two Greek verbs for forgiveness: *charizomai*, derived from *charis* (meaning 'grace'), and *aphiemi* which means 'to release'.[1] To forgive is to extend grace, and release a person from the debt they owe us; and as we forgive, we too are released. We begin to experience healing for our wounds, and freedom from the person who has hurt us. In *The Book of Forgiving*, Desmond and Mpho Tutu summarise these extraordinary dynamics of forgiveness:

> The invitation to forgive is not an invitation to forget. Nor is it an invitation to claim that an injury is less hurtful than it really is. Nor is it a request to paper over a fissure in a relationship, to say 'it's okay' when it's not. It's not okay to be abused. It's not okay to be violated. It's not okay to be betrayed. The invitation to forgive is an invitation to find healing and peace.[2]

Avoiding Forgiveness

To a greater or lesser extent, we have all experienced rejection, betrayal, disappointment, deception, injustice, ingratitude and misunderstanding – and it hurts! Sometimes we are hurt unavoidably or unintentionally, yet this still causes us pain. At other times, we are hurt deliberately – anything from being excluded or criticised to a serious crime being committed against us. Whatever the nature of our hurts, God's strategy for dealing with them is the same: forgiveness. However, because it is so difficult to face up to the pain that has been caused, we often find alternative ways of dealing with it. We might, for instance:

Whitewash sin

We might overlook sins against us, even though deep down we know that damage has been caused. Often people say things like, 'My parents did the best they could. I had everything I needed. I had a good home, and a good education.' All these things may be true, but they can be used to whitewash the hurt or neglect we may have experienced in our families. Maybe we were left wanting in terms of affirmation, inclusion, unconditional love or acceptance. If we come from a Christian family and a 'reasonable' home, it can be particularly difficult to acknowledge that family members have hurt us.

Make excuses

We often make excuses for people when we are trying to understand what happened, reasoning that they had a difficult childhood, were acting out of their own hurt, or were just having a bad day. Again, there may be truth to these statements, but they do not excuse the offence or minimise the pain. We must recognise sin as sin: whatever the reasons for a person's behaviour towards us, there is still sin that has caused damage, and that has to be dealt with.

Switch responsibility

We may respond to pain by thinking we were somehow at fault or have caused the situation. While in some cases we may be partly responsible for the pain that has been caused, we also need to recognise where we have been sinned against in order to forgive. A heightened sense of guilt is often linked to perfectionism (the idolatry of the ideal) and is compounded when the enemy joins in and brings condemnation.

Build a defensive wall

We sometimes build a defensive wall to avoid owning and feeling the depth of our pain. We simply blank the pain out, suppressing it by pretending it doesn't hurt. In more extreme cases, we totally bury bad memories, but tend to bury the good ones with them, so we can 'lose' whole chunks of our lives. Alternatively, we might cover our pain with humour and party pieces. In this case, we become the group clown, but it is very hard for people to penetrate our defensive wall and get to know the real us.

Anaesthetise pain

We can also anaesthetise pain with addictions that might involve harmful substances or behaviours like alcohol, drugs or pornography, but can also manifest as quite ordinary things, such as food, shopping, work or ministry. These things become addictive when we use them as a means of comfort, but can be quite hard to spot, especially if the activity is not inherently wrong. In addition, we frequently have several addictions that we play around with – so we can pretend to ourselves that we are not *really* addicted, because we can stop one thing and start another. It is a good idea to ask God to show us how we comfort ourselves and dull our inner pain.

Why We Develop Avoidance Strategies

Avoidance strategies prevent us from feeling the depth of our pain and anger, but they also distract us from facing the issues causing our hurt. In turn, this blocks us from beginning the hard work of forgiveness. Sometimes, our avoidance of pain is fuelled by faulty theology. For instance, if we do not have a robust theology of suffering (which comes from understanding that we live in a broken world), when bad things happen we can either get angry with God and get stuck in self-pity, because we are unable to accept that life is 'not fair', or we deny the pain we are experiencing, because it doesn't fit with our understanding of how the world works.

Patterns from our childhood may also encourage us to suppress pain and anger. If our parents habitually minimised pain, saying things like 'Don't make a fuss', or they constantly made excuses for other people's behaviour, this may inhibit our ability to own our pain or recognise others' sin in the present.

As a child, when I came back from school complaining or upset, my mother would always listen, but would quickly find an excuse for the other person's behaviour. So I ended up thinking that I mustn't make a fuss; that it wasn't important, and therefore, somehow, I wasn't important. If you think like that, you end up seeing yourself as a doormat for others to wipe their feet on, and I certainly became very skilled at minimising my wounds and making excuses for others, thinking that I was being a 'good Christian' by doing so.

I took these patterns of thinking into my marriage – I thought everything was my fault and that I mustn't make a fuss, so I buried all the anger I felt towards Andrew. One day at the kitchen sink, the emotional pain became too much.

Somehow, I knew that everything wasn't my fault and I also knew that I needed to forgive, but I couldn't. I just said to God, 'I cannot do it.' I felt him say: 'Ruth, I took what's been done to you so seriously that I went to the cross and I was crucified for it.' That truth impacted my heart; it felt like for the first time in my life somebody was taking me seriously. As that happened, God's love started to flood into my heart, which was deeper and stronger than the offences I had suffered. That meant forgiveness could start flowing out, and this began to have a positive effect on our marriage.

Commonly, Christians wrongly believe anger is sinful, and so they try to suppress it. Certainly, unrecognised and undisciplined anger can lead to sinful actions, but the emotion of anger itself is not sinful, and can in fact be 'righteous', such as Jesus' anger over exploitation in the temple (John 2:14–16). The Bible does not say, 'Don't feel anger,' but rather, 'In your anger do not sin' (Ephesians 4:26), and getting in touch with angry feelings is often part of the process of healing and forgiveness.

Often people don't recognise anger as a problem they have; we can avoid such feelings by casting particular people or situations out of our mind for the most part. This is very different from deliberately forgiving someone, and is an avoidance strategy that is often used when we fear the emotions which might be provoked if we were to confront the pain. In these cases, getting in touch with the anger can be very useful, as it can prompt us to ask God: 'Would you lead me back to the source of the pain?' It is when we begin to acknowledge and articulate our pain that we are able to move on to the work of forgiving.

Finding Freedom

Forgiveness opens up the path to freedom and is essential to our own health and wholeness. Refusing to forgive can feel like getting revenge, but, in reality, it hurts us more than the person who has offended us. The effects of unforgiveness are so toxic that it has been described as 'taking poison and waiting for the other person to die'.[3] Desmond and Mpho Tutu describe the crippling effects of unforgiveness:

> Until we can forgive, we remain locked in our pain and locked out of the possibility of experiencing healing and freedom, locked out of the possibility of being at peace. Without forgiveness, we remain tethered to the person who harmed us. We are bound with chains of bitterness, tied together, trapped. Until we can forgive the person who harmed us, that person will hold the keys to our happiness; that person will be our jailor. When we forgive, we take back control of our own fate and feelings. We become our own liberators.[4]

The journey of forgiveness

While freedom is the destination, a journey of forgiveness is required to get there, and the journey of forgiveness is exactly that – a journey! It may be long or short, depending on the depth of the pain, but it is always a process. In addition, this is a journey we make very intentionally. Forgiveness is not an emotional response, but a deliberate choice, and often one which we need to make over and over again.

The journey of forgiveness can be broken down into several steps with which we need to engage. As a simple aide-mémoire, you can use your hands to remind you of five steps of forgiveness. Begin by making a fist, punching outwards. This is a good symbol of unforgiveness, which is really about wanting to hit out at somebody else for the pain they have caused. Then extend each digit until the hand is open for you to bless the other person. Each digit represents a part of the process of forgiveness, which will be considered in more detail below:

- Thumb – Acknowledge the pain
- First finger – Name the sin
- Middle finger – Recognise your own sin
- Ring finger – Pray for the willingness to forgive
- Little finger – Release forgiveness.

Approaching forgiveness in this way can feel somewhat 'mechanical', but this reflects the fact that forgiveness is a choice rather than an emotional response.

Acknowledge the pain (thumb)
The process of forgiveness begins when we are really honest with ourselves and with God about the pain that has been caused. Rather than allowing our minds to rationalise the pain, we need to get in touch with the wounds in our heart. When we minister to others, we need to help them access this heart pain, because we cannot even begin to forgive until we acknowledge that it hurts. The psalms are a useful resource in this process, because the psalmists are brutally honest about their own pain and anger, and using their words can help us to own our feelings.

As we acknowledge the pain, we will also begin to realise that there are layers to our wounds, and the deeper the pain, the more time it takes to reach the core. Minor hurts are a bit like scratches and bruises which require simple and immediate attention. These types of hurts can be quickly forgiven immediately after they happen, as memories come to you, or as you recall the events of the day before you go to sleep. But if we have deep wounds of betrayal or abuse, it can take a lot of skilful pastoral care, counselling and prayer to become fully aware of the extent of the damage to our hearts. In these cases, it is a bit like somebody needing to go into the Intensive Care Unit, followed by a long-term rehabilitation.

When we are processing deep pain, we may simply have to say that we want to forgive the perpetrator, but are not yet ready. Forgiveness is the ultimate route to healing, but it is not a quick fix or a plaster to stick over a deep wound; we need patience with ourselves and those we are journeying with, to allow the pain to be fully acknowledged. Sometimes, other things also need to be in place, such as a deeper knowledge of God's love, before we are able to return to the issue of forgiveness.

Name the sin (first finger)

The second step in the process of forgiveness is to name the offender and how they have hurt us. We need to be as specific as possible: when we pinpoint exactly how we have been hurt, we know what we have to forgive. On the other hand, if we fail to do this honestly, or if we make excuses for a person, or minimise their sin against us, it leads to confusion. We are not sure whether we have actually forgiven them for the offence or not. Sometimes we will need to look below the surface of a situation and ask what really hurt us, praying that God would bring his light and truth to help us clearly recognise and acknowledge sins against us.

Because our culture rejects moral absolutes, it can be difficult for us to label things as being wrong, and many Christians also get stuck at this point because we think we should not judge others. The Bible does say, 'Do not judge, or you too will be judged' (Matthew 7:1), but *naming* sin is very different from *judging* it.

Recognise your own sin (middle finger)

When we have been hurt, we often sin in response. Perhaps we have lashed out in anger at the other person, gossiped about them, or avoided them. Sometimes, our wrong reactions are more internal – we hold on to unforgiveness by constantly replaying the offence, plotting our revenge, or fantasising about all the clever things we could say to put down the person in question. At other times we let our unforgiveness bubble to the surface: we may bring up a historic grievance during an argument about something totally different, or find ourselves secretly pleased when we hear that something has gone wrong for the person who has hurt us. Commonly, when we have been belittled, criticised or shamed, we believe the lies that have been spoken against us, and internalise a negative self-image which does not match how God views us. While all these reactions are completely understandable, they are actually sinful responses, and so they need to be acknowledged and confessed.

Pray for the willingness to forgive (ring finger)

Being made in God's image, we have been created with the desire and capacity to forgive. However, as we are also fallen human beings, this impulse towards forgiveness has been replaced by an impulse towards judging others, and focusing inwards on our own pain. Being ready to forgive means being willing to let go of both.

Releasing others from our judgement does not mean we condone or overlook the wrong that has been done. Rather, we choose to give up our desire for revenge or retaliation, and instead trust the situation and the person to God's justice, which is very different from human justice.

Moreover, by choosing to focus outwards in forgiveness, rather than focusing inwards on our pain, we avoid sinking into destructive emotions like self-pity and rage, or indulging the desire to run away. When we choose to meet pain with forgiveness, we set free 'a great healing river'. Sister Margaret Magdalen writes: 'Pain in itself is morally neutral. It is how it is used that either sets free a great healing river or lets loose a destructive force far worse than any poison gas leak or nuclear explosion.'[5]

These choices run counter to all our instincts, because we are walking away from our own ways of dealing with pain, and releasing those who have hurt us to God. Regardless of how we feel, we can decide to extend grace. Jesus modelled this perfectly on the cross when he prayed, 'Father, forgive them, for they do not know what they are doing' (Luke 23:34). When we echo this prayer, we are joining Jesus in his passion for forgiveness. If we are not yet able to do this, we can begin by praying, 'Lord, please make me willing to be willing to forgive.'

Release forgiveness (little finger)
Now, with an open hand, we release forgiveness to the person who has wounded us, by praying a simple prayer like this:

> Father, I forgive (name) for sinning against me by (name the ways they have hurt you) and I choose to cancel the debt I feel they owe me by releasing them to you.

This is a conscious choice and may not immediately be accompanied by any desire to forgive. We can therefore choose to forgive someone whether or not they choose to apologise to us, and can release forgiveness to someone who has hurt us today, many years ago, or even to someone who has died. It may be helpful to write this prayer out in your journal, and then, particularly if you are forgiving something deeply painful, you can go back and remind yourself that you have started and will continue on a journey of forgiveness. Praying this prayer of forgiveness with trusted others, like a prayer partner, minister or counsellor, can also help to 'ink it in'.

Releasing forgiveness in this way frees both others and ourselves. Jesus said, 'Whatever you loose on earth will be loosed in heaven' (Matthew 18:18). When we forgive, it not only releases people from our judgement, but also releases us from the prisons others have put us in. Ultimately, it brings us into the experience of freedom Christ won for us on the cross. As forgiveness and healing are so closely linked, when we keep on forgiving those who have hurt us, we will experience more and more restoration in our own lives.

This is rather like an oyster producing pearls: something painful or uncomfortable gets inside the oyster's shell, and to deal with this, the oyster coats it in beautiful mother of pearl, which builds and builds until something very precious is produced from the pain. Forgiving can be both painful and hard work. But, once we decide to respond to the source of pain with forgiveness, it builds and builds until something beautiful is produced in our lives.

I knew I needed to forgive a group of people who had hurt me, and so I meditated daily on scriptures about God's forgiveness and restoration. I then prayed, 'I choose to forgive . . .', and would name each person who had been involved in the situation. I repeated this process week after week, month after month. While I was beginning to forgive others, Jesus began to heal me. Over time, the more I was able to forgive, the more I was able to receive restoration, peace and joy. It was a cycle of giving forgiveness and receiving healing.

Completing Forgiveness

Forgiveness is primarily a spiritual transaction, but the process can be completed in different practical ways, according to our circumstances. Having journeyed through the process of forgiveness, our hand is fully opened, and we can use it to bless the person who has hurt us. This is the position that God wants us to be in, but it is difficult. We can begin with prayers of blessing, and then ask God to open up practical opportunities for us to bless the other. Joseph is a great example of this. He was in prison and beset with trouble for many years after his brothers had sold him into slavery. Then the day came when they appeared before him again (Genesis 45), and it seems that, amazingly, Joseph had forgiven his brothers because he was able to bless them practically. Like Joseph, we may have to wait a long time to complete our forgiveness with blessing, but God's timing is always right.

Sometimes, there can be real reconciliation with the person who has hurt us, which is powerful and liberating. However, where we have been deliberately hurt, especially when there has been a very bad breakdown of trust, reconciliation takes time and bridges need to be rebuilt.

At other times reconciliation is not possible or appropriate. While Jesus urges us to continue forgiving those who repeatedly offend us (Matthew 18:21−22), this is very different from putting ourselves in a position where we can continue to be hurt. Forgiveness is in no way incompatible with setting good boundaries, and we must be particularly careful to protect ourselves from people who choose consistently or deliberately to hurt us.[6] Sometimes, we may choose to end a relationship completely to protect our own safety. In other cases, reconciliation cannot happen because the person has died, or we do not actually know who the offender was. Where reconciliation is not possible, for whatever reason, we can complete the process of forgiveness by using our open hand to release the person to God, trusting them to his justice, and, if they are alive, to pray prayers of blessing for them.[7]

As we practise forgiveness, we are bearing the image of a kind and merciful God, and witnessing to the very heart of the gospel – the forgiveness of sin. The image of God in us is gradually being restored, and the wounds that have damaged us are being healed.

Exercise: Forgiveness

These prayers and ideas are designed to help you in the process of forgiveness. Several things are suggested here, which can be adapted for use with a group or an individual. You may choose to use some or all of them, and will find that some are more appropriate for a group context than others.

PREPARATORY PRAYER

Sometimes we know exactly who and what we need to forgive. At other times, especially if the idea of forgiveness is new or we are working with groups, we may need the Holy Spirit to show us where to begin or to pinpoint key memories of times we have been hurt. The following prayer can be helpful:

> Holy Spirit, please show me where you want me to start on this journey of forgiveness – not where I think I ought to start, but where you want me to start. You are very gentle and patient, so please just give me one place where we can start today on the journey of forgiveness.

FORGIVE SIN

Write down the name(s) and the specific sin(s) of the person who has hurt you. Fold the paper over so that nobody else can see it, and place it at the foot of a cross or pin it onto a cross as a symbol of your decision to let go of this person and situation, and release them to God. As you do so, pray a simple prayer of forgiveness like that on page 158. As you continue the process of forgiveness, it may be helpful to pray the Lord's Prayer regularly, bringing to mind the specific people and situations you are forgiving.

TAKE COMMUNION

It can be very powerful to take Communion during or after the process of forgiveness. As we receive Christ's forgiveness for ourselves, we are empowered to extend forgiveness to those who have sinned against us.

RECEIVE HEALING

Forgiveness is necessary because we have been wounded, so we also need to allow Jesus to meet us in our pain and heal our wounds. You could pray along these lines:

Lord Jesus, through the power of your cross, please begin to release me from these offences and their effects on me. Amen.

You may find it helpful to visualise giving your wounds to Jesus on the cross, as discussed in Chapter 6 (under 'Exercising our Imagination' on page 121).

CELEBRATE THE EXCHANGE OF THE CROSS

Use something symbolic to celebrate the positive exchange that happens at the cross – where Jesus takes our sin, shame and pain, and lavishes us with his forgiveness, freedom and healing love in return.

If you are praying for others, it may be appropriate to use holy water as a symbol of Jesus cleansing their wounds (Psalm 51:7), or oil as a symbol of him giving them the 'oil of joy instead of mourning' (Isaiah 61:3).

Another idea for use with a group is to provide a bowl of roses or rose petals and encourage people to take one home. This is a symbol of the beauty of forgiveness and freedom Jesus gives us in exchange for the ashes of pain and resentment we are dealing with (the MSG version of Isaiah 61:3 says the Messiah will 'give them bouquets of roses instead of ashes').

Further Resources

Kendall, R. T., *Total Forgiveness* (London: Hodder & Stoughton, 2001).

Tutu, Desmond and Mpho, *The Book of Forgiving* (London: William Collins, 2014).

PART 3

Emotional Aspects
of Restoration

Spiritual maturity is vitally linked to emotional wholeness, and so it is important to explore the impact of the foundational relationships in our lives. Our parents were intended to image God to us and to establish in us a secure identity as his children. However, because of the fall, they have loved us imperfectly, and this will have inevitably caused some degree of emotional damage. Sometimes the damage is extreme, even intentional, but most of us had good parents who nevertheless 'wounded us not because they wanted to wound us, but because they also were people who were loved imperfectly'.[1] As we consider our relationship with our parents, we are not blaming them for their imperfections (which we all have), but instead recognising the impact of their limited love, so that we can bring our hurt to God and receive his limitless love, which is the key to our restoration as self-portraits of God.

In this section, exercises to help you process the material are included as we go along, so that where particular ideas or insights resonate with your own story, they can be captured immediately. Completing these exercises will help you to pray through any issues that arise for you, and specific prayers are presented at the end of each chapter to help you do this. These are followed by a list of relevant scriptures for meditation and prayer.

8

Receiving Mother Love

Our mother's love is the first experience of life, and as we will see, it is intended to reflect God's love to us, and lay a secure foundation of love in our lives. This puts us in a strong position to receive God's love and relate to him as children. Having this core foundation of love can be described as having a 'sense of being'.[1] This is really a sense of our own personhood. It means that we feel deeply loved and completely accepted. We have a fundamental and profound sense of safety and security – the deep confidence that, whatever we face in life, we will ulti-mately be okay. We also have a core sense of our own legitimacy and significance, which is not dependent upon anything other than our 'being' – we know we have a right to be here and that we matter as much as anyone else. When we have a strong 'sense of being', we know who we are, have a secure sense of identity (not related to gifts or achievements), and a feeling of solidity inside. As a result, we will be relaxed and at ease within ourselves, whether still or active, alone or in company. We will also be able to 'be still' and at rest, not needing to prove anything to ourselves or others.

Having this sense of being enables us to receive God's love and to relate well to others. We can engage with others, know-ing that we are already loved, rather than desperately seeking love and approval. Jesus summed up all the Old Testament law by calling us to love God, to love others and (at least implicitly) to love ourselves (Matthew 22:37–9). In this Great Commandment, he seems to be saying that our purpose and effectiveness as human beings springs from our relationships with God, with others and with ourselves, so it stands to reason that if our capacity to relate is damaged, then we are in trouble.

This sense of being is also the key to fruitfulness, because when we are confident in God's love for us, we are free to obey him, and act 'in step with the Spirit' (Galatians 5:25), rather than being driven by our own need for affirmation or approval. Western culture is easily impressed by activity, so we often get trapped into *doing*. But Jesus delights in our trusting obedience, and this comes from a place of inner stillness – being with him. Jesus said, 'I am the vine; you are the branches. If you remain in me and I in you, you will bear much fruit; apart from me you can do nothing' (John 15:5). So being with Jesus comes first, and from there we are able to start doing things in partnership with him. Indeed, without a strong sense of being, our doing quickly becomes distorted either by passivity (where we lack confidence to do anything with or for God, because we are unsure of our value and purpose) or by over-activity (where we are driven to do things by our own need for purpose or recognition).[2] But when our doing comes from a strong sense of being, we are able both to *receive* God's strength and love (through being with him) and to *assert* God's strength and love (through our doing), and self-reliance is replaced by radical reliance on God. This posture is the basis of true obedience and authority, and is therefore critical for leadership.

Having a sense of being lays the foundation for us to develop an intimate connection with God, and to be at rest in his love. David described this experience when he said, 'Truly my soul finds rest in God ' (Psalm 62:1). Jesus too knew the deep rest of being intimately at home in God's love (John 17:20–3), and invites us to experience this rest by coming to him (Matthew 11:28–9), and finding our home in him (John 15:4). Being intimately at home in God's love is the key to experiencing 'life in all its fullness' (John 10:10), and our mother's love has an important role to play because, ideally, it provides the basis for receiving it.

Establishing a Sense of Being

Life begins in relationship with our mother, and her unearned, unconditional love and nurture[3] is fundamental to establishing a sense of being in us. According to Frank Lake, 'human personal BEING arises in a relationship between an attentive mother and a responsive baby'.[4] It is by receiving her love and acceptance that the baby perceives itself as a person and develops a sense of being. This maternal nurture also creates the basis of secure relationship, setting the pathways of love which enable us to relate securely to others, self and God in later life. The loving connection between mother and child, which we call bonding, begins in the womb. God is already active in the life of the unborn child (Psalm 139:13–16), and happy parents will talk about and focus on their expected child, preparing for his or her arrival in various ways. They will probably already feel a deep love for and connection with their unborn child, and for the mother this is a particularly physical connection.

The bonding process continues as the child is born and develops, especially during the first eighteen months of his or her life. In the womb, the baby is strongly connected with the mother. When the umbilical cord is cut there is a degree of physical separation, but emotionally the child perceives itself as 'an extension of the mother, without clearly perceptible border'.[5] The umbilical cord is replaced by the mother's touch, her breast and milk, her voice, her warmth, and her comfort. As the newborn baby is held to the mother's breast or in her arms, it can see the mother's face, from which it feeds emotionally. The child is receiving not only milk through the breast or bottle, but all the love and acceptance its mother is pouring in through her touch, eye contact, nurture and attention. Safe in her arms the child can lie still, quietly and at rest.

It is now widely accepted that the newborn and infant needs to attach securely to their mother (or mother substitute) and receive her love in order to flourish emotionally, feeling accepted, safe, welcomed and confident.[6] For the baby, security is fundamentally associated with the presence of the mother, because she is his or her life-giver and 'source of being'.[7] Therefore, dramatic psychological, emotional and even physical problems can occur in children who are washed and fed but completely deprived of motherly affection.[8] It is this mother love which imparts a sense of value and worth, relationship, security, well-being, protection and identity to the child, providing the bedrock of love on which the rest of life and all relationships can be securely built. The psychologist Henry Cloud concludes that 'God has ordained the mothering process to literally "call the infant to life"'.[9]

Mother Wounds

If the mother is not able to meet her child's physical and emotional needs, or if the bonding process is interrupted, problems occur. These 'mother wounds' may happen for a variety of reasons and occur at different stages of development. Because of the close connection between mother and baby, even when a baby is in the womb, maternal stress, anxiety or depression may have a negative impact,[10] and perinatal events such as foetal distress, forceps delivery or emergency Caesarean section may also impact the child.[11] Even once the baby has made it into the world, the mothering process can be disrupted or distorted in some way.

Disrupted mothering

The bonding process between mother and baby will be disrupted if the mother is physically absent through illness, work, adoption or even death, or if she is unable to hold or feed her child (perhaps through a need for intensive care). She may be emotionally absent as a result of depression, addiction or an unhappy marriage.[12] Such interruptions to the 'love process' can damage a child's sense of being, which is sometimes called separation anxiety. This is not the temporary separation anxiety of certain phases in a child's development, but a more lasting sense of being ill at ease.

Distorted mothering

Where a mother is broken somehow or relates to her child in broken ways, this can distort the mothering process. One way to understand the mother's impact on her baby is to see her as a mirror in which the infant sees its own reflection. Because of the importance of eye contact in communication,[13] 'when a baby looks into the eyes of his mother and sees joy and pleasure, he identifies with that. But when he sees "anger" or "sadness" or any other negative emotion he will identify with that'.[14] If the mother is deeply depressed or chronically ill the baby may perceive themselves as a burden. If she herself does not have a strong sense of being, she will be unable to impart this to the child. If the mother is absent, the baby may receive the message that they are unworthy of love. If she is anxious, abandoned, overwhelmed or alcoholic, the baby's early experiences and foundations may be fear, danger or anger. This is not a straightforward equation where a particular issue in the mother automatically leads to a particular problem in the child, but these are all ingredients which might create the possibility of a child receiving distorted messages. Sometimes, an insecure, unhappy mother may be seeking to fulfil her own needs for love and security through the child; instead of pouring life and love into them, she distorts the love process by trying to draw these things out of the child. And in extreme cases, the mother may be pouring something toxic into her child, in the form of physical, verbal or sexual abuse, which seriously distorts the way the child sees him- or herself.

If, for whatever reason, we did not receive our mother's love successfully in early life, this hinders our ongoing capacity to receive and contain love. Of course, we will not remember all our early experiences, particularly before the age of three, but they are stored in the unconscious mind,[15] and affect our present expectations and behaviour. In particular, these early experiences have a huge impact on our ability to respond to and trust others, including God. If our foundational experience of love was deeply flawed, we will find it especially difficult to imagine what God's perfect, unconditional love is like, and so we struggle to have the kind of deep confidence and trust in God's unfailing love that the psalmist expresses: 'God is within her, she will not fall . . . Be still, and know that I am God' (Psalm 46:5, 10).

A Damaged Sense of Being

When our sense of being is damaged as a result of our mother wounds, we often feel empty, and may even experience a physical sense of emptiness within. It can feel as if we have an empty chasm inside which nothing seems to fill, or that there are a lot of little 'holes in our soul' so that, like a colander, we cannot hold what is poured in. No matter how much another person tries to give us love and belonging, it never seems to be enough. Even the love we seek from God does not seem to fill our inner emptiness, because our capacity to receive it is damaged. Sometimes, we demand more and more reassurance from God that he loves us, but ironically, our anxiety about this makes it difficult to simply accept and trust in his love, which means we struggle to grow up and become mature.

Alternatively, such emptiness may manifest itself in the form of panic attacks, a 'free floating' anxiety which can attach to anything, or a constant feeling of being on 'high alert'. Without a sense of being, we lack the ability to simply *be* – to feel at home with God, with others, and with ourselves. We may experience deep loneliness (even in group settings) or social discomfort, where we feel insecure and unsure of who we are. In more extreme cases, we feel that we have nothing real inside. This is sometimes described as 'nonbeing'[16] – where we feel 'shadowy', transparent, fake or even that we don't really exist.

These kinds of emotions and experiences can be particularly frustrating for Christians, because we know in our heads that we are loved by God and feel that we should be secure in that love. So, we easily become experts at hiding or masking the pain in different ways. Some of us put on an identity, like 'clown' or 'expert', to hide the emptiness inside, while others assume an attitude of defensive anger as a way of protecting ourselves from feeling the inner emptiness. Very often, we learn to present a competent and confident exterior in social or professional situations, but continue to feel empty inside.

Plugging holes

We may try to deal with our inner emptiness, or the 'holes in our soul', by plugging them in unhealthy ways. First, we may try to fill the void with relationships, where we look to other people (including our spouse, children or friends) to meet our need for love and to complete us. In such relationships, we make the other person an idol. We are then unable to relate to them as an equal, and easily become dependent on them for love, acceptance and affirmation. When we are 'solid inside', we have the capacity for meaningful and healthy relationships, but when we are hungry for love, we are susceptible to trying to fill this emptiness through unhealthy emotional or sexual entanglements.[17]

Second, we may seek to fill the emptiness inside through addictions. An addiction is really anything that is misused as a comfort blanket to deaden the pain of our inner emptiness, and may include food, work, alcohol, drugs, social media, shopping or sport. Also, because we are sexual beings, our need for love can become sexualised and may be expressed through a range of unhealthy behaviours including compulsive masturbation, pornography and other sexual addictions. This can be very frightening for Christians, and lead to shame, because we know these things are wrong. It can also be deeply confusing and alarming to experience strong impulses that we do not want or understand, but Jesus promises that 'you will know the truth and the truth will set you free' (John 8:32). Often, asking God to reveal the roots of our unhealthy sexual compulsions can help us begin the journey to freedom.[18]

Restoring a Sense of Being

Our early life experiences provided the foundations on which a sense of being could be built, but often these foundations were cracked, and so our sense of being suffered damage. Whatever our childhood experiences have been, God longs to restore the bedrock of love in our lives. He does this by healing our wounds and filling us with more and more of his perfect love. As we drink in God's love, we experience the security of being deeply loved, fully accepted and utterly safe. In this way, we gradually become 'rooted and established' in God's love (Ephesians 3:17), and our sense of being grows. We are then secure enough in God's totally accepting love to be still in his presence, like King David, who said, 'I have calmed and quietened myself . . . I am like a weaned child with its mother' (Psalm 131:2).

In order to enter this place of deep well-being and rest, we need to ask God to restore our sense of being. The elements explored below will probably be significant in this, and exercises are included to help you process this material as we go along, with suggested prayers at the end of the chapter.

Identify mother wounds

Because an insecure sense of being usually stems from difficulties in the mothering we received, we first need to identify areas of damage (bad things we received) or deprivation (good things we failed to receive) in our relationship with our mother. This is often very difficult because of the natural loyalty we feel towards her, and is even more complicated if she has died. The Bible commands us to honour our parents, but this is not the same as saying they were perfect! Every parent has imperfections, so while we can be genuinely thankful for the many good things we received from our mothers, we can also be honest about any damage or deprivation we experienced.

Sometimes we minimise childhood wounds by relegating them to the past and saying it doesn't really matter any more, but Jesus takes children and their wounds very seriously (Matthew 18:5−6; 19:14). We may certainly be able to explain and rationalise our mother's behaviour towards us, or even recognise she was not at fault. However, we do need to acknowledge honestly any damage or deprivation because, whether it was intentionally or unintentionally caused, it still leaves wounds which God wants to heal.

In order to identify 'mother wounds' we must recognise what God intended us to receive at the beginning of our life. This includes the need for a secure home in the womb, cradling and comforting arms to receive and welcome us, the physical and emotional presence of our mother, and healthy communication with her through an investment of time, talking, appropriate touch, and eye contact.[19] Where, for whatever reason, these things are missing, it causes damage, as one of Ruth's clients shares:

> My parents were trapped in a loveless marriage, and during my mum's pregnancy there were many violent rows. I believe that when I was in the womb I was afraid of my dad's voice shouting and therefore didn't feel safe. My mum gave all her love to her firstborn, my older brother, who meant everything to her. When I was born there was not the same excitement that had been there for his arrival. There was little mother–baby bonding between us, and I have no memory of being loved or cuddled. When Mum spoke to me, it was only to issue orders, and her tone was cold and strict. Yet she would speak and laugh with my older brother for hours. If I

was hurting, there was nobody to run to for comfort. Home was a very frightening place and I used to have frequent nightmares.

EXERCISE: IDENTIFYING MOTHER WOUNDS

This exercise helps you to identify possible areas of damage or deprivation in your relationship with your mother, even if this was caused unintentionally or unavoidably. Reflect as honestly as you can on the three main questions; the subsidiary questions may help prompt your thinking.

What was your relationship with your mother like?
- What words would you use to describe her?
- Can/could you sit comfortably with her/hug her/kiss her?
- Do you want to be like her in any way?
- As a child, did you feel she loved you unconditionally?

Were there any interruptions in the bonding process?
- Hospitalisation (you or your mother), including being in an incubator?
- Adoption, fostering or being in care?
- Mother's illness or post-natal depression?
- Going to boarding school?
- Parents' divorce?
- Physical absence of mother (e.g. through prison, work)?
- Emotional absence?
- Physical, verbal or sexual abuse?
- Mother's death?

Did your mother make it easy or difficult for you to relate to
God as Comforter, Carer, Nurturer and Generous Giver?

- In what ways did your mother model these attributes of God
  to you?
- Were there ways she failed to model these attributes of God
  to you?
- How did your mother relate to God? (e.g. Was a relationship
  with God central to her life or missing altogether? Was it close
  or distant? Fearful or secure? Motivated by duty or joy?)

Sometimes, it is easy to see where damage has occurred. At
other times, it is much easier to recognise the present effects of
any damage or deprivation than to identify where we have been
wounded, particularly if these wounds occurred in our early
life, or even in the womb. Where this is the case, we can begin
by acknowledging current areas of brokenness, and ask God to
show us any connections with our early experiences. We will
also be greatly helped by processing this with someone who is
able to help us make the links.

Forgive your mother

Having identified any mother wounds, it is important to forgive
our mother, as this clears the ground for us to receive God's
healing and love. One way to begin this process is to write a letter
to your mother, identifying ways in which you feel she damaged
you or deprived you of what you needed. State how this made
you feel or how this has affected you. Such a letter is *not* to be
given to your mother, but is for you to bring these things to the
cross and give them to Christ. You can then forgive your mother
in prayer, specifically naming and releasing to God areas of
damage and deprivation in your early experiences. A suggested
prayer of forgiveness is offered at the end of this chapter.

In some cases, there is clearly no culpability on the part of the mother (for instance, when she is hospitalised or dies). In these cases, we need still to acknowledge the profound impact that this has had on us, to grieve it, and to seek healing for it. A prayer of lament is offered on page 188.

Break unhealthy ties

When we are sinned against, we often sin in response, and sometimes this involves developing unhealthy ties with our mother, which can stop us entering fully into our identity as God's children. For instance, a painful relationship with our mother can cause us to make 'inner vows', such as 'I will never be like her', or conversely, 'I will always be just like her'. In this case, our identity is still bound up with our mother, rather than being defined by God and his view of us. Where we have made such inner vows we need to repent of them and renounce them in prayer, asking Jesus to break any hold they have over our lives. A suggested prayer is included within the prayers of confession at the end of this chapter.

We may also be bound by wrong beliefs about our mother, including things like 'I can't live without her' (or conversely – 'She needs me to live') or 'I am the source of her happiness' (or conversely – 'I was the reason she was unhappy'). These lies can bind us to our mother in an inappropriate way, so that we behave like conjoined twins. When we recognise that we are a separate person, we can live out our own God-given identity freely, and relate to our mother in a healthy way.

Remove false plugs

As God is restoring our sense of being, we can ask the Holy Spirit to show us where we have plugged the 'holes in our soul' with unhealthy relationships, addictions or other idols. It is helpful to write these down, so that we can then begin the process of unplugging the holes through confessing them and letting them go at the cross (there are prayers at the end of the chapter). Unplugging the holes in this way is painful, sometimes even excruciating, because it feels in some cases as though our life-support machine has been switched off. In fact, the opposite is true: by getting rid of these false comforts we are opening ourselves up to receiving real life. God does not simply ask us to give things up, but runs to meet us with something far better – the real and satisfying love we were made for in the first place.

Having begun to break free from unhealthy behaviours, we will need to make ongoing choices, both to give up these idols and to take hold of God's love. Overcoming addictive patterns can be a long process in which we will usually experience setbacks. For this reason, it is helpful to find someone you can be honest with and accountable to, and with whom you can pray, as you continue this journey into real life.

One of Ruth's clients shares her story of learning to depend on God, rather than others, for the love she needed:

I came to realise that I had maintained patterns from childhood of striving for others' affection and approval as a way of gaining worth. I was ambitious, highly disciplined and worked hard at music, having trained as a violinist from a young age. Music became the place where I earned my self-worth and received the affirmation of others. I was a freelance musician (performing and teaching), but the Lord started speaking to me in my restlessness, telling me to 'lay it down'. I had to let go and receive God's love in the place of having 'no props'. I started to hear what Jesus was saying about me and my worth. Through an increased intimacy with the Father, I learnt about loving others from a new place of freedom, secure in God's redeeming and healing love.

After many years of having laid down playing violin, the Lord then called me quite clearly into music therapy. Now I am working in a red-light district in India: serving, living and working alongside vulnerable women and children. I use the gift of music to help others find freedom and healing in him.

Receive healing

When we understand more about how we have been damaged, we can ask God to heal and restore us. This takes place at the cross, where Jesus takes onto himself all our pain and suffering, as well as the sins done to us and by us, and offers us healing in return. God is able to reach and restore all our experiences, whether they are known or unknown to us – so even damage that occurred in the pre-language phase can be healed through the cross, although inevitably this kind of damage can be harder for us to grasp and to process.

When we pray for God to restore our sense of being, we are essentially asking him to fill us with the welcome, comfort and love that we have not absorbed in our infancy and childhood. A prayer for doing this is suggested at the end of this chapter. Ruth often encouraged people to imagine 'cuddling' or 'snuggling' up to God – this language may initially sound sentimental and syrupy, but it relates to the kind of affectionate love we all need to begin life with so that we can feel totally accepted and secure.

Practising God's Presence

As our sense of being begins to be healed, we need to nurture it. We do not move from non-being to well-being through a 'magic prayer', but must position ourselves to receive God's love and hear his loving words to us on a daily basis. One of the best ways to do this is regularly to 'practise the presence of God'; this means reminding ourselves of the truth that God is with us and placing ourselves in his loving presence. Practising the presence of God is not necessarily the same as experiencing the presence of God, and involves consciously turning our hearts and minds to God, irrespective of our feelings.

In practical terms, it can be helpful to pray the Jesus Prayer, or simply repeat the name of Jesus, to place yourself in his presence.[21] Meditating on a scripture, such as 'The Lord is my shepherd' (Psalm 23:1), is a simple and effective way of connecting with God.[22] You might prefer to use something physical, like a pebble in your pocket or a reminder on your phone, as a prompt to stop and consciously practise God's presence, thanking him that he is present with you and that he loves you.

Practising the presence of God helps us to connect ourselves with God, moment by moment. We begin to dwell in his presence, responding to Jesus' invitation: 'Live in me. Make your home in me just as I do in you' (John 15:4, MSG). As we receive his love on an ongoing basis, our experience of being loved, safe and secure grows. When this strong foundation of love is in place, the emptiness in our hearts is satisfied, and we face life knowing that we are deeply loved and valued, made in God's image, and cherished as the 'apple of his eye'.[23]

Ruth experienced great healing in this area. This is her story.

When I was just setting out on my healing journey, I sensed there was a huge black chasm inside me, and I felt an excruciating emotional pain. I had begun journeying with God in my healing, and some of the compulsive habits and addictions I had previously used to stop me feeling empty had been exposed and stripped away. For instance, as a child and a teenager, and even at college, I used to suck my thumb – it was a comfort blanket. A lot of these things had already gone, but they had not yet been replaced by the real comfort I needed. It felt as if I was in a small boat, and the engine had been turned off – I was stranded in deep water. I could appear very calm on the outside, with everybody thinking everything was all right, but inside I was anything but calm.

At that point I had a sense of God's strong right arm being plunged down inside me through my head, into my chest and right into the core of my being. I said to God, 'Don't you dare take this out or I will die!' Then he showed me that he was planting a seed deep within me – it was the seed of being known and loved, which was going to take root and grow slowly but surely, like an oak tree, into something that was solid, stable and completely satisfying. There was also a sense of God making his home within me, and creating a place of rest so that the inside could be as calm as the outside. I sensed that as this seed grew within me into a solid oak, he would know when he could gradually pull his arm out, and I would then be able to lie quietly in his arms, like a weaned child.

Now, years later, I know that has certainly happened, but there are still times when I can feel that emptiness again. For example, during my cancer treatment I was lying on the radiotherapy table and had a horrendous sense of being alone, accompanied by that same emptiness and anxiety. So it is not as if this was 'done' and then I sailed through life. However, whenever the anxiety reappeared, because my sense of being had been firmly established and nurtured, I could always quickly access a sense of inner stillness again.

Exercise: Prayers for Mother Wounds

The following prayers are suggestions for personal use. Find a quiet place without distractions, and set aside plenty of time to pray. Tune in to God and your own emotions, and be as specific as possible as you recall particular events, both for forgiveness and confession. Remember that healing is a process, and you will probably need to pray through these issues on further occasions. Consider inviting a trusted confidential friend or experienced church worker to be with you on at least one occasion.

FORGIVENESS

Perfect God, thank you for your unconditional love and welcome [Psalm 27:10]. Thank you for my mother and for all the love she was able to show me.

I am aware of the ways and times in which my mother sinned against me: by the way she treated me . . . the negative words she used . . . I choose to forgive her for each of these.

I think of the ways and times in which she failed to give me the affection and sense of belonging that I needed . . . I choose to forgive her for each of these.

I recognise that much of this came about because she too had areas of brokenness in her life. As I choose to forgive, I ask you to bless her, and show me how I can do the same.

LAMENT

You may have suffered mother wounds for which your mother was in no way culpable (e.g. as a result of her death or hospitali-sation). Where this is the case, it is important to lament what you have lost. In some cases, there will be a need for both forgiveness (for wounds that *were* caused by your mother) and lament (for wounds you suffered through her unavoidable absence), and you may need help untangling the two.

Compassionate God, thank you for my mother, who carried and birthed me, and loved me in the following ways . . .

I recognise that because of . . . [name the reason], and through no fault of her own, I did not receive all the mother love that you intended for me.

I lament this deep loss. I name the particular losses I have suffered as a result . . . and I grieve before you.

Thank you that you promise to comfort me 'as a mother comforts her child' [Isaiah 66:11–13]. I ask that as I pour my pain out to you, you will begin to pour your true comfort into me.

CONFESSION

Merciful God, I recognise that I have reacted wrongly and behaved sinfully in my response to these wounds. I have looked for things and people to fill up the holes in my soul.

I now name these sins before you . . . and confess them to you.

(Where I have made a vow that I will never be like/always be like my mother, I repent of that vow and renounce it now . . . Please enable me to become the man/woman you created me to be and increasingly to relate well both to men and women.)

Thank you that I am now forgiven freely and completely.

SENSE OF BEING

As you pray, you may find it helpful to put your own hand over your heart or over any places where you feel pain or emptiness (e.g. stomach, tight chest), and ask God to fill you up with his love and affection. You may want to incorporate this prayer into your daily routine for a season (e.g. when you clean your teeth or are about to go to sleep) which is rather like setting up an intravenous 'spiritual drip' as a way to cooperate with God's ongoing process of healing.

> Life-giving God, thank you for knowing all about the emptiness . . . the loneliness . . . the worthlessness . . . the abandonment . . . the hunger for love . . . that has crippled me for so long (and which I even feel physically).
>
> Please will you come into my broken heart with your infinite love and begin to fill it with life, warmth, light, and beauty. Place your loving hand on where it hurts so much.
>
> Wherever, as a baby or child, I lacked love, affection or acceptance, or felt fear, deep-seated dread, anxiety, anger or hurt, please now fill me with your perfect, satisfying love. Establish in me a sense of being deeply loved.
>
> I choose to believe that you have answered, and will continue to answer, this prayer. Please set up within me a drip of your life-giving presence, and continue to infuse it day by day.
>
> Thank you for doing this for me. I look forward to that time when I truly know and feel it, and can fully grasp your word 'You are my child. I love you. I am pleased with you' [based on Mark 1:11].

More detailed prayers can be found in Signa Bodishbaugh, *Illusions of Intimacy* (Ellel: Sovereign World, 2004), pp. 211–20.

Maternal Images of God:
Scriptures for Meditation

A number of biblical passages use maternal imagery to convey God's care for us. While we are in the process of being healed from mother wounds, it can be helpful to meditate on these and incorporate them into our prayers as we ask God for the foundational love we did not receive in childhood.

Isaiah 66:11–13: 'For you will feed and be satisfied at her comforting breasts; you will drink deeply and delight in her overflowing abundance . . . you will feed and be carried on her arm and dandled on her knees. As a mother comforts her child, so will I comfort you.'

Psalm 27:10: 'If my father and mother should abandon me, you would welcome and comfort me' (TLB).

Hosea 11:3–4: God is described as a mother 'who taught Ephraim to walk . . . led them with cords of human kindness . . . ties of love', and who 'bent down to them and fed them'.

Deuteronomy 32:11–12: God is pictured as a mother eagle that 'stirs up its nest and hovers over its young'.

Luke 13:34: 'O Jerusalem, Jerusalem, you who kill the prophets and stone those sent to you, how often I have longed to gather your children together, as a hen gathers her chicks under her wings.'

Isaiah 49:15:   'Can a mother forget the baby at her breast and have no compassion on the child she has borne? Though she may forget, I will not forget you!'

Further Resources

Bowlby, John, *A Secure Base* (Abingdon: Routledge, 2005).

Brother Lawrence, *The Practice of the Presence of God* (London: Hodder & Stoughton, 1981).

Gerhardt, Sue, *Why Love Matters* (Abingdon: Routledge, 2014).

Guinness, Lisa, *In The Beginning* (London: Living Waters UK, 2009).

Lees, Stuart, *Will the Real Me Please Stand Up* (London: Hodder & Stoughton, 1997).

MacNutt, Francis & Judith, *Praying for your Unborn Child* (London: Hodder & Stoughton, 1988).

Nouwen, Henri, *Life of the Beloved* (London: Hodder & Stoughton, 1992).

Payne, Leanne, *The Healing Presence* (Grand Rapids: Baker Books, 1995).

Payne, Leanne, *Restoring the Christian Soul through Healing Prayer* (Eastbourne: Kingsway Publications, 1991).

Pytches, Mary, *Yesterday's Child: Understanding and Healing Present Problems by Examining the Past* (London: Hodder & Stoughton, 1990).

Receiving Father Love

Both men and women are made in the image of God, and so both parents reflect God to us, but because the name given to us in scripture for God is 'Father', our human fathers play a particular role in shaping our heart understanding of God. Where our relationship with our father has been loving and positive, the idea of God being Father is comfortable for us. But where our relationship was deficient in some way, or missing altogether, it will profoundly affect the extent to which we are able to receive God's father love and relate to him. In this chapter we will consider the impact of our relationship with our human fathers and explore how we can receive more of God's unconditional, unlimited, father love.

'Our Father'

The concept of God as our personal Father is present throughout the Old Testament,[1] but is brought alive by Jesus – especially when he connects it to his own relationship with God (John 20:17). The Bible presents a number of maternal images of God[2] – all telling us something important about God's character and action – but the primary name given is 'Father'. This is how Jesus addresses God, and how he invites us to address him in prayer (Matthew 6:9). The invitation to call God 'our Father' is not to do with gender, because God is Spirit (so neither male nor female);[3] neither is it saying that fatherhood is superior to motherhood.[4] Rather, this is about how we are *related to God* and how we *relate to him*.[5]

Theologically, we can think of God as our Father both through creation and through adoption. God gives us life, and in this sense is the Father of all people.[6] But believers are also children of God by adoption, and the apostle Paul uses this metaphor to enrich our understanding of our relationship with God as Father.[7] Writing in a Roman culture, where families in need of an heir would buy the child of a slave to become their adopted son, Paul uses the idea of adoption to express the truth that through Christ's death on the cross we have been bought out of slavery to sin, into freedom, and into an intimate relationship with God.

So while Jesus is uniquely the Son of God from eternity, we too can call God 'Abba, Father' (Romans 8:15), as Jesus did (Mark 14:36), and have the status and privileges of sons, which includes being heirs and inheritors of the kingdom of God (Galatians 4:7). Of course, all these benefits are available to women, who are 'sons' of God in the same way that men are part of Christ's 'bride', the Church.

His Children

Knowing God as our Father goes way beyond understanding a theological concept; it enables us to embrace our core identity as his children, and to experience the joy of this relationship. Theologian Tom Smail points out: 'Knowledge of God's fatherhood implies knowledge of our own sonship. When we become confident about who he is, we also become confident about who we are.'[8]

Jesus has this confidence in his own sonship. At his baptism, the Father says: 'You are my Son, whom I love; with you I am well pleased' (Mark 1:11). Even before Jesus begins his public ministry, the Father explicitly affirms him, giving him security, identity and approval. As a result, Jesus knows that he belongs to God ('you are my Son'), is unconditionally loved ('whom I love'), and totally accepted ('with you I am well pleased'). Assured of the Father's love, Jesus is able to trust him and be obedient to him – to the extent that he does only what he sees the Father doing (John 5:19–20). Having received his Father's approval, Jesus is not seeking this elsewhere and is therefore able to minister to others in humility (John 13:3), and to do the will of God irrespective of what others think of him.

As we explored in the first part of this book, we have a tendency to seek identity and value through what we do or what we own, and often look to others for approval and a sense of belonging. But God has already given us an identity as his beloved children, and he longs for us to find the love, approval and affirmation we crave *in him*. When we know we are already loved by God, and are significant in him, we no longer need to seek approval, belonging or identity elsewhere. Instead, we are free to love others and serve God, not out of fear or duty, but with confidence, authority, humility and joy. We can even embrace our mistakes and the imperfection of our efforts, because we know that our identity does not depend on our performance.

The Role of the Human Father

Just as with good mothering, a child's emotional, cognitive, linguistic and social skills are enhanced by fathers who are nurturing, close, supportive and warm.[9] Although there are many aspects to God's love,[10] and both parents are involved in modelling and providing these things, Ruth's experience with many clients suggests that there are some key areas in which fathers have a particularly important role. These include:

Protection

God the Father protected Jesus, not least by warning Joseph in a dream of Herod's plot to kill Jesus (Matthew 2:13). Similarly, human fathers reflect God's love by protecting their children. This love involves not just physical protection and provision, but also protection from emotional harm.

Boundaries

Good boundaries protect us and promote a sense of safety. They provide a space in which we can flourish and from which we can relate to others in healthy ways.[11] When we are small, boundaries are mainly about what is safe and unsafe, but in adolescence they need to be expanded, and are not only about safety, but also about relating to ourselves and others in a healthy way. As we grow up, transgressing boundaries has bigger repercussions, and we need both discipline to help us understand the costs of crossing them, and support to make good choices and establish healthy boundaries. Ultimately, our parents need to encourage us to take responsibility for ourselves, and enable us to develop self-control from within, rather than relying on a fear of punishment to control us from the outside.

The parable of the prodigal son offers an insight into this process. The father gives his son freedom to choose, freedom to risk and freedom to fail. He endures the pain of letting his son go, and allows him to live with the consequences of his poor decisions, but he doesn't give up on him, and is actively waiting to receive him home, forgive him and help him start again.

Both parents need to be involved in setting and maintaining boundaries for their children, but Ephesians 5:21–6:9 teaches that husbands and fathers have a particular responsibility to exercise loving authority within the family in a way that reflects the sacrificial love of Christ, and enables different members of the family to flourish.[12] This responsibility includes 'training' children (Ephesians 6:4),[13] especially with regard to their discipleship. Developing boundaries is critical to this task, and fathers have an opportunity to exercise the kind of loving authority which will enable their children to flourish and provide the foundations on which they can respond to God in obedience for themselves.

Affirmation

At his baptism Jesus was affirmed by his Father (Mark 1:11), and this imparted a sense of security and significance, from which he was able to minister confidently. If Jesus needed the Father's affirmation then so do we, and our human fathers have an important role to play in this. When they communicate delight in us, they reflect the delight God feels for us, and a sense of significance develops within. Doing this involves giving affection and attention, speaking words of approval, unconditional love and belonging, and affirming our skills, abilities, achievements and physical appearance through their praise and encouragement.

When we have gained strong affirmation from our fathers, we not only receive such affirmation more readily from God, but can also face the world knowing we have something valuable to offer and that our contribution matters. Again, although many people have a role in affirming us, anecdotal evidence suggests that the father's voice particularly matters.[14]

Empowerment

Jesus took initiatives in unity and harmony with the Father, doing only what he saw his Father doing (John 5:19). We too are invited to 'keep in step with the Spirit' (Galatians 5:25), which involves actively taking initiatives in line with God's purposes for our lives, both general and specific. Human fathers have an important role in empowering us to fulfil these purposes, by cultivating confidence within us to step out and take initiative.

While a mother is uniquely able to provide her child with security, nurture and sustenance in the first months and years of life, fathers can call their children out of the shelter of secure childhood and into the adult world, encouraging them to take responsibility and to mature into the people God created them to be. When a father is interested in his child's world, listening to their dreams, and affirming and encouraging their unique gifts, skills and preferences, they will gain a clear sense of the person they are becoming.

As a father calls his children into their destiny and purpose, he is also able to empower them by journeying with them, believing in them, backing them and championing them. A father can tackle things with his children, and provide the guidance, confidence and support which then enables them to push out and make good, courageous choices for themselves. He can also encourage adventure and risk, which in turn builds strength and robustness in his children. When we are confident that our father is supporting us, we can take risks, make mistakes and learn from them. So, in very simple and general terms, we might say that while receiving mother love gives us the capacity to *be*, receiving father love gives us the capacity to *do*.

Father Wounds

We all need protection, healthy boundaries, affirmation and empowerment when we are growing up. However, all our fathers are limited to a greater or lesser extent in their ability to give us what we need and accurately to reflect God, and this creates 'father wounds'. Before we explore the impact these father wounds may have on us, it is important to recognise that there are a number of causes:

Absence

Some fathers are *permanently* absent, either because of death, abandoning a pregnant mother, or leaving the family entirely. In Britain, 1 in 6 families are single parent, with mother being the lone parent in the vast majority of cases (6 out of 7),[15] and divorces peaking 4 to 5 years after marriage[16] (which may or may not lead to the father being permanently absent). Other fathers are *temporarily* absent as a result of illness, working elsewhere, serving in the Armed Forces, the impact of separation or divorce, or sending the child to boarding school at an early age. Sometimes, fathers who are physically present are *effectively* absent due to emotional shut-down, which leaves them unable to connect with their children. Historically, the two world wars resulted in the absence of whole generations of fathers, and even those who returned often came back spiritually and emotionally broken, which understandably affected their ability to be fully present to their children. Today, factors such as illness or over-work are more likely to cause fathers to be effectively absent.

In all these situations, to a greater or lesser extent, the child fails to receive the unique gifts that a father can model and impart, especially if there is no other effective 'father figure'.

This can then be passed on to the next generation who are fathered by men who themselves had no model of good fathering.

Abuse

Our father is intended to reflect God's love, kindness and protection towards us. Where he intentionally inflicts physical, emotional, verbal or sexual abuse, he totally distorts the image of God, and deeply wounds us, causing great harm.

Ineffective fathering

Ineffective fathers have not done anything actively wrong, but have left a gap by failing to give their children what God intended. This includes fathers who failed to provide adequate affirmation, who may have been critical, over-indulgent, controlling or authoritarian. Similarly, where fathers were insecure, apathetic, passive, driven by achievement or unreliable, this will distort our view of God and damage the image of God in us.[17]

Misogyny

Many children experience or observe misogyny within their parents' marriage or as part of their experience of being fathered. Although literally meaning 'hatred of women', misogyny is really a deep-seated belief that men are inherently more valuable than women. It is a refusal to appreciate the image of God in women, and often expresses itself in very subtle ways. Where these attitudes are absorbed, they prevent us from relating to others, and even to ourselves, in the whole and healthy ways that God intended.

Daughters may feel belittled, undervalued, or 'incomplete' without a man. They may also take on misogynistic attitudes themselves, leading to poor self-image, failure to fulfil their potential and subservience towards men, possibly under the smokescreen of 'submission'. Alternatively, some women respond by acting against men, and exhibit misandry (literally meaning 'hatred of men'). Misogyny is also, of course, toxic to sons. Fathers can (consciously or subconsciously) undermine God-given characteristics that are often perceived as 'feminine', such as the capacity to feel or express emotion. This is sometimes revealed in statements like 'boys don't cry', and can inhibit their sons' healthy emotional development. If a father models wrong expectations of and attitudes towards women, his sons may perpetuate these, or may fear intimacy with women.

The Impact of Father Wounds

Father wounds vary in their degree, but the more gaps we have in our experience of being fathered, the greater the impact on us and on our relationship with God. Our father wounds can manifest themselves in different ways,[18] including:

A distorted view of God

Our perception of God as Father is greatly influenced by our experiences of human fathering. For example, if our own father was absent, we may have great difficulty even relating to God as Father, or see him as remote. If he was authoritarian, we may see God as critical or unfair, and struggle to receive his mercy. If our father was over-indulgent, we may have difficulty coping with suffering. If he was passive, we may see God as helpless, or if he was capricious (often true of alcoholics), we may fear that God is unpredictable, unreliable and untrustworthy. We quickly make God in the image of our father. We do not necessarily believe in our heads that God is like this, but this is how our hearts perceive him, and it seriously impacts our ability to love and trust him, to receive from him, and to obey him.

In some cases, just using the word 'Father' can trigger major problems, because of the negative associations built up around it. Until this is healed, it may be helpful to use a different biblical name for God that you are more comfortable with, like 'Friend', 'Saviour', 'Redeemer' or 'Good Shepherd'. The more intimate ones, like 'Abba' (the Aramaic word for 'Daddy'), can provide a way of becoming close to God for someone whose human father was distant.

Distorted relationships with others

Wounds from our relationships with our fathers commonly lead to difficulties in how we relate to others, especially male authority figures, including leaders, clergy and bosses. We often project our experience with our fathers onto such people, viewing them through the lens of our own hurt. Thus a woman who had a tyrannical father may feel angry or rebellious towards all male authority figures. Alternatively, we may put great expectations onto male authority figures, subconsciously wanting them to be everything our father wasn't, in the shape we would like our father to be, which might in itself be a damaged view.

While a childlike search for fathering is often transferred to men in leadership, difficulties in our relationship with our father may also cause problems and ambiguities for us with relationships with men in general, either driving us away from them or driving us towards them in unhealthy ways to get our needs met.

Distorted relationship with ourselves

Our father wounds can also lead to a range of issues within ourselves. For example, if we did not receive the affirmation we needed, we may experience low self-esteem, including uncertainty about our physical appearance or abilities, or a more general lack of self-worth or significance. Similarly, if we have not been taught how to establish good boundaries, we may find that we are unable to say 'no' and set healthy limits for ourselves in areas such as work, eating, spending, drugs or sex. Our weak boundaries might mean that we tolerate behaviour that is disrespectful or abusive, or mean that we fail to respect other people's boundaries. If we received inadequate empowerment, we may become quite passive, lacking courage and the ability to take initiative to realise our full potential or follow our godly desires. This can even result in a frustrating and disabling feeling of being 'stuck' so that we are left wondering who we really are and what we were made for.[19]

Restored Children of Our Heavenly Father

Whether our experience of fathering has been generally positive or missing altogether, God longs to redeem any negative experiences in this area and restore us, and this is likely to involve the steps explored below (although not necessarily completed in this order). An exercise is provided to help you process this material as we go along, and more prayers are included at the end of the chapter.

Identify father wounds

As with our mother wounds, we first need to acknowledge and identify areas of damage or deprivation in the fathering we received, and bring these wounds to God. These may be extreme and obvious or they may be more subtle. They can be especially hard to acknowledge and identify if we had a generally good father, particularly if he was a Christian. However, in naming our wounds we are not being critical or disloyal, but, rather, realistic, in recognising that no human parent is able to offer perfect love.

EXERCISE: CHARACTERISTICS OF FATHERS[20]

This exercise helps you to begin identifying father wounds. The words in the left-hand column of the list describe some of the characteristics of a great father, while those in the right-hand column represent the opposite. Reflect on how you perceived your own father, and give each characteristic a score from 1 to 5 (1 = bad, 2 = poor, 3 = average, 4 = good, 5 = strong) in column A (ignore column B for the moment; we will return to it later). Try to do this as honestly and dispassionately as possible. Respond to your discoveries by thanking God, specifically, for the good aspects of your father, and noticing where there has been a lack.

Scores 5	Scores 1	A	B
Warm and affectionate	Cold		
Accepting and encouraging	Critical		
Approachable	Distant		
Unconditionally loving	Conditionally loving		
Releasing	Controlling		
Consistent	Capricious		
Available	Absent		
Trustworthy	Unreliable		
Forgiving	Condemning		
Generous	Stingy		

Affirming	Ignoring
Accepting	Judgemental
Emotionally engaged	Emotionally frozen
Gentle	Violent
Solid	Vague
Responsible	Lazy
Self-controlled	Out of control
Protective	Abusive
Strong	Weak
Initiating	Passive
Providing	Not providing
Loving disciplinarian	Authoritarian

Forgive your father

As you identify specific areas where the fathering you received has been in any way deficient, you can begin the work of forgiving your father, and repent of your own sinful responses to the pain. Prayers to help with this are included at the end of the chapter, although the more dysfunctional a father has been, the more likely it is that you will need help with this.

Develop new pictures

There is often some disparity between our theological beliefs about God as Father and our heart's picture of him. We need to identify where our picture of God has been distorted by our experiences of human fathering, and ask God to replace these damaged views and expectations of him with truth about who he is and what he's like. Then we can begin to relate to God as he truly is, rather than through the distorted lens of our flawed experience.

Return to the exercise on the characteristics of fathers and in column B score each one according to your perception of

God as Father. It is important to differentiate between what your head tells you God is supposed to be like (all scores would be 5!) and how you actually perceive God. So, although your head understands that God is approachable, kind and faithful, he might *feel* distant, critical or unreliable to you. By comparing these scores with the previous ones, you may begin to understand where your misconceptions of God come from.

Now you can talk to God about the distorted picture you have in your heart, and ask him to replace it with an accurate one. Meditating on truth about what God is like is important here, and a list of relevant scriptures is included at the end of the chapter. By reading and dwelling on these Bible verses we allow the truth about who God is and how he fathers us to take root in our hearts in such a way that it transforms us. If, for instance, we take the phrase 'Never will I leave you; never will I forsake you' (Hebrews 13:5), we already know, in our heads, that God is like this, but by meditating on this truth (without over-analysing), we allow God to minister it to our hearts – which is where it really counts – and as a result we begin to really believe and *experience* it.

Once a true picture of Father God is in place, we can build on it by bringing any wrong thinking or broken behaviour patterns into alignment with it. For example, Ephesians 2:4 tells us that God has 'great love for us' and is 'rich in mercy', so we can choose to reject any negative thoughts that say we are unlovable or unforgivable because of our background or failures. This is hard work and takes discipline, but it opens the way for us to receive more of God's restoring love.

One client of Ruth's explains how her broken picture of God, informed by her earthly father, was transformed through prayer.

I loved my dad so much and I knew that he loved me, but he never once expressed the words to me: 'I love you . . . I am so proud of you.' Somehow, I comforted myself with the knowledge that he didn't have to say them, as I knew it in my head to be true. But when no such words materialised on my wedding day – boy, did that hurt. The sting of their absence haunted me for years.

Some ten years later, this hurt really caught up with me; I understood that how I viewed my earthly father was how I viewed God. I had believed that somehow I must have been a disappointment to my earthly father, and I had projected this onto God. My relationship with God was not intimate and I certainly didn't think that I was the apple of his eye.

There was a very significant event at a parish weekend when we were asked if we wanted to be prayed for and anointed with oil. Ruth prayed with me and the verse she spoke over me has never left me, nor has its impact:

The Lord your God is with you . . .
He will take great delight in you,
he will quiet you with his love,
he will rejoice over you with singing.

Zephaniah 3:17

Since then I have, at a greater and deeper level, understood how much God loves me and that he could not be more delighted about me, and that I was chosen by him before the creation of the world. This love has made a journey from my head to my heart and is taking root there.

Receive God's father love

Ultimately, we are restored as we allow God to impart more of his father love to us through the Holy Spirit (Romans 5:5). Tom Smail writes: 'In Christ God has made himself our Father and us his children. For that to come home to us in the power of the Spirit is one of the most healing things that can ever happen to us.'[21] God's love may 'come home to us' through the Bible, or as he speaks more directly to our hearts through words and pictures. It is this heart-revelation of God's love, rather than a theological belief in God's fatherhood alone, that enables us to experience and enjoy God's father love. One of Ruth's clients shares how God's love came home to him in the power of the Spirit:

My mother's pregnancy was shrouded in secrecy, and she was sent away. So I grew up with a lot of shame and the label 'illegitimate', and never believed anyone could want me. During our prayer time, as Ruth invited Jesus to give me a picture, I saw him dressed in hospital garb pacing up and down in a waiting room, eagerly awaiting a baby's birth. He then picked me up from the cot into his arms and carried me into the corridor: he marched up and down, parading me and exclaiming, 'This is my son! This is my son!', with a great beaming smile. Sometimes he would carry me aloft as if showing off a treasured trophy. Or he would carry me close to his breast; I could feel the roughness of the cotton of his tunic, I could feel his ribs. He was just like any elated father – thinking his son is the best. Secrecy and ignobility were replaced by the knowledge that I was the precious child of a proud father.

Because our parents, as well as ourselves, were broken and damaged image bearers, they inevitably reflected a distorted view of God to us. Henri Nouwen concludes that 'their love was limited and conditional, but it set us in search of that unconditional, unlimited love'[22] which is only found in God. So, whether we had parents who damaged us deeply, or parents who did the very best they could, ultimately only God knows how to meet our deepest longing for love. He parents us perfectly and the homesickness of our hearts is cured, as Jesus promises: 'I will not leave you as orphans; I will come to you . . . Anyone who loves me will obey my teaching. My Father will love them, and we will come to them and make our home with them' (John 14:18–23).

Exercise: Prayers for Father Wounds

The following prayers are suggestions for personal use, and can be combined with the discoveries made throughout this chapter. Find a quiet place without distractions, and set aside plenty of time to pray. Tune in to God and your own emotions, and be as specific as possible as you recall particular events, both for forgiveness and confession. Remember that healing is often a process, and you will probably need to pray through these issues on further occasions. Consider inviting a trusted confidential friend or experienced church worker to be with you if you are struggling.

If there has been serious abuse and you cannot face this yet, put it on hold and pray that God will show you the right time to revisit the process. At that time, pray with someone else who you sense knows how to support you, or seek professional counselling. Remember: you are not required to re-establish a relationship with the perpetrator.

FORGIVENESS

Perfect Father, thank you for your unconditional love and utter trustworthiness. Thank you for my father and the love he was able to show me.

I am aware of ways and times in which my father sinned against me: by the way he treated me . . . His negative words . . . His actions . . . I choose to forgive him for each of these.

I think of the ways and times in which he failed to give me what I needed: the time . . . affection . . . sense of safety . . . and for failing to encourage and bless me . . . I choose to forgive him for each of these.

I recognise that much of this came about because he too had areas of brokenness in his life. As I choose to forgive, I ask you to bless him, and show me how I should now relate to him.

LAMENT

If you have suffered father wounds for which your father was in no way culpable (e.g. as a result of his death, illness, prolonged depression or hospitalisation), it is important to lament what you have lost. In some cases, there will be a need for both forgiveness (for wounds that *were* caused by your father) and lament (for wounds you suffered through his unavoidable absence), and you may need help untangling the two.

> Compassionate Father, thank you for my human father, and for the ways in which he loved me . . .

> I recognise that because of . . . [name the reason], and through no fault of his own, I did not receive all the father love that you intended for me.

> I lament this deep loss. I name the particular losses I have suffered as a result . . . and I grieve before you.

> Thank you for adopting me as your child (Romans 8:14–23). I ask that, by the power of your Holy Spirit, this truth would become real to me so that I can call you 'Abba, Father' with confidence.

CONFESSION

Merciful Father, I recognise that I have reacted wrongly . . . and behaved sinfully in response to these wounds.

I now name these sins before you . . . and confess them to you.

(Where I have made a vow that I will never be like/always be like my father, I repent of that vow and renounce it now . . . Please enable me to become the man/woman you created me to be and increasingly relate well both to men and women.)

Thank you that I am completely forgiven.

RECEIVING GOD'S FATHER LOVE

As you pray, you may find it helpful to put your own hand over your heart or over the place where you feel the pain of father-lessness, and ask God to fill you up with the particular form of father love you lacked (e.g. affirming love, protecting love). This prayer, based on Mark 1:11, can also be incorporated into your daily routine for a season, as you cooperate with God's ongoing process of healing.

Life-giving Father, thank you for knowing all about the loneliness . . . the worthlessness . . . the drivenness . . . that have debilitated me for so long.

Holy Spirit, please bring the father love of God to all the areas where I lacked love, attention, protection, affirmation, encouragement, delight from my earthly father. Place your loving hand on where it hurts so much.

I choose to believe that you have answered, and will continue to answer, this prayer. Please set up within me a drip of your father love, and continue to infuse it day by day.

Thank you for doing this for me. I look forward to that time when I truly know and feel it, and can fully grasp your words 'You are my child. I love you. I am pleased with you.'

Characteristics of God as Father: Scriptures for Meditation

In order to relate to God as our Father, we need both to *believe* and to *receive* the truth about who he is and what he is like. The following scriptures are useful resources for meditation, and you might like to begin by choosing a characteristic which was minimal or missing in your own experience of being fathered. For example, if your father did not adequately affirm you, you could meditate on and memorise a scripture about God's affirmation. Ask God to heal you from your father wounds in this area and enable you to believe in and receive his affirmation of you.

Faithfulness	Deuteronomy 7:9; Psalm 27:10; Lamentations 3:22–3; 1 Corinthians 10:13; Hebrews 10:23; 13:5b; 1 Thessalonians 5:24; 2 Thessalonians 3:3; 2 Timothy 2:13
Trustworthiness	Psalm 93:5; Proverbs 16:20; Jeremiah 17:7
Unchanging nature	Psalms 62:11–12; 71:1–5; James 1:17; Hebrews 13:8
Justice	Deuteronomy 32:4–5; Jeremiah 9:24
Forgiveness	Psalm 103:12–13; Luke 15:17–24
Patience and mercy	Exodus 34:6; Psalms 103:8; 147:11; Lamentations 3:23; Luke 23:29–43; 2 Peter 3:9
Leads and guides	Exodus 15:13; Hosea 11:3–4; Nehemiah 9:19; Psalm 48:14; Isaiah 58:11

Provision and generosity	Psalm 37:3−5; Malachi 3:10−12; Matthew 7:11; Luke 12:31−2; Matthew 6:26−32; John 16:23−4; James 1:17
Love and kindness	Psalm 103:13; Jeremiah 31:3, 20; Hosea 11:1−4; Luke 19:1−10; 2 Corinthians 1:3−4; 1 Peter 5:7
Strengthens us	2 Samuel 22:33; Isaiah 41:10; Habakkuk 3:19
Delights in us	Psalm 45:10−11; Zephaniah 3:17
Intimacy with us	Psalm 139
Constant presence	Psalm 86:15; Isaiah 41:10; Jeremiah 31:20; Ezekiel 34:11−16; Matthew 28:10; Hebrews 13:5
Affirmation	Matthew 3:16−17; Mark 9:7
Protection	Deuteronomy 1:31; 33:12; Psalms 28:1; 118:5−17; Isaiah 41:10; Zechariah 2:8
Correction	Deuteronomy 8:5; Proverbs 3:12; Hebrews 12:5−11

Further Resources

McClung, Floyd, *Father Heart of God* (Eastbourne: Kingsway, 2007).

Nouwen, Henri, *The Return of the Prodigal Son* (London: Darton, Longman & Todd, 1994).

Nouwen, Henri, *Home Tonight: Further Reflections on the Parable of the Prodigal Son* (London: Hodder & Stoughton, 1992).

Payne, Leanne, *Crisis in Masculinity* (Eastbourne: Kingsway, 1985).

Payne, Leanne, *The Broken Image* (Eastbourne: Kingsway, 1981).

Pytches, Mary, *A Father's Place* (Berkhamstead: New Wine, 2000).

Smail, Tom, *The Forgotten Father* (London: Hodder & Stoughton, 1992).

Stern, Karl, *The Flight from Woman* (London: George Allen & Unwin, 1966). Provides a fuller discussion on misogyny.

PART 4

Practising and Sustaining Restoration

The process of being restored into the image of God often involves looking at areas where we have been damaged, and allowing God to heal our wounds. It is important to address these issues, but also important not to get stuck in the past. The aim is to 'live life forwards' by enjoying the freedom and life God is giving us. Indeed, the goal of our restoration is to become fully alive in Christ, and as this happens, we will reflect more of his character and love to those around us. The prophet Isaiah says that, because of the Messiah's ministry, the people of God 'will be called oaks of righteousness, a planting of the LORD *for the display of his splendour*' (Isaiah 61:3, italics added). This is a wonderful picture of God's people being mature and firmly established, reflecting his glory to others.

In this final part of the book, then, we consider some of the attitudes and habits which will help us to maintain a healthy relationship with God, ourselves and others, and we also explore how we can live well right up to the very end of our lives.

Living Well

Living well is all about living 'in Christ'. When we come to
Christ, we are 'born again' (John 3:5–8). Like babies, however,
we need to grow up, and scripture invites us not only to start a
relationship with Christ by placing our faith in him, but also to
mature in him.[1] Theologically, it is true that 'if anyone is in
Christ, the new creation has come' (2 Corinthians 5:17), but
despite this profound truth, we still need to be cleansed, healed,
restored and sanctified by God – and this process takes time.
That said, maturity is not just a natural by-product of the
passage of time, but rather the *work* of a lifetime, involving the
kind of steady growth which produces character. As we commit
ourselves to this lifelong process, each of us will mature in
different ways and at different rates. However, there are some
general but discernible stages as we grow spiritually from
infancy to maturity that can be compared to our physical
growth from babyhood to adulthood.[2]

When we are new to faith, we are like babies – totally dependent on others for (spiritual) nourishment, and often needing to
be comforted or reassured a lot of the time. We then reach the
weaning stage, where we are increasingly able to feed ourselves,
transitioning to more 'solid food' (Hebrews 5:12–14). Just as
children begin to explore the world and discover new things, as

we reach childhood in our faith journey, we develop in our understanding and experience of God, often learning discipline too. As spiritual teenagers, we grapple with the complexities of faith and with fundamental questions like 'Can I really trust God?' and 'Is he good after all?' This stage may well involve rebellion, pain and emotional storms, but through all this there is an opportunity to grow in our relationship with God and discover more of his grace. Finally, as we mature into spiritual adults, we start responding to and obeying God out of love and trust, rather than need or fear. We also learn discernment and good judgement to meet our growing responsibilities. It is here that we begin to display more of the fruit of the Spirit in our lives.

Of course, we may be grown up in some areas, but still babies or teenagers in others; maturing involves opening up every area of our lives to Christ's love and restoration. It means making a daily and active choice to keep growing in him so that we don't get stuck as spiritual babies or teenagers in any part of our lives. As we commit ourselves to maturing in Christ, two biblical metaphors can help us think about what maturity looks like and how it is achieved.

A Fruitful Vine

Jesus compared a maturing life with a vine, which requires ongoing pruning in order to become more and more fruitful: 'I am the true vine, and my Father is the gardener. He cuts off every branch in me that bears no fruit, while every branch that does bear fruit he prunes, so that it will be even more fruitful' (John 15:1–2). As we commit ourselves to knowing Christ and growing up in him, God commits himself to cutting out the unfruitful areas of our lives. This can happen when we are reluctant to grow up, when pride and unruly ambition appear, or when we become too independent. When this is the case, we may be brought to the end of our own resources or humbled in some way. But God is so committed to our growth that he not only cuts out the unfruitful parts of us, he also cuts back the parts that *are* fruitful, so that they will be even more fruitful. We might be using our gifts, doing something really well and seeing positive results, but have to stop for some reason. Being pruned in this way is uncomfortable, even painful, but it is essential for growth, because while this area of our life may be unfruitful for a season, the pruning means it can be even more fruitful later. A rose that has been pruned often looks dead, but the following summer it produces even more wonderful blooms, whereas a rose that has not been pruned doesn't produce many flowers at all. Likewise, when God cuts us back, it can sometimes feel as though we are going to die, but we need this pruning in order to flourish and grow into mature, healthy and fruitful people.

Sometimes God's pruning happens through circumstances, as we find ourselves restricted through ill health, or while caring for young children or elderly relatives. God can use this season of 'lying low' to sift our motivations and develop our faith and character. At other times, we more actively participate in the pruning process. We may discern that God is calling us to cut back or scale down in some area. For instance, leaders who sense that their 'front stage' ministry is bigger than their 'back stage' relationship with God[3] may choose to cut back their ministry commitments in order to focus on strengthening that life-giving relationship with Christ.

Pruning forces us to put our roots deeper into Christ, and to find our security and significance in him, rather than from any ministry we do 'for' him. It can be agonising to our ego, but is critical for our future fruitfulness. Whether we are being pruned through our circumstances or through our own choices, we can always ask God, 'How do I cooperate with you so that I can mature through this experience?' In this way we embrace God's pruning process, confident that it will produce the kind of growth that leads to fruitfulness.

The fruit produced by pruning is seen not primarily in our achievements, but in our character. Just as a mature tree is fruitful, so a maturing person will be one in whom the fruit of God's Spirit is ripening (Galatians 5:22–3). For example, joy is part of the fruit of the Spirit, so as we mature in Christ, we can expect our capacity to enjoy life, even in the midst of pain, to grow. Similarly, the other fruits of the Spirit – love, peace, patience, kindness, goodness, faithfulness, gentleness and self-control – will grow within us as we mature in Christ. A direct outworking of this is that we reflect God's image more fully to others, and so we are more fruitful as we relate and minister to them – not because our *doing* has expanded, but because our *being* is becoming more Christ-like.

A Marathon Runner

A second biblical metaphor which can help us to visualise the process of maturity is that of a marathon runner. Paul describes the Christian life as a race (1 Corinthians 9:24; Galatians 2:2; 5:7; cf. Hebrews 12:1), but it is a lifelong marathon rather than a sprint. This suggests that maturity is not a destination at which we arrive, but a process in which we are engaged for the whole of our lives; whatever our age or experience, there is always more of Jesus to discover and grow in. When we think of maturing in Christ as a marathon, it is clear that we will need to develop perseverance, strength and stamina to stay on track and go the distance. Above all, we will need to stay focused on the goal, which Paul expresses so clearly in Philippians:

> I want to know Christ – yes, to know the power of his resurrection and participation in his sufferings, becoming like him in his death, and so, somehow, attaining to the resurrection from the dead. Not that I have already obtained all this, or have already arrived at my goal, but I press on to take hold of that for which Christ Jesus took hold of me. Brothers and sisters, I do not consider myself yet to have taken hold of it. But one thing I do: forgetting what is behind and straining towards what is ahead, I press on towards the goal to win the prize for which God has called me heavenwards in Christ Jesus.
>
> Philippians 3:10–14

Paul's stated goal was simply to know Christ more and more – in his power and in his sufferings. We are usually keener to experience more of the former than the latter, but suffering is an inevitable part of life in a fallen world. Just as pruning increases our fruitfulness, so our anguish can draw us into a closer union with Christ, who has gone before us into every imaginable form of human suffering. Paul writes out of the experience of deep suffering, and shows us how to develop a healthy attitude towards it. He does not seek suffering or exalt it as achieving something in and of itself, but neither does he avoid or run from it. Rather, in the midst of suffering, he holds unswervingly to his life goal of knowing Christ more. Suffering is not what God intended for us – it is a result of the chasm that opened up between the whole of creation and God at the fall. But while God is not the source of suffering, he can use every circumstance – even our own mistakes and others' sin against us – to achieve good in our lives (Romans 8:28). As we involve

God in our pain, trusting that he is good (even when our circumstances seem to suggest the opposite), we will discover that Christ, the 'crucified God',[4] is present to us in our suffering, and we will get to know him more deeply.

Paul admits to not having arrived at this goal, but he is committed to keep striving towards it, with his eyes focused on Christ. We too will have setbacks and make mistakes. We may be overwhelmed by anxiety, pride or hatred, and be ashamed of our struggles. However, these setbacks do not put us out of the race. God invites us to get back on track, focus on the prize of resurrection life, and renew our commitment to following Christ.

Building Spiritual Fitness

Just as an athlete prepares for a marathon through regular training and physical care, we too must consciously put wise practices in place that will sustain our spiritual lives and promote further growth in Christ. In short, we need to establish habits that help us live well. At first, this will require effort, but as we persist, we gain momentum until we reach a place where these practices become instinctual. These habits – sometimes called spiritual disciplines – have been practised throughout the Church's history. They root us more deeply in God's love, so that we can enjoy a rich and satisfying relationship with him, and they enable us to be restored and transformed on an ongoing basis. In the rest of this chapter, we focus on six life-giving practices which help us to build spiritual fitness and live well.

Prayer and Bible reading

Prayer is the communication that keeps us connected to God and growing in Christ. It is intimately connected with Bible reading, which opens us up to God's perspective and to an encounter with him. Developing a rhythm of personal prayer and Bible reading, therefore, is vital in sustaining our spirituality. Prayer is simply conversation with God, so there are as many ways to pray as there are people. Our prayers will often be spontaneous as we talk naturally with God about what is in our hearts, but resources from the Church's rich tradition of prayer can provide structure and open up new ways of communicating with God. We have seen how the discipline of practising the presence of God can be particularly helpful in keeping us anchored to God, while Lectio Divina and Ignatian meditation (discussed earlier on pages 104 and 109)[5] offer a doorway to meeting Christ through scripture.

Liturgical prayer may be useful, especially when we are facing sickness or suffering, and struggle to pray. We might sometimes think of liturgy as being formal and rather lifeless, but by taking other people's words – words of truth that are soaked in scripture – we can be led into Christ's truth and presence. In liturgical prayer, we are joining in the prayers of the Church, prayed over many years and in many nations, and are reminded that our journey of faith is not taken alone but in the company of God's people, past, present and future.[6]

In developing a deeper prayer life, we may also benefit from seeing a spiritual director, who will accompany us on our spiritual journey, helping us to discern where God is at work in our lives and what he is saying. A spiritual director will encourage us to respond to God and to grow in intimacy with him. They will introduce us to a variety of forms of prayer and

meditation,[7] and challenge us to grow as a disciple of Christ.
Finding a suitable spiritual director can take time, and it is wise
to ask your church leader for suggestions. Although your spiritual director may well be from a different Christian tradition
(which can be very enriching), you will want to find someone
who is Christ-centred, theologically orthodox, wise and
discerning. Above all, you will be looking for someone whose
relationship with God you respect, whom you trust and with
whom you can feel an affinity.

Community

When we come to faith in Christ, we become part of the
community of faith (the Church). This is a theological reality[8]
and should be a source of great joy. But relating to others in
Christian community can also be one of the most challenging
aspects of the Christian life. It means living and worshipping
not only with those who are like us, but also with those who are
different and whom we may find difficult.

We must learn to see these people as our brothers or sisters,
not on the basis of any social similarity or shared interest but
purely on the basis that we are each made in the image of God,
redeemed by Christ and adopted into his family. This alone, as
Bonhoeffer points out, is the basis of our community:

> Our community with one another consists solely in what Christ
> has done to both of us . . . I have community with others and I
> shall continue to have it only through Jesus Christ. The more
> genuine and the deeper our community becomes, the more will
> everything else between us recede, the more clearly and purely
> will Jesus Christ and his work become the one and only thing
> that is vital between us.[9]

In Christian community we taste the grace of God, receiving kindness, forgiveness and generosity from others, and also extending these gifts. However, journeying with others often exposes the woundedness and sin in our own hearts, including our pride, selfish ambition, self-hatred, impatience and ungodly anger. As we acknowledge and face these sins, it is in community that we can begin to develop humility, trust, forbearance, compassion, patience and love: attributes that simply cannot grow in isolation, but need the soil of human relationships in which to be cultivated. This growth can be painful – it is much easier to be offended and to withdraw from people. However, it is as we persevere in community that we develop maturity of character. This is needed for us to be able to live in unity with others and therefore to reflect the gospel of reconciliation (2 Corinthians 5:18) to the world.[10]

The Bible envisions the Church as a community built on humility, mutual submission and service[11] and this is totally counter-cultural in our highly competitive, ambitious and individualistic society. Jesus, of course, was the servant par excellence who washed his disciples' feet as an example for them to follow (John 13:14–15). And in his letters, Paul encourages the early Christians to imitate Christ's humility and service (Philippians 2:1–11), and presents a vision of Christian community in which each member is using their gifts for the good of all (Ephesians 4:1–16). In community, we have endless opportunities to serve others, not only by using our gifts, but through mundane acts of service with no recognition or reward. We can also allow ourselves to be served, and, together, can serve those beyond the Church. As we serve, our sense of community is strengthened, God's kingdom is demonstrated in the world, and, perhaps above all, we are changed. Serving others forces us to say 'no' to self-actualisation and self-promotion, and the humility which Christ desires, and which enables his power to flow, is gradually formed within us. Like any community, Christian communities are full of imperfect people, and it can be tempting to opt out. But there is no such thing as solitary Christianity, and the writer of Hebrews urges us not to give up meeting together (Hebrews 10:25). As we pursue our goal of growing in Christ within the context of Christian community, we will probably also be helped by investing in a smaller group of three or four people with whom we can find honesty, accountability and support.

Communion

Holy Communion, or the Lord's Supper,[12] is at the heart of Christian worship and supports our growth in Christ, as through it God encounters us in a particular way. Communion has often been seen by evangelicals as simply an act of remembrance, and by Roman Catholics as much more than that, but for both it is a 'sacrament'. Viewed in this way, Communion is a meal in which the very presence of Christ is mediated to us through the material elements of the bread and wine.[13]

Communion speaks all at once to our bodies, minds, spirits and senses, and through it we can experience Christ in a real and powerful way. It is a healing meal, in which we receive the life and presence of Christ to forgive our sins, heal our wounds and restore our brokenness. This is not magic, but it is effective, as we trust that God is present to us through the bread and wine. Jesus did not say 'Take and understand', but 'Take and eat' (Matthew 26:26). Communion also connects us powerfully to one another. We are a community on the basis of Christ's work for each one of us, and in Communion we both express and experience this unity, accepting one another in all our differences and weakness.[14]

We will normally share Communion within the church community, but it can also be helpful to share bread and wine with a small group of believers, a family, or even to take it alone,[15] as a way of receiving the life of Christ and 'feeding on him'.

I encouraged some clients, particularly those who lived alone, to regularly put out some bread and some wine at mealtimes, and use it as a way of having communion with Jesus. Sometimes this would include using the best tableware, setting an extra place, disconnecting electronic distractions, and having a conversation with Jesus. This action enabled God to become more real to them.

Training our feelings

Maturing in Christ is a holistic process involving emotional, as well as spiritual, growth. This means that we need to bring our emotions into alignment with God's truth. Although our feelings certainly need to be acknowledged, listened to and understood, we should not allow them to rule us, because feelings do not always reflect what is true about God, ourselves, others or indeed any part of life.

We usually assume that our feelings always tell us the truth, but they simply *don't*! They are rather like children – sometimes they are wonderful to have around, but at other times they can be naughty, grumpy, confused, argumentative, sick, hurt or frightened. Feelings frequently get the wrong end of the stick, and when they do not correlate with biblical truth, they need to be educated and corrected.

We can do this by speaking to them, rather like children. By memorising relevant scriptures, we can reassure our feelings of the truth and correct our misunderstandings in an area. We may also need to repent of any lies we have believed based on our feelings. For example, although we may believe that we are victims of our circumstances and that they or we will never change, we must *choose* to trust that God is always working for our good (Romans 8:28), and that he will complete the work he has begun in us (Philippians 1:6). Feeding on our negative emotions is like eating junk food – it can feel satisfying at first, but an over-indulgence leads to all manner of problems. God's truth, however, nourishes us and helps us grow up strong and healthy.

Praying the psalms can help us to notice and train our feelings. They give us the inside story of the psalmists' lives, and it is clear from their thoughts, feelings and God-conversations that they struggled with the whole range of human emotions and experiences. Taking time to dwell in the psalms helps us to be honest. They expose the ugly things in our hearts, and they nurture what is good and true and beautiful, because they point us back to God and put him firmly at the centre of life.[16]

As we train our feelings by rooting them in God's truth, we are becoming emotionally mature, so that our 'centre' is secure and anchored solidly to Christ, whatever our feelings tell us. This takes persistence and practice, but it is how we ground ourselves in Christ, choose to listen to his perspective, and actually begin to *experience* his truth, rather than being at the mercy of our own turbulent emotions.

The other night I was thinking about my cancer: 'It's not fair . . . I don't need this right now!' I realised that these feelings needed to be acknowledged – if you try to suppress your emotions, you run into trouble. However, I also knew that if I fed on them it would get me nowhere. Training your emotions isn't about shutting down, but rather it's about

dealing with them from a mature perspective. This allows
the Father to come in, giving us the strength and comfort
that we need, without us being reduced to whining children
again, taking out our hurt on everybody else.

Celebration

Growing maturity in Christ is marked by a growing capacity to
celebrate. This comes from an inner attitude of joy, which is
part of the fruit of the Spirit growing in our lives (Galatians
5:22), and celebration both expresses that joy and actually
creates more joy.

Philippians 4:8 encourages us to focus on things which are
right, pure, lovely, admirable, excellent or praiseworthy, and on
one level celebration involves simply enjoying the physical
things God has created for our pleasure, including good food,
beautiful art, the created world, faithful friends, and a loving
family. Sometimes, we assume that a truly spiritual person has
little concern for these things, because we have inherited a
dualistic understanding of the world, in which we divide life
into that which is 'spiritual' and that which is 'fleshly' and
somehow unspiritual. This is essentially a Greek worldview,
whereas in Jesus' Jewish worldview there was a holistic understanding of life: God was concerned with every aspect of life,
and the physical and spiritual were intimately connected with
one another.

Celebration also involves rejoicing in the goodness and faithfulness of God. This is not always instinctive, but sometimes
more of a deliberate decision, particularly in difficult times.
However, as we celebrate the goodness and gifts of God, we
choose the path of joy. We do not forget or deny our sufferings;
rather, we choose to focus on what *is* good in any given situation. Making this choice will not change our circumstances,

but it might change our outlook, as we increasingly see things to celebrate in the midst of our broken world.[17]

So celebration produces joy, which in turn gives us strength (Nehemiah 8:10). Israel regularly celebrated the goodness of God in festivals, and finding opportunities to celebrate will help us live well too. These may include festivals like Christmas and Easter, family events like birthdays and anniversaries, and achievements such as a new job or a child's first year at school. When appropriate, it is good to extend our celebrations beyond the nuclear family, and especially to consider including single people, to whom our culture often assigns fewer occasions for celebration, and people who are poor, who can be easily excluded. Whatever shape our celebrations take, they are powerful statements of our gratitude towards and trust in God, and they help us to experience more of his joy and strength, as we anticipate the eternal wedding feast of the Lamb which is to come (Revelation 19:6−10). One of Ruth's friends recalls how she modelled a life of celebration, even in the midst of pain:

Ruth always found ways to celebrate the good things of life, and this was especially powerful during the time of her illness, when she showed how genuine celebration can coexist with genuine grief and mourning. She regarded the cancer in her body as an evil thief, but at the same time chose to see and find ways to celebrate God's goodness, kindness and faithfulness to her and those around her. At her funeral the coffin was carried out of church to the popping of champagne corks, reminding us to celebrate the joy of resurrection life in the midst of our mourning.

Affirming our humanity

Maturing in Christ means that we become more, not less, in touch with our humanity. As we know, God created us in his image, so when Irenaeus said that 'the glory of God is a human being fully alive',[18] he affirmed that it is when we are being most truly and fully ourselves that we best reflect our Creator. As we discover and express more of the unique person God created us to be, with our unique personality, preferences and desires, we will best reflect his image. There are several aspects to this.

Affirming our humanity involves, first, honouring and caring for our own bodies. Our culture idolises the body. As a result, vast amounts of time, energy and money are expended in achieving a particular body shape, while we are simultaneously witnessing self-hatred on an unprecedented scale, manifested in alarming rates of eating disorders and self-harm from a very young age.[19] By contrast, God wants us to accept ourselves as being 'fearfully and wonderfully made' (Psalm 139), and to honour our bodies as a temple of the Holy Spirit (1 Corinthians 6:19). This means developing habits of getting enough sleep, eating well and exercising. Without these things in place, it is hard to live life fully and joyfully. Of course, we all have periods in which these habits are difficult, and some face long-term health challenges, but consciously taking care of our physical and mental well-being will promote our ability to live well.

One of the practices God has given to enable us to care for our bodies and minds and to live well is a day of rest, or Sabbath, and this principle is enshrined in scripture. God rested from the work of creation on the seventh day to enjoy what he had made (Genesis 2:3), and he commands his people to have a weekly rest day.[20] Jesus upholds the Sabbath, but denounces a legalistic interpretation of it, instead pointing to its heart by saying that 'the Sabbath was made for man, not man for the Sabbath' (Mark 2:27). Having one day off a week is a gift to us! Sabbath offers us the physical rest we need to live well, it invites us to anticipate the rest we will have with Jesus in the new creation,[21] and it encourages us to rest in Christ, by trusting in him rather than our own efforts.

Slowing down to rest is deeply counter-cultural in our busy, work-addicted world, and so Sabbath needs to be practised consciously. It will look different for different people and families, and in changing seasons of life, but we can shape our Sabbath habits by asking ourselves and others questions like: 'What restores you and gives you life?', 'What is the work from which you need to rest?', 'What helps you disengage from work?' and 'What helps you connect with God?' The answers to these types of questions will help us to find ways of practising Sabbath which are not legalistic, but which actually lead us into God's rest. Israel often missed the rest offered by Sabbath – not least by approaching it legalistically. We are in danger of missing it by conforming to the pressure of our busy culture (including our busy church lives), but practising Sabbath will lead us into the rest we need to live well.

A second aspect of affirming our humanity involves being in touch with and pursuing the God-given 'desires of your heart' (Psalm 37:4). Desires are sometimes considered to be at worst bad, or at best unspiritual. Some of them may be, but many of our desires are good, and an integral part of who God has created us to be. Sometimes it can be helpful to identify our desires before God and ask him to help us pursue the godly ones, as a way of recognising and celebrating our God-given humanity. (There is an exercise on page 329 to help you with this.) As we explore and express our God-given desires and gifts, we are being true to his image in us, and can recognise that he delights in the way he has made us. This is illustrated in the film *Chariots of Fire* when Eric Liddell unashamedly delights in his ability to run fast – he sees this as a gift which is given by God, and through which he experiences a connection with God. As we explore and express our God-given desires and gifts, we are being true to his image in us, and can recognise that he delights in the way he has made us. God is making us more, not less, human, and as we humbly use, develop and celebrate the gifts he has given us, his image in us is being revealed.

The habits we have explored in this chapter will help us in this lifelong process of growth towards maturity, enabling us to live well. Jesus offers life in all its fullness (John 10:10), which is defined not by our outward circumstances, but by our inner relationship with him. It is this relationship which enables us to live life fully – with purpose, meaning, joy, and the knowledge that we are completely loved. So, as we nurture our relationship with Christ and pursue our goal of knowing him, we experience more and more of the fullness of life he offers.

Exercise: Maturity in Christ

Consider each of the six habits we have discussed which lead to greater maturity in Christ. The following questions and suggestions are intended to help you reflect on how you are already engaged in each of these habits and examine how you might develop your practice in each area.

PRAYER AND BIBLE READING

Do you have a regular rhythm of prayer and Bible reading that sustains your relationship with God? If not, could you carve out a specific time of day to touch base with God or read his word?

If you need resources to help with this, Lectio 365 and the Bible in One Year apps are both excellent. You could also try exploring a form of prayer that is unfamiliar to you and which we discussed in Chapter 4, such as Lectio Divina, Ignatian meditation, liturgical prayer or spiritual direction.

COMMUNITY

Are you part of a church? What situations within that community is God currently using to develop character in you, and how can you cooperate?

If you are not already in a small prayer group, consider inviting two or three other people you trust to form one with you. Make room for honest sharing, confession, support, challenge and prayer.

COMMUNION

Do you approach Communion solely as an act of remembrance or a sacrament through which Christ meets you?

When you next receive Communion at church, or break bread informally at home, take a moment to bring any unconfessed sin, unforgiveness or pain to him, and expect Christ to meet you as you receive the bread and wine.

TRAINING OUR FEELINGS

In general, do you control your feelings or do they control you?

Whenever you notice negative feelings, take time to stop and listen for God's truth. Say to God, 'Lord, I am feeling . . . What is your truth in this situation? How do you see me?' Listen to God's perspective – drawing on scripture if possible – and then choose to believe and feed on that truth.

CELEBRATION

How easy or difficult do you find it to celebrate? What are the reasons for this?

Why not think of an event to celebrate and go the extra mile (it doesn't need to be expensive, and you can get creative with home-made decorations, silly games, or in-house entertainment)? Consider including others in your celebration.

AFFIRMING OUR HUMANITY

How much attention do you pay to the 'desires of your heart' (Psalm 37:4)?

Try writing a list of your desires. Think about activities you love or would love to have a go at, like painting, making music, sport, practising hospitality, learning a language or writing poetry. Be bold in naming your buried dreams and anything

you would love to do but have never had the opportunity.
Submit these to God and ask him to show you the next step in
pursuing one of these.

Further Resources

Bonhoeffer, Dietrich, *Life Together* (London: SCM, 1954).
Foster, Richard, *Celebration of Discipline* (London: Hodder & Stoughton, 1989).

Dying Well

We saw in the previous chapter that the apostle Paul made it his goal to 'know Christ' (Philippians 3:10), and that this really is the key to living well. Paul goes on to say that he wants to 'experience his resurrection power, be a partner in his suffering, and go all the way with him to death itself' (Philippians 3:10–11, MSG).[1] The natural fruit of living well is dying well – it is a continuation and 'culmination of a life lived for the glory of God'.[2] So at the close of this book, we consider how we might run the Christian race well, right to the very end.

The subject of death is feared and avoided within our culture, and sometimes even within the Church. When an Illinois geriatrician ran four church seminars on the subject of ageing, 250 attended each one, compared to only sixty who attended the seminar on dying, which several people confessed they found too uncomfortable to think about.[3] As a result of this attitude, the dying and their families are often unprepared for death, and even clergy may be ill-equipped to 'prepare the dying for their death'.[4] Previous generations of Christians gave much more serious attention to the business of dying, and from around the fifteenth century a body of works known as the *ars moriendi* ('art of dying') literature grew, to help Christians prepare for death. Later, in the eighteenth century, John Wesley invested significant energy in preparing people for death, and could confidently reflect that 'our people die well'.[5]

The Church's focus on helping Christians die well might have diminished, but death remains an inevitable fact of life, so it is worth thinking about how we might finish our earthly journey 'in Christ'. This chapter presents a practical approach to dying, in which scripture, theology and testimony are interwoven. It is not a full theology of dying, by any means, but it explores some experiences of dying, both those of Jesus in the Gospels, and those of various Christians who have reflected on the process. In particular, it draws on Ruth's story of facing her own death. On learning of Ruth's terminal diagnosis, my husband said to me, 'Ruth has shown us how to live well. Now she is going to show us how to die well.' That proved to be true, and sharing Ruth's 'final gift'[6] of a good death is the focus of this chapter.

This, of course, is Ruth's story. Each person is unique and will face their own death differently. Additionally, none of us knows exactly how or when we will die, and many will not even know that their own death is approaching. Not all will have the benefit – as well as the burden – of an extended period of preparation for death, and not all will have the mental faculties to engage with their impending death. However, keeping our end in view helps us to receive life as a gift and to order our priorities. So, while Ruth's story is a personal and subjective account of her own dying, we can take from it some principles for living life in the knowledge that death is certain, and in the hope that it is not the end. Additionally, for those currently living with serious or terminal illness, or walking with someone in this position, Ruth's story may offer some encouragement and support for the journey.

The final chapter of Ruth's story begins with a diagnosis of terminal cancer. She sets the scene by describing the impact it has:

> One Friday in June 2011, seven years after having been treated for breast cancer, my surgeon broke the news to us that I had advanced cancer of the neck, spine and sacrum. That evening we began teaching on 'Restoring God's Masterpieces' in a local church. Wondering how on earth I would manage, I knelt at the altar rail as the worship group sang the words 'Who can know the mind of the Creator?'[7]
>
> That weekend, the empowering of the Holy Spirit was awesome, and once again we could testify that the ways of Creator God are perfect, even in the face of that arch enemy – death.
>
> Facing a terminal illness is not dissimilar to finding yourself in the middle of an earthquake. Discovering whether your foundations will survive the initial impact and the inevitable after-shocks is pivotal. However, since receiving this terminal diagnosis, I can see how God has prepared me and laid deep, solid foundations to equip me for the journey of dying, and to ensure that my faith would not fail – even when I thought it had!

The foundations of faith that God had already built into Ruth's life proved vital, and several principles that characterised her life also characterised her journey of dying:

Following the Example of Jesus

Just as we seek to follow Jesus' example in how we live, we can also look to him for clues as to how we might die. Jesus' death is central to the gospel accounts, and the final week of his life occupies 40 per cent of the narrative, so we can see in some detail how he faced death. Jesus' death is, of course, different from ours in its vital theological significance for all humanity. But it is similar in that it was very much a *human* experience, and so provides an example which can help us face death. Following her initial diagnosis of cancer, Ruth prayed for healing, but, after receiving news of widespread secondaries, she instead chose to pray, 'Show me how to die.' In contemplating this, she returned again and again to the example of Jesus, finding in his final statements from the cross seven principles which helped shape her dying.[8] These were as follows:

1. **Total forgiveness**: 'Father, forgive them, for they do not know what they are doing' (Luke 23:34).
2. **A concern for family**: He said to his mother, 'Woman, here is your son,' and to the disciple, 'Here is your mother' (John 19:26–7).
3. **A concern for others**: 'Today you will be with me in paradise' (Luke 23:43).
4. **Doing what one can for one's physical needs**: 'I am thirsty' (John 19:28).
5. **Turning to God in all circumstances**: 'My God, my God, why have you forsaken me?' (Matthew 27:46).
6. **A burning desire to finish God's work**: 'It is finished' (John 19:30).
7. **Entrusting ourselves, including all our emotions and fears, to God**: 'Father, into your hands I commit my spirit' (Luke 23:46).

These principles, along with reflection on Jesus' passion as a whole, provided real encouragement and guidance to Ruth as she sought to face her own death in a Christ-centred way:

As I prepare for death, I keep looking at how Jesus did it. I have found that there is no shame in owning the doubts and fears with the one who withstood the temptations and experienced Gethsemane as my mentor. There is no problem in expressing the anger and asking, 'Why? It is robbery! Death is hideous and unjust! It hurts the people I love the most, and I am powerless to protect them or myself from this enemy.' But Jesus, who defeated death, knew his Father. He knew the heart of the Father he was relinquishing his life to. He knew the Father he was entrusting his family, friends and followers to. He knew the Father whose plans are always redemptive and restorative. He knew the Father whose love throws out those usurping fears. And I have begun to know and trust this infinite Father too.

Surrendering to the Father

Knowing the Father is the key to surrendering everything to him. Facing an agonising death, Jesus surrendered his own will to the will of the Father. In Gethsemane he prayed that, if possible, the cup of suffering might be taken from him. Ultimately, though, he surrendered to God's will in trusting obedience (Luke 22:42), and his final prayer on the cross was one of surrender – 'into your hands I commit my spirit' (Luke 23:46).

Christian discipleship is characterised by surrender, as Jesus calls us to surrender our hearts, our wills, our money, our desires, our work, our relationships – our whole lives – to him. Through these, which can each feel like 'mini-deaths', we surrender more and more of our own lives and hearts to God, and yet we actually discover more and more *real* life, for, as Jesus said, 'Whoever finds their life will lose it, and whoever loses their life for my sake will find it' (Matthew 10:39). Death is the final act of surrender, as we let go and entrust everything we are, along with everything and everyone we know, to God's love. Henri Nouwen describes death as 'a great struggle: the struggle to surrender our lives completely', and reflects that 'in the end, I will have to let go of everything and be carried into the completely unknown'.[9]

Catherine Marshall explores this theme of surrender more fully, making a clear distinction between *resignation*, which is passive and negative, and *acceptance*, which is active and positive. It is acceptance, she argues, which offers the key to surrender:

> Only in acceptance lies peace – not in forgetting nor in resignation nor in busy-ness . . . Resignation is barren of faith in the love of God. It says, 'Grievous circumstances have come to me. There is no escaping them. I am only one creature, an alien in a vast unknowable creation. I have no heart left even to rebel. So I'll just resign myself to what apparently is the will of God; I'll even try to make a virtue out of patient submission.' So resignation lies down quietly in the dust of a universe from which God seems to have fled, and the door of Hope swings shut . . . Acceptance says 'I trust the goodwill, the love of my God. I'll open my arms and my understanding to what he has allowed to come to me. Since I know that he means to make all things work together for good, I consent to this present situation with hope for what the future will bring.' Thus acceptance leaves the door of Hope wide open to God's creative plan.[10]

Ruth found these words particularly helpful earlier on in her life when her baby daughter's life was in danger. She recounted how, through this experience of suffering, she began a journey of surrendering to Christ, which enabled her to surrender more easily to him in dying:

I first read these words of Catherine Marshall in 1981, and soon afterwards our baby daughter was rushed into hospital, struggling to breathe with severe croup. As I held her on my lap in the middle of the night, doctors made various attempts to find a vein to put up a drip, but I was told she would have to be transferred to Great Ormond Street Hospital for a tracheostomy. At that moment I 'knew' for certain that God's love for my baby was even greater than mine and so I found myself able to say, 'If you want her, I will give her back to you, but please don't let her suffer any more pain.' Her eyes were wide open with the terror she was unable to voice. Immediately, the doctor got the drip into her vein and a tracheostomy was no longer necessary. So I think it is vital that we learn to pray prayers of surrender and relinquishment throughout our lives, not just at the finish, and doing this helps us to be able to pray them at the end.

Certainly, as I have faced my own death there is a need to continually surrender to the love of God. It seems to me that surrender hinges not on what I am surrendering, but on whom I am surrendering to. Jesus knew and trusted the Father he was relinquishing his life to. When we know and trust the infinite love of God, we are more easily able to surrender our lives into his loving hands. St Augustine said, 'We must fly to our beloved homeland. There the Father is, and there is everything.'[11] From this perspective we are returning to a Father who loves us.

Remaining Rooted in Christ

We are God's beloved sons and daughters – this is our fundamental identity. Yet our *sense* of identity – our heart's belief that we really are God's beloved children – is often challenged by our life experiences and circumstances. We have also seen that we are constantly tempted to derive our identity from other sources, and that one of the most important aspects of God's restorative work in us is to root our identity firmly in him. As Jesus approached death, his identity was challenged by the high priest ('Tell us if you are the Messiah, the Son of God': Matthew 26:63), by Pilate ('Are you the king of the Jews?': Matthew 27:11), and by those who stood around his cross ('Come down from the cross, if you are the Son of God': Matthew 27:40). In a different way, for Ruth the process of dying presented both a challenge to her sense of identity, and an opportunity to appreciate more fully who she truly was in Christ:

Living with a terminal illness has challenged my identity, as more and more of 'me' gets stripped away. I am no longer the homemaker who loved practising hospitality, enjoyed gardening, and being the grandmother who could leap in the car and take over at a moment's notice, scoop my grandchildren up in my arms and cuddle them. I am no longer the counsellor or the missionary who revelled in the challenges of life in Egypt and seeing God gently transforming broken lives. I am no longer the wife I long to be as I become less and less mobile and need a wheelchair. I am no longer able to stand and teach alongside my husband. I am no longer the friend who can offer support and practical help. In the midst of these circumstances, I find myself asking, 'Who am I?'

But I know more than ever that I am a deeply loved daughter of the eternal Father. Nothing I do can add to that. Nothing I fail to do can change that. No doubts or fears can reverse that. The one thing I become more and more sure of is his abiding presence, cradling me and bending over me with the most profound compassion in his eyes.

In May 2012, I was on my way for more tests at the Marsden Hospital, where I was to discover that the cancer had spread to my hip and right arm. In the car, I became aware that the real me, that is to say my true identity, was getting stronger and stronger as my body was deteriorating. I had the sense that the real me was being enlarged and would soon be bursting out of this tired, sick body. I remembered watching a dragonfly crawl out of our pond, climb up a reed and shed its old body. It clung weak and vulnerable to the reed as the sun shone and we watched its wings develop until the moment it let go and soared upwards with such grace and beauty. Instead of death diminishing me, I knew that, through it all, the Restorer was at work, and I wanted to shout from the mountaintop, 'How great is our God!'

The process of dying is often seen as a diminishment of the person, as we refer to people as 'a shadow of their former selves'. But in our journey towards death, we can *experience* the Christian hope of God's ultimate restoration of ourselves, including our bodies. N. T. Wright presents the biblical vision in these terms:

A Christian in the present life is a mere shadow of his or her *future* self, the self they will be when the body which God has waiting in his heavenly storeroom is brought out, already made to measure, and put on over the present one – or over the self that will still exist after bodily death.[12]

Leaning on God

The Christian life is a relationship of trusting God, and as we are restored, we grow in trust, and learn to lean on him in the midst of joy and sorrow, as the beloved disciple leaned on Jesus' breast at the Last Supper (John 13:25). Even at his point of greatest suffering, Jesus addressed his pain to God – 'My God, my God, why have you forsaken me?' (Matthew 27:46), and we too can turn to and lean on God in our suffering. God's embrace is the place of comfort and safety, and 'when we know that God holds us safe – whatever happens – we don't have to fear anything or anyone but can walk through life with great confidence'.[13] Indeed, there are rarely answers that can adequately meet our pain, and all that remains is simply to *be* in God's presence. Ruth discovered that leaning on God in the midst of terminal illness brought her into the presence of Jesus where she found deep peace:

I often return to Psalm 146:3, which I read the day before I received the devastating news. *The Message* version reads, 'Don't put your life in the hands of experts who know nothing of life, of salvation life.' That doesn't mean I am not grateful for all the medical treatment and care – I am – but I don't put my trust in them! It's the eternal Father who is in charge.

Of course, there are bad days and sleepless nights when I experience fear as new pains appear. There are times when I beat my fists on God's chest saying either, 'It's too hard! I can't do this! Let me die now!' or, conversely, 'There's not enough time!' In these times tears are shed. Despair is looked full in the face. Envy and anger are acknowledged. But in the midst of this, I am learning to practise gentleness towards myself, and recognising that pain pulls the plug on every-thing – my energy, my ability to communicate, my desire to make the effort, even my will to live. Yet it throws me more onto leaning on Jesus' chest and gripping his nail-pierced hand so tightly and just being with the only One who can walk all the way with me to the beyond that is shrouded in mystery. The questions evaporate and all that matters is he is fully present, fully capable, and I can sink into him.

Walking with Others

Ultimately, Jesus faced death alone, but he journeyed towards the cross with his closest family and friends. The night before the crucifixion, he shared the Passover meal with his disciples, and indicated the nature and significance of his impending death through the elements of bread of wine. He took his three closest disciples with him as he wrestled with God in Gethsemane (Mark 14:33–34). His mother and the beloved disciple were there at Calvary, supporting him throughout his awful death. However, his friends proved to be far from perfect – Judas betrayed him (John 18:3), the disciples fell asleep when he most needed them (Mark 14:37–41), and Peter intervened violently to try to defend Jesus (John 18:10), then denied even knowing him (John 18:17–27). Jesus had to cope with betrayal, misunderstanding and abandonment from those closest to him, even at the end of his life. But despite their imperfections, he chose to approach death in the company of friends, and he also remained connected to the wider community of faith by pray-ing for his disciples, and for all believers, as he prepared for death (John 17:6–26).

The Christian life is lived in community, and as Ruth walked through terminal illness she learned to accept and draw on the support of friends, while continuing to serve other people, especially through her prayers:

One of the things I have found especially helpful is having several very precious companions who are able to let me express fears and my doubts about what comes next. I have recognised that most people can't walk this with me, and fear that I am losing my faith, or find these questions too threatening. But I have found just two or three in whom I can confide, including Michael Lloyd who helped me by saying, 'If our eternal hope was wishful thinking we wouldn't be struggling and grappling with it – we'd be in denial, not asking the hard questions.'

It is also important to keep the needs of others in mind, and not become too self-focused. On a very practical level, I keep reminding myself of the persecuted Church to keep perspective, and I am praying more for others than for myself. One day, as I was worshipping, pictures of people and places flashed into my mind and I realised that as I was worshipping, I was also interceding. It just flowed. Jesus said, 'My yoke is easy and my burden is light'! What extraordinary kindness God was showing me in my weakness and what a gift to treasure and value in the days to come.

Preparing for an Adventure

The Christian life is a faith adventure, and many Christians have thought of death itself and the journey of dying in these terms. Grace Sheppard, the widow of Bishop David Sheppard, described it like this:

Living with David's dying was certainly an adventure. We both
felt like explorers in a new world which was full of surprises,
both welcome and unwelcome. This new world was dangerous
and called for courage. It was distressing and comfort was
needed. Emotional and physical exhaustion took its toll. It was
frightening yet love came to our rescue. Plodding on with
people for company, and resisting the urge to look down, was
certainly a major part of the action. We knew where we were
heading.[14]

When Jesus appeared to Mary Magdalene after his resurrection, he forbade her to hold on to him, saying, 'I am returning
to my Father and your Father, to my God and your God' (John
20:17). The Bible teaches that, through death, we, like Jesus,
are returning to the Father, and it gives us many clues about
the nature of our future hope: we will inhabit resurrected
bodies (1 Corinthians 15:35−58)[15] in a new earth (Revelation
21), where there will be no suffering (Revelation 21:4).[16] What
we do not know, and cannot imagine, is what shape our resurrection life will take. The details remain shrouded in mystery.
For this reason, death can be seen as a journey into the
unknown, even as an adventure. All we know as we venture
into the unknown is that the destination is God himself, for
'we believe that we go to a person and a place where we belong,
a place in which there is no more sorrow or pain, a place where
we will receive a welcome from someone who loves us unconditionally . . . That God will be a place of safety and security
when we die'.[17] Death, then, is a homecoming to the Father,
and Ruth expanded on these themes of adventure and homecoming as she prepared for the journey from this life to the
life ahead:

I am coming more and more to see this time as preparing for the biggest adventure of my whole life. As I reflect on my short-term mission trips to Egypt, I know that while I have often felt fear about travelling to an unfamiliar country and culture, I have also experienced some of the happiest and most deeply satisfying moments of my life in this 'foreign' country! So as I prepare to step into the 'unknown' territory beyond death, I am confident that joy and adventure awaits me.

As I contemplate my own death, I am also coming to see the things I have most enjoyed in life as just a foretaste of heaven and the relationships that are waiting to be explored within the Godhead himself. I am beginning to see that in dying I am coming home and that there will be so much to be explored within the vastness of God. This is captured by C. S. Lewis as he describes the entry into Narnia in *The Last Battle*: 'I have come home at last! This is my real country! I belong here. This is the land I have been looking for all my life, though I never knew it till now . . . Come further up, come further in!'[18]

Leaving Things in Order

Throughout his life, Jesus was preparing and training his disciples to continue his kingdom work. At his death, he made specific provision for his mother and his closest friend by instructing them to care for one another. He also prayed for the Church and instituted the sacrament of Communion for his disciples in every generation. In such a way, 'he was equipping them for his departure, and for their mission when he had left'.[19] Leaving our affairs in order when we die will look different for different people, depending on our particular

circumstances, responsibilities and personalities. It may be
straightening out relationships through apologies, 'thank
you's, and honest conversations about the past and future. It
may involve the ordering of finances and possessions, or it may
entail making arrangements for the future provision of our
family, friends and communities. When Ruth made short-
term trips to Egypt, she ensured that life at home would
continue to function smoothly while she was away. Similarly,
as she approached death, she made preparations for leaving,
by putting things in place (including material for this book)
that would continue to bless and equip her family, friends and
fellow travellers in her absence:

I have always loved planning and preparing for special events,
and so I have even enjoyed planning my own funeral as a way
to glorify God! I have also left things in order. I have passed
on treasured possessions and even left presents for grandchildren and godchildren.

In December 2012, we moved back to Oxford, as we had
always wanted to do after retirement. It seemed madness at
that stage of my illness but God appeared to be in it, and I
was able to help Andrew to settle into a home he will love
and which I have put my 'stamp' on, and it is a bonus to
have a few months enjoying being close to my grandchildren after moving. However, as we prepared to drastically
downsize, emotions of feeling utterly bereft hit me. Things
were not just objects, but were loved, cherished, and
imbued with precious memories. Faces flashed before me
of folk I'd held as they wept with their pain and had
profound healing encounters with Jesus on my sofas. My
mind drifted back over twenty-five years of rich conversations around our table with family and friends – at

Christmases, Passovers, Sabbath meals, and birthday celebrations. Many prayers had been prayed and answered
around our table. How could I leave these things behind?
How could I make home without them? Who would love
and cherish them and carry on the legacy of healing, hope
and restoration around them?

With tears pouring down my cheeks, I rang one of my
closest friends who really understood my pain. This call
utterly transformed things for me as I discovered she and her
husband not only had need of and room for my 'spare' sofa
but would 'continue to love people into the kingdom seated
on it'. I discovered God does care about the details, and, as it
says in Zechariah 14:20, 'Every pot in Jerusalem and Judah
will be holy to the Lord Almighty.'

Finishing with Hope

Perhaps the most important aspect of finishing well is to finish
with hope. Jesus endured the cross 'for the joy set before him'
(Hebrews 12:2), and Paul kept his eyes focused on the prize of
resurrection life (Philippians 3:14). Finishing with hope does
not mean that we deny the pain and suffering involved in death,
but that we *focus* on God and on the resurrection life to come.
When we are confident in the hope of resurrection (John
14:1–4), we can see death as 'the gateway to new life',[20] and
prepare to 'walk through the gates of death with the self-
confidence of heirs'.[21] The Puritan preacher Richard Baxter
encouraged Christians to practise hope as they prepared for
death, urging us to 'enter heaven in our imagination, picture its
glories and tread its streets.[22] He advised that 'we should spend
some time there every day'[23] and Ruth certainly faced death
with a clear vision of her future hope.

When Ruth was diagnosed with terminal cancer, she was very honest about the suffering and robbery caused by her death. There was no denial. But neither was there self-pity or despair. Sorrow and grief were balanced by faith and hope as she trusted both in the promise of resurrection life, and – most importantly – in God himself. True hope is, very simply, hope in God. It is not even hope in what he might do, but hope in him as a person. It is a 'ruthless trust'[24] that he *is* good, whatever our circumstances might seem to tell us. Hope built on circumstances is easily eclipsed when those circumstances change, but true hope is built on the solid foundation of God himself, and it is this trust in the person of God which opens up the possibility of hopeful living and hopeful dying. Moreover, Paul describes God as 'the God of hope' (Romans 15:13), and so as his image in us is restored we can expect our capacity for hope to grow. Ruth reflects on how suffering develops this kind of hope, and how, in turn, hope changes our perspective on suffering:

Hope develops in the most difficult times of our lives, not in the easiest. It is in suffering that we learn how to wait. We learn not to focus on trying to prevent it, but to ask the hard questions, to voice the anguish, and to search for God in that mysterious darkness. And in suffering we also learn how to watch for what God is doing. We believe that God's word and character is as it says in the Bible and not as our feelings may be telling us, so we choose to harness our imaginations to faith not to fear, and we choose to expect that redemption will come out of suffering – because it will.

Waiting and watching like this is what produces hope – true hope. Hope in God himself is not wishful thinking. Wishing is like a line that comes out of me with an arrow pointing to the future – it tries to twist God's arm and get him to give me what I want. But true hope is actually a line that comes from God out of the future towards us. Hope means being surprised because we don't know what is best for us or how our lives are going to be completed. And to cultivate hope, we need to stop this wishful thinking for what we want and live in anticipation of what God is going to do next in our lives and in the lives of those people around us. Living in this kind of hope sustains me on the journey, so that I can testify:

> Strength for today, and bright hope for tomorrow,
> Blessings all mine with ten thousand beside.
>
> Great is thy faithfulness, great is thy faithfulness,
> Morning by morning new mercies I see.
> All I have needed your hand has provided,
> Great is your faithfulness, Lord, unto me![25]

Homecoming

A month before Ruth died, Andrew shared with prayer partners a picture he had of walking hand in hand with Ruth, her right hand in his, up a path to the heavenly city. Jesus opened a door, smiling as he came towards them, and gently took her by the other hand; then the two of them walked together towards the open door. The night before Ruth died, she was comatose and unrousable, but at 9.35 a.m. the next day she lifted up her left hand for about fifteen seconds, then it dropped as she took her last breath. It was the same hand which Jesus had taken in Andrew's picture. She had truly walked 'all the way with him to death itself'.[26]

Ultimately, Jesus is calling each one of us home to himself. In the meantime, the God who made us in his image is utterly committed to restoring that image within us, so that we might enjoy greater intimacy with him and with others, and fulfil our vocation to reflect his glory. If we are willing, he will use every circumstance to accomplish his work of restoration in us, right to the very end of our lives. His desire for us is to live well, and so to finish well, clothed in hope as we enter into the full restoration of resurrection life. We can be confident that God, who has started a great work in us, will keep at it and bring it to a flourishing finish: 'God is the one who began this good work in you, and I am certain that he won't stop before it is complete on the day that Christ Jesus returns' (Philippians 1:6, CEV).

Further Resources

Dunlop, John, *Finishing Well to the Glory of God* (Wheaton: Crossway, 2011).

Gawande, Atul, *Being Mortal: Illness, Medicine and What Matters in the End* (London: Profile Books Ltd, 2014). Not written from a Christian viewpoint, but offers a helpful perspective on ordering priorities at the end of life.

Giddings, P., Down, M., Sugden, E., *Talking about Dying: Help in Facing Death and Dying* (London: Wilberforce Publications Ltd, 2016).

Goodall, Janet, *Children and Grieving* (London: Scripture Union, 1999).

Lewis, C. S., *The Last Battle* (London: Bodley Head, 1956); *A Grief Observed* (London: Faber & Faber, 1961).

Nouwen, Henri, *Our Greatest Gift: A Meditation on Dying and Caring* (London: Hodder & Stoughton, 1994).

Sheppard, Grace, *Living with Dying* (London: Hodder & Stoughton, 2010).

Stickney, Doris, *Water Bugs and Dragonflies* (Cleveland: Pilgrim Press, 2004). A picture book for children, intended to help children process grief.

Varley, Susan, *Badger's Parting Gifts* (London: Andersen, 1984). Also a picture book for children, intended to help children process grief.

Wright, N. T., *Surprised by Hope* (London: SPCK, 2007).

Appendix 1

Ministering Restoration to Individuals – In Conversation with Ruth

During the last year of her life, we interviewed Ruth about her experience of being a prayer counsellor. We hope that her insights will encourage and help you to minister God's restoration to others, whether in a professional, lay or ordained capacity.

Tell us about your first steps into healing prayer.
When we were living in north London in the late 1970s, various things were emerging about inner healing. The first book that any of us in the church read was by President Jimmy Carter's sister![1] I led a group for women where we decided to explore this a bit further, and so read and discussed these kinds of books. The group was quite charismatic; I wasn't and had some reservations. Then my husband Andrew, who is a doctor, had a Christian patient who was suicidal, and for some reason he told her, 'You should speak to my wife', which she did after having been discharged. She turned out to have a very damaged background with horrendous abuse. She came to stay with us for several days, and was indeed very disturbed. I didn't really know how to help her, so I rang somebody who had a lot more skill in listening to God and ministering healing. As we started

to pray with her, I found myself praying in tongues. I thought, 'Ah! I can understand why I need this [tongues],' because until then I was completely stuck, so obviously it was a gift from God to enable me.

But at that time, you had no professional training?
No! God began to heal me directly without anybody being involved, and as I later heard others describing healing prayer, I would think, 'That happened to me several years ago directly from God, so I know that this is genuine.' You've got to be in a place where you are engaging in this with God for yourself before you start to do it for somebody else. So it's not a formula, but instead came out of my experience. If God wants to train somebody up, he can do it in his unique way.

So why did you then take a course?
Around 1994 I felt that God said to me, 'You need to get a piece of paper', and that it should be a course that had secular accreditation. Then as I was food shopping, I bumped into a woman who was the wife of a psychiatrist, and she mentioned she was about to embark on a pastoral counselling course, so we went together. It had a Christian base, set up by a chaplain in a psychiatric hospital who had got it accredited with Roehampton University. The course sharpened me up about what I really did believe; it challenged a lot of my evangelical presuppositions (making me believe many of them more firmly), and also enabled me to recognise some of the naivety of things I had seen as black and white.

How do you make people feel safe?
Safety comes from various things: from clients feeling assured that what they're saying is totally confidential, knowing that

you're not in a rush, being able to reflect back to show that you have listened and thought about things, and from emitting warmth and empathy. Trust is the foundation for healing prayer to work. I often succeeded because I worked from home, and so from a warm environment, whereas when you go to formal therapy/counselling it can be in a very bare room with nothing human in it. Sometimes I would take people into the garden when I sensed they needed to walk around it, or we would have sessions on the patio. I remember one woman who had just lost a baby: we sat on the patio and she cried the whole session while I held her, and she just looked at the flowers, which was what she needed. Sometimes I'd offer a warm drink, or if I discovered that they hadn't been eating – a ham sandwich. Why not? Humanity is an important part of it. Without empathy you're not going to get anywhere.

What are some things that stop people feeling safe?
You have to be very careful not to put your 'stuff' onto your clients, or even to presume you know how they feel. I find a helpful phrase is 'I cannot imagine the impact of that' which may encourage them to say more about it. Completing a listening skills course can be helpful, because you learn these kinds of phrases, and are taught how to reflect back to the other person. It is very easy to put your foot in it so that a client doesn't feel understood. This happened with one person I thought I was doing quite well with, and whom I was going to use as a case study for my professional course. I said something in a session which triggered how her mother used to speak to her, and since I had not understood this from her perspective, she got quite angry. I knew I had lost the connection, but I didn't know exactly why. The next time she came, I began by saying, 'I really need to apologise for what I think I got wrong

last time', and we were able to move on. You've got to be honest
when you twig that somebody has slightly pulled back, and
then find a way to sort that out.

How do you enable people to be more honest?
People never ever come out with everything in the first session. I
wouldn't! There are always layers to our pain – like an onion – and
you have to trust God that what needs to be revealed will come out
as and when. You don't rip somebody's mask off, because that
causes damage. God is incredibly patient – we have to remember
what he is like with us and show that same patience to others. Often
clients try to minimise wounds and say that 'it doesn't really
matter' – but if we want to encourage them to share their pain, it's
important to validate what they are saying and feeling.

**How do you listen to what God is saying during your
sessions?**
I pick up a lot through sensing things – I'm more of a feeler
than an observer – and I think it's the same when I'm listening
to God. When I start to pray with somebody, I've not necessarily actually heard God say something; instead an idea will form
in my head, and I'll feel my way with it. Of course, other people
will be different – some will get a very clear word from God, or
a picture. Because I often don't, it makes it easier for me not to
spoon-feed people. But when I do get one of these, I will wait
until they have also heard this from God, and only then say,
'That's great, because it's also what I sensed/saw/heard',
which confirms and underlines what they have received from
God themselves. If they can personally connect with Jesus
(either by hearing him or by seeing or sensing things), that
creates a far more powerful and lasting impact in their lives
than if I give a word or picture to them.

An important key in enabling this connection with Jesus is to find some way to help a person visualise, because that is the language of the heart rather than the mind. Once they have had that initial encounter, they can start to connect with God as he really is, but often they need a lot of reassurance. People regularly come back and have forgotten what they have heard from God or think they have imagined it, so they need to be given confidence to hold these things and build on them.

How do you unravel what might be at the heart of a client's issue(s)?
Usually clients present with a particular problem, which may well be where you start because you need to take it seriously. However, you may immediately realise that there is something underneath this. For example, under depression there is often a lot of anger, even though there are other things feeding into it. Getting a client to talk about their family and their background can be very revealing. For example, they might spend a lot of time talking about one parent but never the other; it's as much what they don't say as what they do say that's important. Most people hide the parent that they are more defensive about in what they share initially; so, if they start by talking more about their mother, they are often more defensive about their father.

I sometimes get them to write down their story, then I ask *them* to read out this story, even when they expect *me* to read it. This is often very effective because the emotions come out as they recite it. Then you can reflect certain parts back to them using slightly different words, which may help them recognise things they perhaps haven't seen before.

I often find that when clients return, God has been at work in between sessions, and they have started to make their own connections. At this point you can ask, 'Do you think that may in some way tie up with what you told me before about . . .?' This way you give them the two ends to see if they connect them. You need to discern when that is appropriate to risk, otherwise they may become very defensive.

How do you know whether it's right to pursue a particular issue?
As you try to explore something, if a client conveys that it is a no-go area, you must respect that (even though you may be right to assume it's important), otherwise trust disappears. Indeed, by backing off you may be respecting their boundaries in a way that they have never experienced before. Using the mask analogy again, trying to take a person's mask off prematurely may rip off the skin, which could be horrific. If on the other hand trust is built up over time, the mask is gradually soaked to such an extent that it can be lifted off without causing any damage.

However, if somebody is trying to avoid coming into the light, there are times when you have to quietly but firmly challenge this. Somebody I'd seen for quite a number of years had struggled with various sexual things and had made some progress, but was very much stuck in self-centredness. I can remember thinking, 'If I don't challenge this, he's going to stay stuck for ever.' I said something to the effect of, 'You can continue in self-pity, feeling sorry for yourself, carrying this for the rest of your life, in the same way that I could walk around saying, "Poor little me, I've got cancer." Or you could say "Okay, it's happened, but that doesn't define me".' He was really shocked, yet knew I was speaking from a very authentic place. He didn't like it though, and didn't make any more appointments – but it later turned out that he really shifted, and we had some good email correspondence.

How do you help people change?

Here there are two streams: one is to change thought patterns by the renewing of the mind, and choosing to *think* truthfully. The other is to move into prayer for healing, which concerns the *heart*. Although the latter allows the former to be realised, I also have to educate my feelings until they believe the truth. You can't make a method out of this, but often wounds will keep sabotaging the cognitive progress. I usually explore the healing of the heart route first, otherwise you can slip into what is just positive thinking and self-help; this can get you part way, but it doesn't really allow God to heal in a way that enables you to become free, no longer striving. Someone I know very well has gained a lot from exploring the cognitive approach, but hasn't sought God's healing. Her approach is, 'I'm going to manage this', believing that she has the answers, whereas doing it God's way leads to a dependence that is healthy and gives true security and appropriate humility. Undoubtedly, people can do well with a non-Christian approach and finish up in a much better place, but it doesn't lead to the full freedom that Christ offers.

What have you learned as you reflect on how Jesus ministered to individuals?

Jesus met people where they were at.[2] He gained their trust. He didn't do the same thing twice. He brought them into a better place. But he didn't say, 'I'm going to make you comfortable here.' A lot of counselling and therapy attempts to make clients more comfortable, so that they are essentially just rearranging their room, as it were. What we as Christian counsellors are doing in gaining their trust is saying: 'The door is open; let's bring you out to where there is freedom, where there is so much more for you to see.'

What is the place of the cross in what you do?

For many evangelicals, the cross is the doorway that leads into the kingdom, but then it's left behind, rather than being central to the whole of your Christian life. There is, of course, truth in the 'once and for all' of the cross — for example in terms of guilt. But with respect to transformation within us, we need to engage with the cross over and over again. It is 'the place of exchange' where you can leave your grot and shame, and in return, receive restoration in an ongoing way.

I learned early on that some people carry baggage about this – one client had formed a 'hellfire view' of the cross having endured frightening sermons as a child. When I attempted to bring her to the cross, she freaked out and I quickly realised I had to find a new approach. In the next session, I invited her to visualise Jesus taking her somewhere that she would like to go. He took her on a journey where she started to fly out through space, and as she described this I was wondering, 'What have I done?!' But he took her towards the New Jerusalem, where she saw all the light, streets paved with gold, and so on; yet she had no idea that this was in the Bible. I then read that section from Revelation to her, which is also linked to our names being written in his Book of Life. So Jesus used this vision to show her his forgiveness and acceptance of her, and her eternal security with him.

At some point for every single person the cross does have to come in, but sometimes other healing may be needed beforehand. Ultimately, I don't believe anybody can make progress without the cross. I have noticed that liberals tend to try to hold on to compassion, but don't hold on to the cross. As a result compassion leads them down the route that God loves everybody, so let's forget about sin as long as people are happy and don't hurt others. This means there is nowhere to go and deal with sin. On the other hand, I see evangelicals who are not showing mercy, because they have not understood the transforming power of the cross. So the cross is the centrepiece of freedom and healing.

What do you recommend people do between sessions?
First, to practise listening to God, and to start a listening prayer journal.[3] Second, to take Communion regularly, the Church's most healing sacrament. Third, to work through a healing prayer book like Signa Bodishbaugh's *The Journey to Wholeness in Christ*.[4]

Do you pray for people in between sessions?
Rarely! My attitude is that when clients walk out of the door I can say 'bye-bye' because they are in Jesus' hands, and it's up to him. I always make it clear that clients should not contact me, but rather develop their own network of support in their church or prayer group, for example. However, if somebody were suicidal it would, of course, be different; on occasions I have phoned on a daily basis, but that would be rare.

How do the tools of healing ministry compare with prayer ministry after a church service?
There is a difference between this and most other models of prayer ministry, such as those based on prophetic insight – although both have an important place. The biggest difference is between ministry being done *to you* and learning to use the healing tools *for yourself*. The first can be like being spoon-fed – it runs the risk of keeping people at an immature level, depending solely on others, and not necessarily pursuing God for themselves. So, despite all the benefits of prayer ministry, there can be dangers in having ministry done 'to you', both for

the person receiving it and for the person administering it. There is something in us that likes those we pray with to be dependent upon us, because it makes us feel good, and important, and of value.

For me, the key thing is that people learn how to use the tools for themselves; this is an apprenticeship – discipleship in the truest sense of the word – where somebody comes alongside another person until they have learned which tools are appropriate, how to use them, and when to use them. Then off they go! It's like good parenting – one of the overriding things that I realised in having children was that they had been given to me to train and teach, so that one day they would walk in God's ways. So it's a process of training and letting go until they grow into maturity in their relationship with God.

How do you set boundaries with clients?
If they are coming purely as a paying client whom you see only during sessions, that's relatively easy, but within your own church, or when you are not involved in formal counselling, you have to be very clear about what you can and can't offer. This may mean offering to see someone for a limited number of sessions and defining what these meetings will involve, so everyone has the same expectations.

If the person doesn't have many friends, the temptation to try to meet that need by becoming one is strong – this is a massive learning curve for all of us. Some people are so needy that they start to resent the fact that you are not always available to them, and relationships get messed up because you haven't spelled it out beforehand. For example, you might want to say that weekends and evenings are reserved for your family time. I learned a very good phrase to use when somebody rings at a time which is inappropriate (say a Saturday afternoon): 'Thank you for calling. I haven't got the time you deserve to give it my full attention at the moment, but if you could ring again on Monday morning at 10 o'clock, I will do then.' This gives them something to hang on to – it's not rude, and it's true. Once somebody rang me as I was getting the kids out of the door for school, saying, 'I'm just about to turn the gas taps on so that I can blow myself up', and I knew that she had young children in the house. I took a deep breath and heard myself saying 'Do you think you could possibly wait until 9.15, and I'll come round when I've dropped off the children?' She said 'Oh. All right.' I drove along thinking, 'Am I coming back to see a fire engine and a massive explosion?', but she was sitting there waiting for me. That must have been God, mustn't it?

With respect to confidentiality, it's also important to define the boundaries you are working within. I would always say to clients, 'You do realise that the way this works is that sometimes I will need to discuss things with my supervisor in order for me to get the best help for you.' The client also needs to be aware of what confidentiality means in terms of safeguarding (i.e. what they share might need to be passed on).

How do you know a client no longer needs to attend counselling?
The timing often comes from both sides, or sometimes the person will say that they don't feel they need to come any more. Even if there is an anxiety about this, when you unpack it there is often an elation about a client realising they have enough of a handle on their issues, and a map, so that they can have a go at engaging more in the healing and restoration process themselves. As in the weaning process, the child looks forward to having more exciting nourishment and is ready for the change. We might then make an appointment for three months' time

for review and to see how they're doing, but if they don't want to come they can phone and cancel it.

What are some of the signs of emotional health you would want to see developing in your clients?
I would want to see them:

- having a relatively healthy view of God;
- becoming integrated into some form of Christian community *during* that journey;
- looking outwards, rather than everything always being about them – this is key;
- beginning to think how to serve others more than themselves – being able to put someone else first;
- keeping some sort of journal and/or having a prayer partner;
- having some sort of accountability;
- developing healthy pursuits such as a hobby, and expressing talents, rather than having a very limited world;
- having a sense of humour, including being able to laugh at themselves – damaged people don't laugh easily, and take themselves too seriously.

Appendix 2

Ministering Restoration in the Local Church

Hennie Johnston is currently vicar of a church and Area Dean in the Chester Diocese. She met Ruth Miller three decades ago at a Leanne Payne conference in Swanwick, and became first a client, then a colleague, companion, and dear friend. Ruth's ministry of healing and restoration was an important part of Hennie's own walk with God, as she was led out of places of darkness into the light of Christ.

Here, Hennie explains the need for restoration and healing prayer in the local church based on her own experience over the past twenty years, first as a lay member, and then as an ordained minister of a local church. She will look at the principles and good practice of healing prayer, addressing questions such as: '*Why* should a local church think about the ministry of healing prayer?' and '*How* might it be introduced into the church?'

Why we need this kingdom ministry
Many churches today do not have a ministry of restoration and healing. There may be magnificent worship, powerful preaching, fabulous fellowship and friendship, small groups and prayer meetings, even effective evangelism and mission, and prayer ministry (by this I mean a team of people who are

available to pray for a person after a Sunday service). And yet, there may be no healing ministry of the type which brings emotional restoration of feelings, attitudes, outlooks, beliefs, behaviour or expectations.

This is a tragedy, because the Church is a hospital for sinners – not a sanctuary for saints. Jesus said: 'It is not the healthy who need a doctor, but those who are ill. I have not come to call the righteous, but sinners' (Mark 2:17). So a church that lacks the ministry of healing remains a broken body of Christ.

As has been discussed earlier in this book, complete restoration does not happen as soon as we are converted – even if we have had a Damascus Road experience. It is often a gradual and gentle process. My stepsister is a picture restorer and many years ago my stepfather asked her to restore a huge painting hanging in our drawing room. It is a beautiful painting and I can remember wondering what it would look like once she had spent months carefully and delicately working on it. What I did not expect was that previously hidden characters in the painting would emerge from behind the grime: there were the figures of a little girl and boy playing in the background, and fishermen along the riverside to the right of the painting – it was an amazing transformation. The painting looked awesome before it was restored, but now it hangs in its full glory.

This is similar to churches that lack the ministry of healing – they can look and feel amazing, but they are not fulfilling their God-given potential, because lives remain broken and unhealed, marred from the years of grime that life has thrown at them. As Christians, we are not called to walk alone, and most of us need someone to help us out of the place where we are stuck, into a place of freedom and healing. Today there are so many different therapies and secular counsellors on offer, and people are desperate to be healed from depression, addictions, habits, and bad attitudes. But none of these secular sources will bring God's full healing. However, where there is a channel for God's healing and restoration, lives will be restored and healed – and these transformed lives will also signpost others towards Jesus.

Personal need of restoration

I had been brought up as a Christian, but it was not until my early thirties that I was taken to a small church plant in London of about forty people, and it was there that I learned about the possibility of having a real and intimate relationship with Jesus. I asked him into my life, and was filled with the Holy Spirit. Certain things in my life did dramatically change, but I was very aware that I still carried a lot of baggage within me, like a heavy rucksack on my back.

Soon after asking Christ into my life, my stepbrother suggested two books that I might find helpful – *The Healing Presence* by Leanne Payne and *Yesterday's Child* by Mary Pytches. Both were about inner healing. I read them immediately, and they spoke and ministered to me powerfully, but there was no one I knew with whom I really could share what was beginning to happen in my heart and head. So when I saw that Leanne Payne was coming over from America to run a conference in Swanwick, Derbyshire, I knew I had to go. I took one of our churchwardens with me and a young intern who had joined the church, both of whom were interested to learn more about healing ministry. (Just as an aside, if you can take others with you to healing conferences, do!) It was at this conference that I met Ruth, and it was also here that I started to get very interested in the ministry of healing, relating it to Jesus' ministry and therefore the ministry of the Church.

The Church's need for restoration

Not only was I in need of this ministry, but so was my church. It was an amazing time of exponential growth for the church, as many young Christians joined having just moved to London. Many people also came to know Christ through the Alpha course, which was just getting under way at the time. The average age of those in the church I attended was around twenty-five for the first few years of its growth, and it was very exciting to see God at work in the lives of these young people.

However, as I got to know them and listen to them, I also realised that there was much pain behind their personal stories – addictions, eating disorders, lack of self-worth/esteem, anger, unforgiveness, masks, pornography, misogyny, abuse, avoidance of one's past, and ungodly attitudes and reactions. I soon realised that as Christians mature in both age and faith, we can still carry these unhealed wounds throughout the whole of our lives, unless there is a place for them to be treated. So I felt passionately that healing prayer was needed in the local church – my next obstacle to tackle was 'How can I introduce it?'

As I was not a leader in church, I had to pray hard and 'manage upwards' to convince the leadership of the need for this ministry. Having said that, the church where I was a lay member of the congregation, progressing on to the church leadership, was the one that in my twenty years of being involved in healing prayer was the most receptive, and we saw great healing, restoration, and transformation in people's lives.

I was later ordained and have since been involved in bringing healing prayer into various different churches. The church where I was curate had in the past cultivated a thriving ministry of healing and restoration, and had even been a resource for other churches in the UK and abroad. However, when I arrived, there was only a remnant of the team left who, although disillusioned, were keen for this ministry to be empowered once again. So the vicar and I began to encourage and equip these team members through teaching, preaching and training courses. It was an exciting time as people embraced this ministry again, allowing the Holy Spirit to minister to them, and in turn equip them to help others be healed and restored.

The two other churches that I have ministered in as an ordained priest had a history of offering prayer ministry after Sunday services, and introducing healing prayer proved more of a challenge. However, yet again there were a few people who were moving in the spiritual gifts of healing and prophecy, and the ministry began to catch fire. As I write, the church where I now minister is in a transitional place – alongside offering prayer ministry on a Sunday, we are teaching and training people for the ministry of healing, reconciliation and restoration, and are seeing lives transformed through the power of the Holy Spirit.

Whether you are the leader or a lay member of the pastoral/prayer ministry team, a small group leader, or member of the congregation who is convinced that God is calling your church to embrace healing ministry, I think the key principles and processes in introducing healing ministry are the same. Those that I have discovered are:

1. *Immerse yourself in the teaching that is available on healing ministry.* Look at the Further Resources sections in this book to help you start.
2. *Speak to others experienced in healing ministry and ask who they would recommend as speakers or teachers.* This ministry evolves and develops; those who were speaking and teaching

in previous decades may have now passed their baton on to others.

3. *Invite people you know and trust to come to your church to run a 'taster session' introducing the concept of healing ministry.* I have found it is good to have a variety of different speakers over the first few years because some of your church members will engage with certain speakers depending on age groups, character and churchmanship. Don't give up if few people turn up for the first taster session – the enemy longs for people to remain imprisoned in their old ways of being, and will try every trick he has to keep people away. Persevere and pray!

4. *Attend as many conferences, residential and day, as you can, taking others with you.* New Wine[1] run pastoral prayer weekends for local churches; residential and non-residential courses are run by Lin Button's Healing Prayer School,[2] as well as Journey UK (formerly Living Waters).[3]

5. *Don't just be knowledgeable about healing ministry: experience restoration for yourself.* If we are really serious about introducing healing ministry into our churches, our flock need to know that we are walking the talk, before they will follow us into this unknown territory. However, we also need discernment and wisdom as to how much we share – I was once advised that leaders need to hang out some of their dirty laundry, but not all of it!

6. *Preach on it.* Begin to bring healing ministry into your sermons. As I write, our church is doing a sermon series entitled 'The Psalmist's Heart', looking at a number of different psalms, including some of the lament ones. It is amazing how the psalms show us that we can come from a place of great darkness, hurt, pain, envy, grief, depression and sin, into a place of hope, light and freedom. Alternatively,

you could preach on the healing miracles of Jesus. If you follow the Lectionary or have other sermon structures, look out for when you can incorporate the healing touch of Jesus into your preaching.

7. *Embrace it*. A church that embraces the ministry of healing and restoration will need to be a church that is okay with mess, vulnerability, transparency and honesty – a church where people can leave their masks behind and model Jesus' ministry of weeping with those who weep, and rejoicing with those who rejoice.

8. *Above all – pray*. Pray for the healing ministry to become part of the DNA of your church's life and ministry.

Practical implementation

Healing ministry can take place in the local church in different ways and is very much dependent on the resources available – human, practical and even structural. One scenario may be that as a leader, you have embraced some of the suggestions above, and you have now trained a team who could begin offering this ministry. As already explained, healing ministry is not the same as prayer ministry offered after a Sunday service, and churches that are experienced in healing ministry usually offer one-to-one prayer outside this context. An appointment is usually made with one or two of the team for prayer during the week – offering three sessions of one-hour prayer slots is good practice. Depending on the team member and those seeking prayer, it may be appropriate to meet in the church building, church centre, or in some other safe setting. The church needs to set up a structure and policy that works for them, and have godly boundaries to protect both the people administering and those receiving prayer.

This appendix has described how I have introduced healing

ministry into the churches I have been a part of, and I continue to use these techniques. However, one cannot be prescriptive, and we must allow the Holy Spirit to lead and guide us in our implementation.

Ruth often described healing ministry as preparing people to be ready for Jesus' return when he comes and claims the Church as his bride. That is why healing ministry is an integral part of being a disciple of Christ, with the power to transform the life of the Church, and to restore individual lives into the image bearers God has created them to be.

Acknowledgements

It has been a privilege to write this book in honour of our dear friend and mentor Ruth Miller, and thereby to capture some of her insights as a gift to the Church. We are particularly indebted to her husband, Andrew, for his teaching material on 'Restoring God's Masterpieces', which was the starting point for this book. He also transcribed the interviews we conducted with Ruth, gathered and collated testimonies from her clients, contributed the prayers for mother and father wounds, checked quotations, and sourced references.

At an early stage in the project, Jackie Arnold transcribed Ruth's recorded talks, which enabled valuable insights to be captured, and we have been faithfully supported in prayer throughout by other friends of Ruth: Bishop Mouneer Anis, Revd Norman Arnold, Sister Margaret Evening, Gail Foot, Alice Laing and Imogen Wolfensberger. We are deeply grateful to each person who has shared their story of God's restoration, and to the team at Hodder, notably Andy Lyon, Sam Sneddon and Jessica Lacey, who have enabled the vision of this book to become a reality.

We wish to express particular appreciation to our families and supporters on the writing journey. For Rachel, thanks especially to Phil, whose passionate pursuit of God's restoration constantly inspires me; to Hannah and Bethany for their patience as I worked on this book, which is a legacy for you both from Hannah's godmother Ruth; to Mum and Dad, who have provided a bedrock of love in my life and helped endlessly with childcare; and to Clare, Jo, and later Charlie, whose thoughtful, astute reflections on the text have shaped my thinking and writing.

For Michael, thanks especially to Abi, who generally finds my writing warming – via the medium of a solid fuel burner – and whose love of beauty and history is an inspiration to me; and to Campion Hall, which provided a community that was wonderfully conducive to learning and writing, and delightfully hospitable to me when I was there on study leave.

Ruth was immensely grateful for the joy and love she shared with her family – Andrew, Ashley, Chloe, Kate, Stuart, Annabel, Maddie, Jos and Jamie. As we talked with her about this book, she also expressed her gratitude to mentors and partners in healing prayer, whose influence may be felt in its pages, including Revd Conlee and Signa Bodishbaugh, Lin and Ron Button, Revd Chris and Dr Lisa Guinness, Revd Stuart Lees, Revd Clay McLean, Leanne Payne, Mario Bergner, Andy Comiskey, Revd Drew Schmotzer and Bishop Keith Sinclair. She was particularly thankful to her friends, Revd Hennie Johnston and Right Revd Dr Tom Wright, for their contributions to the text. Finally, Ruth acknowledged with gratitude her many clients and friends who allowed her 'the immense privilege of stirring God's love into your lives'. We are two of those people, and offer this book back to the Church, trusting that God will use it to stir his love into your life.

Notes

Part 1: The Theology of Restoration

Chapter 1: The Image of God – Created

1 This is a relational riff on the old definition of sin (dating back to Augustine, via Luther) as being bent in on oneself (*incurvatus in se*). See Matt Jenson, *The Gravity of Sin: Augustine, Luther and Barth on 'Homo Incurvatus in Se'* (London: T. & T. Clark, 2006).

2 Sometimes in church history, theologians have believed that 'likeness' and 'image' refer to different things – often that the image was not lost at the fall, but the likeness was. It is now generally acknowledged that the two words are used interchangeably (see, for example, Genesis 5:3).

3 Gerhard von Rad, *Old Testament Library: Genesis* (London: SCM, 2012), pp. 59–60.

4 D. J. A. Clines, 'The Image of God in Man', *Tyndale Bulletin*, 19 (1968), p. 91.

5 It might be possible to mount an argument that the equality of all human beings is implicit in the experience of moral demand. When the Good Samaritan is confronted with a human being in need, he knows instinctively that

this is a neighbour, and that that call upon his compassion transcends the barriers of race, gender, class and creed that are so often used to diminish the set of those to whom we have neighbourly responsibilities. However, the very fact that Jesus felt the need to tell this parable suggests that even the experience of moral demand does not convey the truth of human equality self-evidently.

6 Michael Jensen, *The Christian Revolution 2: Equality* (2008), p. 243. https://biblicalstudies.org.uk/pdf/church man/122-03_243.pdf, accessed 17 January 2023.

7 Of course, some might argue that the defensive and the aesthetic are very closely related – indeed, that the aesthetic has grown out of the defensive, that we find it aesthetically pleasing to have a good view from our house because of what we have 'learned' evolutionarily about being alert to threat. However, the point here is that the aesthetic has developed a life of its own.

8 Again, there is no denying that there is an evolutionary aspect to this. Our desire to look elegant, for instance, is clearly related to animal display and bird plumage. However, there is also no denying that there is more than the desire to attract a mate (or to advertise one's place in the pecking order) going on in the extraordi-nary variety and creativity of the clothing industry. And some of that variety and creativity is done for its own sake. On the day I wrote this, there was an article in the *Daily Telegraph* about some research which showed that, while peacock feathers may attract peahens, flashy cars don't impress those who are look-ing for a long-term relationship. 'Is this an argument for sending the Porsche for scrap?' asks the Editorial, rhetorically. 'Not a bit of it', it answers. 'Unlike for

peacocks, for humans beauty doesn't need to serve an evolutionary purpose' (*Daily Telegraph*, 8/5/18, pp. 5, 17). It is not for me to endorse any particular make of car – there are other models and brands! What I do endorse is the belief that beauty and creativity have got cut loose from their evolutionary moorings and have taken on a (wonderful) life of their own.

9 Hans Rookmaaker, *Art Needs No Justification* (Vancouver: Regent College, 2010).

10 Revd Gerald Ambulance, with Stephen Tomkins, *My Ministry Manual* (London: SPCK, 2002).

11 For an account of how the early Church came to believe the doctrine of the Trinity, see Chapter 8 of my *Café Theology* (London: Hodder & Stoughton, 2020).

12 Jenson, *Gravity of Sin*, p. 1

13 Henri Blocher, *In the Beginning* (Leicester: InterVarsity Press, 1984), p. 97.

14 Sister Margaret Magdalen, *The Hidden Face of Jesus* (London: Darton, Longman & Todd, 1994), p. 152, citing Richard Holloway, *Anger, Sex, Doubt and Death* (London: SPCK, 1992), p. 35.

15 It might be objected that artificial insemination means that there need no longer be any act of intimacy. However, even artificial insemination depends upon voluntary self-giving from the most intimate parts of the female and male body. Even if there is not bodily proximity, there is bodily self-giving for the sake of another.

16 Assuming they are not sinful, obviously.

Chapter 2: The Image of God – Broken

1 Claus Westermann, *Genesis 1–11: A Commentary*, trans. John Scullion (London: SPCK, 1984), p. 148. By 'fall', he

means that rebellion against God, that 'fall' away from his purposes that is depicted in Genesis 3.

2 Theodorus Vriezen, quoted in Hans Urs von Balthasar, *The Glory of the Lord*, Volume VI, *Theology: The Old Covenant*, trans. Brian McNeil and Erasmo Leiva-Merikakis (Edinburgh: T. & T. Clark, 1991), p. 91.

3 Augustine, *Confessions*, Book 1.1.

4 For a defence of the possibility of the fall being in some sense a historical event, see my discussion on 'Theodicy, Fall and Adam' in *Finding Ourselves After Darwin* (Grand Rapids: Baker Book House, 2018), Chapter 16.

5 A personal testimony. We shall see in the next chapter how Andrew was freed from that deep sense of inferiority.

6 I am indebted, here, to a talk I heard at school, by Harry Ferrar, who was one of the teachers.

7 From a sermon to the Baptist Association Meeting at the Friar Lane Baptist Chapel in Nottingham, UK, 30 May 1792.

8 There is, of course, a version of this strategy which tries to get *God* to love us. This tends to take the form of life-denying legalism, or religious workaholism – with a dash of self-deception thrown in, for good measure.

9 I am not denying that governments have, quite properly, a particular and primary responsibility for their own people, just as parents have a primary responsibility for their own children. However, when objections are raised about the use of 0.7 per cent of the UK's gross national income to promote overseas development, it begins to look as if the demand is not just that charity should begin at home, but that it should end there, too.

10 This is a basic principle. See 1 John 4:20; Matthew 18:21–35.

11 Cited by Charlie Haas in *What Color Is Your Parody?* (Los Angeles, California: Price Stern Sloan Publishers, 1984), p. 14.

12 See Tom Andrew, *The Church and the Charter* (London: Theos, 2015) for the role played by Archbishop Stephen Langton in the formation and writing of Magna Carta.

13 First broadcast on *The Frost Report on Class* (BBC, 1966), Episode 1:5.

14 For his flaunting of the rabbinic teaching of his day that men should not address women in public, see John 4:4–42. For his inclusion of women among those who were entitled to sit at his feet and learn as disciples, see Luke 10:38–42. For his flaunting of the fact that the testimony of women did not count in a court of law, see the way in which women were (according to all four Gospels) the first to witness the resurrection.

15 Matthew 19:13–14.

16 Witness the effect that Jacob's favouritism had on relationships between his children (Genesis 37:3–4).

17 For God as having no favourites, see Acts 10:34; Romans 2:11; Ephesians 6:9; Colossians 3:25.

18 See John Blair, *Building Anglo-Saxon England* (Princeton: Princeton University Press, 2018).

19 Charles Dickens, *Hard Times* (Hamondsworth: Penguin Books Ltd, 1976), pp. 51–2.

20 Cf. https://www.london.anglican.org/articles/opening-of-st-mellitus-st-judes-hub, accessed 17 January 2023.

21 Exodus 20:3–6. The iconoclasts argued along these lines. See John of Damascus's three treatises *On the Holy Images* for an Orthodox refutation of the iconoclasts.

22 See, for example, Peter Paret, *An Artist against the Third Reich: Ernst Barlach 1933–1938* (Cambridge: Cambridge

University Press, 2003); Alexander Solzhenitsyn, *The Oak and the Calf*, trans. Harry Willetts (New York: HarperCollins, 1980).

23 Genesis 3 is precisely a story of how cutting ourselves off from God has thereby cut us off from one another (Genesis 3:12; 4:8), from the natural world (Genesis 3:17–19) and from ourselves (Genesis 3:7; cf Genesis 2:25).

24 Jesus' command to love God and to love our neighbour (Mark 12:30–31) makes that clear.

25 C. S. Lewis, *A Grief Observed* (London: Faber & Faber, 1961), p. 8.

26 1 Corinthians 13:12.

27 Song of Songs 5:1, New American Bible.

28 Psalm 63:1, Coverdale translation.

29 Love does, of course, need to be *fed*, but that is different from saying it has to be earned.

30 Assuming, again, that they are not sinful.

31 Galatians 3:28.

32 Isaiah 53:6.

Chapter 3: The Image of God – Restored

1 To give the technical theological terms, the process of restoration is Christological, soteriological and ecclesiological. There are other locations, obviously. It happens first in Israel, it happens fully at death, and it happens finally at the putting right of all things. I have chosen to focus on the three locations of Jesus, the cross and the Church because these are the ones that most shape (and give content and context to) our own process of restoration *now*.

2 Emphasis mine. Notice that the argument only works if the birds of the air have a significant intrinsic value.

3 Matthew 6:32–3.

4 Interestingly, he also seems to identify three important sources of anxiety: first, living in fewer dimensions than we were made for, and ignoring the 'more' to which we are called (Matthew 6:25); second, relying on our own resources alone for our self-preservation and sustenance (Matthew 6:26); third, trying to establish our value by frenetic activity, which is counter-productive and self-destructive (Matthew 6:26–7).

5 John 15:13.

6 Tony Campolo, *The Kingdom of God is a Party* (Word, 1990), p. 5.

7 Ibid., p. 7.

8 Sister Margaret Magdalen, *Jesus – Man of Prayer* (London: Hodder & Stoughton, 1987), p. 21.

9 Ibid., p. 24, commenting on Matthew 6:25-34, cf. 10:29-31.

10 For example, Mark 4:35–41.

11 John 11:35.

12 Not all Christian theologians would agree with me that death as such is contrary to the purposes of God. Tom Wright, for instance, entertains the possibility that the human fall does not introduce death, but changes its character: 'Death, which we may be right to see as a natural and harmless feature of the original landscape, now assumes the unwelcome guise of executioner': see *Evil and the Justice of God* (London: SPCK, 2006), p. 28. It seems to me, however, that Jesus does not help the centurion or the widow of Nain or Mary and Martha to see and experience death differently – he undoes it, and that therefore we should see it as having no place within the purposes of God for his world.

13 Genesis 1:28. Of course, the human fall does not happen until Genesis 3. The fact that there is already something

that needs subduing, and the fact that the serpent is already working actively against the purposes of God even before human beings rebel, persuade me that the world is already fallen, prior to the human fall. I attribute the pre-human fallenness of creation to a prior fall of the angels. See my *Café Theology* (London: Hodder & Stoughton, 2020), Chapter 2.

14 1 Corinthians 15:28.

15 Colossians 1:20.

16 'On the Baptism of Christ', *The Nicene and Post-Nicene Fathers*, Second Series, Volume V (Grand Rapids: Eerdmans, 1988), p. 524.

17 Cf. Romans 12:18.

18 Obviously, many churches are historic buildings, and we need to explore ways of being as sustainable as possible without damaging their historic fabric or diminishing their aesthetic beauty.

19 See, for example, the teaching of Rabi Yose ben Yohanan in m. 'Abot 1.5, discussed by Andy Angel in his *Intimate Jesus: The Sexuality of God Incarnate* (London: SPCK, 2017), p. 3.

20 John 4:7.

21 John 4:27, as translated by Angel, *Intimate Jesus*, p. 1.

22 Ibid., p. 4.

23 John 11:5.

24 Luke 8:3.

25 Mark 14:6−9.

26 Luke 10:39. See Kenneth Bailey's *Jesus Through Middle Eastern Eyes* (London: SPCK, 2008), p. 193: 'To "sit at the feet" of a rabbi meant that one was a disciple of a rabbi.' He cites Acts 22:3 as an example. Malina and Neyrey comment: 'Jesus' remark to Martha serves to vindicate Mary's exceptional presence in space not

expected of her; the story consciously upsets the native
perception of how things ought to be'; cf. Jerome H.
Neyrey, *The Social World of Luke–Acts: Models for
Interpretation* (Peabody: Hendrickson, 1991), p. 62.

27 Luke 24:10–11.

28 Matthew 19:13–15.

29 *The Expositor's Bible Commentary*, ed. Frank E. Gaebelein,
Volume 8 (Grand Rapids: Zondervan, 1984), p. 420.

30 *New International Biblical Commentary* on Matthew
(Peabody: Paternoster Press, 1989; first published 1983),
p. 163.

31 Mark 10:16.

32 Luke 15:1–2.

33 Luke 17:16. Given the Samaritans' perceived religious as
well as racial impurity (2 Kings 17:24–5), we should
include the religiously/theologically heterodox among
those whom Jesus explicitly taught us to regard as recipro-
cal equals.

34 Bernard O'Connor, *The Human Face of Jesus* (London:
Catholic Truth Society, 1986), pp. 21–2.

35 'Sarah Huckabee Sanders and who deserves a place at the
table', *The New Yorker*, 25 June 2018.

36 Matthew 15:24.

37 John 10:16.

38 John 10:15.

39 Ephesians 2:17.

40 Galatians 3:27.

41 Rodney Stark, *The Triumph of Christianity* (New York:
HarperOne, 2011), p. 122.

42 Douglas Hare, *Matthew*, in the Interpretation Series
(Louisville: Westminster John Knox, 1993), p. 224.

43 O. M. Bakke, *When Children Became People: The Birth of*

Childhood in Early Christianity (Minneapolis: Fortress, 2005).

44 See Philemon 16.

45 O. O'Donovan, *The Desire of the Nations* (Cambridge: Cambridge University Press, 1996), p. 185.

46 Stuart G. Hall, *Homilies on Ecclesiastes*, Homily 4 (Berlin: De Gruyter, 1993), pp. 72–4.

47 Cited by Roger Ruston in *Human Rights and the Image of God* (London: SCM Press, 2004), p. 269.

48 Matthew 6:29, KJV.

49 John 2:1–11.

50 Matthew 26:30.

51 Matthew 9:5. Runar M. Thorsteinsson compares Jesus' debate with his opponents in Luke 14:1–24 with the sorts of debates that took place 'at the famous Socratic symposium': 'Unlike Socratic symposia, Jesus begins the meal by healing a sick person, but like Socrates Jesus leads the discussion, rejecting certain opinions and asking rhetorical questions to which his opponents had no answers': see *Jesus as Philosopher: The Moral Sage in the Synoptic Gospels* (Oxford: Oxford University Press, 2018), p. 158.

52 Matthew 9:6, NRSVA.

53 Mark Forsyth, *The Elements of Eloquence: How to Turn the Perfect English Phrase* (London: Icon Books, 2016), pp. 73–5, citing Matthew 7:3–5 and 19:34.

54 Runar Thorsteinsson remains agnostic as to whether Mark, Matthew and Luke knew the writings of Graeco-Roman philosophers, but he does suggest they would have been acquainted with 'some of the philosophical traditions of their closest environment' (*Jesus as Philosopher*, pp. 9 and 11).

55 Isaiah 53:2.

56 *Vitis Mystica* 5 (VIII 168–71), quoted in Hans Urs von Balthasar, *The Glory of the Lord*, Volume II, *Studies in Theological Style: Clerical Style*, trans. Andrew Louth, Francis McDonagh and Brian McNeil, ed. John Riches (Edinburgh: T. & T. Clark, 1984), p. 354. Occasionally, we see that paradox reflected in the way people face death; which can make their death a strange revelation of the glory of God (see John 21:19). I have never seen that more than in the way Ruth Miller faced death.

57 2 Corinthians 5:21.

58 Flannery O'Connor in *Mystery and Manners: Occasional Prose*, selected and edited by Sally and Robert Fitzgerald (London: Faber & Faber, 1972), p. 175.

59 2 Chronicles 3:6, KJV.

60 Luke 2:49.

61 Luke 11:1.

62 E.g. John 11:41–2.

63 E.g. Mark 1:35–37.

64 Romans 12:18.

65 There are times when it seems as if Jesus is being unnecessarily belligerent. For instance, in John 7:19, where he asks, 'Why are you trying to kill me?' In the light of subsequent events, however, his diagnosis that their opposition to him was reaching murderous proportions proved prescient.

66 Mark 10:21.

67 John 13:26. The giving of a morsel of bread was, according to Craig R. Koester, 'a gesture commonly understood to show favour'. See his 'The Death of Jesus and the Human Condition', in *Life in Abundance: Studies of John's*

Gospel in Tribute to Raymond E. Brown, ed. John R. Donahue (Collegeville: Liturgical Press, 2005), p. 149.

68 Luke 23:34.

69 Margaret Magdalen, *The Hidden Face of Jesus* (London: Darton, Longman & Todd, 1993), p. 126.

70 John 15:15.

71 Mark 6:30–4.

72 Luke 10:38–42.

73 John 19:25–7.

74 Luke 23:12, 40–3.

75 John 8:12.

76 John 8:55.

77 Matthew 27:46, trans. Nicholas King (Stowmarket: Kevin Mayhew, 2013), p. 1885.

78 Psalm 27:10, NLT.

79 Cf. the repetitions of 'If you are the Son of God' – Matthew 4:3, 6; 27:40.

80 John Saward, *The Mysteries of March: Hans Urs von Balthasar on the Incarnation and Easter* (Washington: Catholic University of America Press, 1990), pp. 47–8.

81 John 13:23, 25.

82 John 4:27, in Andy Angel's translation.

83 Angel, *Intimate Jesus*, p. 48.

84 Ibid., p. 54.

85 Magdalen, *Hidden Face of Jesus*, p. 154.

86 John 4:34.

87 John 4:16–20.

88 John 4:29.

89 Angel, *Intimate Jesus*, p. 60.

90 Ibid., p. 51.

91 John 1:14.

92 Angel, *Intimate Jesus*, p. 31.

93 Luke 3:7, 10–14.

94 Isaiah 53:12, 9. His actual tomb was 'one in which no one had yet been laid' (Luke 23:53), but it would have been situated among other tombs – hence the angels' question, 'Why are you looking for the Living One among the corpses?' (Luke 24:5, Nick King translation). *The Bible: A Study Bible* freshly translated by Nicholas King, Kevin Mayhew Ltd., Buxhall, Stowmarket, Suffolk, 2013.

95 Herbert McCabe, *God Matters* (London: Mowbray, 1987), pp. 247–8.

96 See the genealogies in Matthew 1:1–17; Luke 3:23–38. See also Hebrews 2:11.

97 *Commentary on the Epistle to the Galatians* (1535) (London: James Clarke, 1953), p. 272, emphasis mine.

98 Please note that I am not holding up Wycliffe as a special example here. We fail in this area as in all others, and there have been high-profile cases of such failure in the past. There almost certainly will be again in the future. My only point is how healing it is when people experience safeness and respectfulness.

99 Luke 2:49. 'Son of God' was a messianic title.

100 From the Te Deum.

101 John 10:20; Mark 3:21.

102 As N. T. Wright points out, in addition to madness, the categories of 'demon possessed' and 'rebellious son' were employed to explain him: see *Jesus and the Victory of God* (London: SPCK, 1996), pp. 439–42. None of these three charges is likely to have been invented by the early Church.

103 For instance, his singleness seems, through later monastic development, to have added singleness as a serious option for the cultures into which the gospel spread.

104 C. S. Lewis, *Perelandra* (London: HarperCollins, 2005; first published 1943), pp. 272, 275–6.

105 Luke 15:3; John 10:11.

106 *Daily Telegraph*, 24 February 2018, https://www.tele-graph.co.uk/women/life/midult-hilarious-guide-middle-age-modern-woman-tinder-anxiety, accessed 12 August 2018.

107 21 July 2018, p. 8.

108 Ruston, *Human Rights and the Image of God*, p. 283.

109 Jane Austen, *Pride and Prejudice* (London: Penguin Books, 1985), p. 100. I am grateful to Fiona Scott-Dawe for correcting my erroneous attribution of this put-down to Elizabeth Bennet in an earlier draft.

110 Obviously, human beings are not there to be worshipped, but they are there to rule the world on God's behalf, and to let the world know what God is like.

111 Colossians 1:15, emphasis mine.

112 George Herbert, 'The Elixir', *The English Poems of George Herbert* (London, Oxford and Cambridge: Rivingtons, 1880), p. 194.

Part 2: Spiritual Practices for Restoration

Chapter 4: Listening to God

1 Francis of Assisi, *The Canticle of the Creatures* (1225).

2 John of the Cross, *The Spiritual Canticle and Poems* (London: Burns & Oates, 1978), pp. 26–30.

3 Evelyn Underhill, *Practical Mysticism* (New York: Dutton & Co., 1914), p. 88.

4 For more on spiritual gifts, see D. Pytches, *Come, Holy Spirit: Learning to Minister in Power* (London: Hodder & Stoughton, 1985).

5 Of course, we need to be mindful of the dangers of taking biblical promises out of context. For example, when God promises Hezekiah that he will recover from his illness and live another fifteen years (Isaiah 38:5), this promise is specific to Hezekiah, and cannot be universally applied. The promises we can appropriate are those that speak of the unchanging character and habitual acts of God.

6 Lectio Divina is a threefold pattern of prayer, consisting of 'lectio', 'meditatio' and 'oratio', and traditionally leading into a fourth dimension, 'contemplatio'. Its origins are ancient, but it was formalised and practised extensively by the Benedictines.

7 Leanne Payne, *The Healing Presence* (Eastbourne: Kingsway, 1990), p. 47.

8 A. W. Tozer, *God Tells the Man Who Cares* (Milton Keynes: Authentic, 1994).

Chapter 5: Rediscovering Heart Knowing

1 In his Latin publication *Principia Philosophiae* (1644), based on his earlier French work *Discours de la Méthode* (1637) which has 'Je pense, donc je suis'.

2 Blaise Pascal, *Pensées*, trans. Alban Krailsheimer (London: Penguin, 1966), 423.

3 It could be questioned whether contemporary society as a whole (including the Church) really does overemphasise reason, or whether it is not actually quite anti-intellectual. Where this is the case, both heads and hearts are undernourished. We have majored here on the dangers of devaluing the heart because Ruth's teaching focused particularly on trying to equip people to see the connections between past hurt and present patterns of behaviour.

4 Ruth describes this incident, from a mother's perspective on p. 248.

5 For more on the link between addictive behaviour and emotional pain see Stuart Lees, *Will the Real Me Please Stand Up* (London: Hodder & Stoughton, 1997), Chapter 8.

6 Eugene Peterson, *Under the Unpredictable Plant* (Grand Rapids: Eerdmans, 1992), p. 171.

7 Ibid., p. 171.

8 C. S. Lewis, whose *Narnia* stories illuminate for us deep truths about Christ and his kingdom, called the imagination 'the organ of meaning': see C. S. Lewis, *Selected Literary Essays* (Cambridge: Cambridge University Press, 2013), p. 265.

9 For more on imagination and the cross, see Leanne Payne, *The Healing Presence* (Eastbourne: Kingsway, 1990), pp. 171–2.

10 Brother Lawrence, *The Practice of the Presence of God* (London: Hodder & Stoughton, 2009).

11 Teresa of Ávila likens the soul of a beginner in prayer to a garden which needs weeding and watering: see *The Life of Saint Teresa of Ávila by Herself*, trans. J. M. Cohen (London: Penguin Books, 1957), p. 78.

12 Signa Bodishbaugh, *The Journey to Wholeness in Christ* (Grand Rapids: Baker, 1997), pp. 153–4.

Chapter 6: Practising Confession

1 N. T. Anderson, *Living Free in Christ* (Regal Books: Ventura, 1993) offers a comprehensive exploration of a believer's identity in Christ. A summary of relevant themes and scriptures can be found at https://vintagelawrence.com/wp-content/uploads/2013/01/

ANDERSON_WhoIAmInChrist.pdf, accessed Jan 2023.

2 Cf. Revelation 12:10.

3 Leanne Payne, *Listening Prayer* (Grand Rapids: Baker, 1994), p. 100.

4 Ibid., pp. 99–100.

5 Bonhoeffer holds that confession to other believers enables us to experience real community as well as an assurance of forgiveness through the cross. Dietrich Bonhoeffer, *Life Together* (London: SCM, 1954), pp. 86–96.

6 The Anglican confession says alongside 'penitence' for our offences, we need 'faith' – in God's character, and his desire and power to forgive us, through Jesus' death on the cross. Find C of E confession at https://www.churchofengland.org/prayer-and-worship/worship-texts-and-resources/common-worship/daily-prayer/forms-penitence, accessed 17 January 2023.

7 This means not disclosing what is shared, unless the other person gives consent, or unless they present a danger to themselves or others. See Appendix 1 on the nature and boundaries of confidentiality.

8 Payne, L., *Restoring the Christian Soul* (Wheaton: Crossway, 1991), p. 151.

9 Ibid., pp. 176–7.

Chapter 7: Forgiving Others

1 Used, for instance, in Matthew 26:28; Colossians 1:14; Ephesians 1:7.

2 Desmond and Mpho Tutu, *The Book of Forgiving* (London: William Collins, 2014), p. 24.

3 First quoted in Susan Cheever, *A Woman's Life* (New York: HarperCollins, 1995), p. 133. Nelson Mandela was

one of several people who adapted it slightly, he most
famously.

4 Tutu, *Book of Forgiving*, p. 16.

5 Margaret Magdalen, *Jesus – Man of Prayer* (London:
Hodder & Stoughton, 1991), p. 137.

6 If a crime has been committed, we can forgive, but it may
still be necessary to prosecute to uphold the law and
protect other people.

7 Tutu talks about 'Renewing or Releasing the Relationship',
pp. 143–60.

Part 3: Emotional Aspects of Restoration

Introduction

1 Henri Nouwen, *Home Tonight* (London: Darton,
Longman & Todd, 2009), p. 103.

Chapter 8: Receiving Mother Love

1 This phrase was used extensively by Leanne Payne: see
especially *The Broken Image: Restoring Sexual Wholeness
through Healing Prayer* (Eastbourne: Kingsway
Publications, 1988) Chapter 4, 'The Search for Sexual
Identity'; *The Healing Presence: Curing the Soul through
Union with Christ* (Grand Rapids: Baker Books, 1989),
Chapter 9, 'Imagery and Symbol: The Imagery Really
Matters'. Frank Lake also uses the term 'being' to refer to
'selfhood ... a steadily functioning "I-myself"': see
Frank Lake, *Clinical Theology: A Theological and
Psychological Basis to Clinical Pastoral Care* (London:
Darton, Longman & Todd, 1966), p. 31.

2 Passivity and over-activity can occur in the same person,
because they are both symptoms of a weak sense of being.

3 C. S. Lewis simply calls this unearned familial love 'affection': see C. S. Lewis, *The Four Loves* (London: Fount, 1960), pp. 33–54.

4 Lake, *Clinical Theology*, p. 31. See also Payne, *The Broken Image*, p. 122.

5 Karl Stern, *Flight from Woman* (St Paul: Paragon, 1985), p. 18.

6 Such views and practices were often frowned upon by Western experts, until the publication of compelling scientific evidence collated by the British child psychologist John Bowlby: see *Attachment and Loss*, Volume 1 (London: Hogarth Press, 1969); the appendix has a useful historical perspective. Controversial at the time, hundreds of scientific studies have since confirmed the importance of 'attachment theory'. See, for example, Margot Sunderland, *The Science of Parenting* (London: Dorling Kindersley, 2006).

7 Lake, *Clinical Theology*, p. 89.

8 This was tragically evident in Romanian orphanages – long-term follow-up showed improvement in those who went into foster care, the earlier the better. For more see Maia Svalavitz, *Measure of a Mother's Love* (2012). https://healthland.time.com/2012/05/24/the-measure-of-a-mothers-love-how-early-deprivation-derails-child-development, accessed 17 January 2023, Charlea Nelson, Nathan Fox, Charles Zeanah, *Romania's Abandoned Children* (Cambridge: Harvard University Press, 2014); Kirsten Weir, *The Lasting Impact of Neglect* (2014). https://healthland.time.com/2012/05/24/the-measure-of-a-mothers-love-how-early-deprivation-derails-child-development, accessed 17 January 2023.

9 Henry Cloud, *Changes that Heal* (Grand Rapids: Zondervan, 1992), p. 70.

10 Michael Kinsella and Catherine Monk, *Impact of Maternal Stress, Depression and Anxiety on Foetal Neuro-Behavioural Development*, Clinical Obstetrics and Gynecology 2009, 52, pp. 425–40; Vivette Glover, *The Effects of Prenatal Stress on Child Behavioural and Cognitive Outcomes Start at the Beginning* (2019). https://www.child-encyclopedia.com/pdf/expert/stress-and-pregnancy-prenatal-and-perinatal/according-experts/effects-prenatal-stress-child, accessed 17 January 2023.

11 M. Ross-Davie et al., *Bonding and Attachment in the Peri-natal Period*. The original article is no longer available but a recent and much fuller article can be found here: https://www.nes.scot.nhs.uk/media/x4lmfskd/final_imh_interactive_pdf__3_.pdf, accessed 17 January 2023.

12 For further exploration of disruptions to the bonding process see M. Pytches, *Yesterday's Child: Understanding and Healing Present Problems by Examining the Past* (London: Hodder & Stoughton, 1990), pp. 15–18.

13 Ibid., pp. 12, 13; Frank Lake, *Clinical Theology: A Theological and Psychological Basis to Clinical Pastoral Care* (London: Darton, Longman & Todd, 1966), p. 22.

14 Pytches, *Yesterday's Child*, p. 13.

15 Bowlby, *Attachment and Loss*; Margot Sunderland, *The Science of Parenting* (London: Dorling Kindersley, 2006); Stuart Lees, *Will the Real me Please Stand Up* (London: Hodder & Stoughton, 1997), pp. 84, 85.

16 Leanne Payne, *The Broken Image: Restoring Sexual Wholeness through Healing Prayer* (Eastbourne: Kingsway Publications, 1988), p. 122.

17 For more see Lees, *Will the Real Me*, Chapter 9, 'Easing the Pain'.

18 For more see Payne, *Broken Image*; Lees, *Will the Real Me*, Chapter 10, 'Hungry for Love'. Journey UK are able to provide further help in this area (https://www.journey-uk.org).

19 Pytches, *Yesterday's Child*, pp. 9–21.

20 For more on breaking free from addiction see Lees, *Will the Real Me*, Chapter 4, 'Kicking the Habit'.

21 The Jesus Prayer ('Lord Jesus Christ, have mercy on me, a sinner') can be shortened simply to a repetition of the name of Jesus. This prayer is inspired by passages including Matthew 9:27 and Luke 17:13; 18:13, 38–9, and has been used throughout Christian history. For more on the Jesus Prayer see Simon Barrington-Ward, *The Jesus Prayer* (Oxford: Bible Reading Fellowship, 1996); Kenneth Leech, *Soul Friend* (New York: Morehouse, 2001), pp. 180–1; Tony Jones, *The Sacred Way* (Grand Rapids: Zondervan, 2005), pp. 59–66.

22 This is the practice of Lectio Divina (divine reading). Repeat a biblical phrase over and over again, emphasising different words, using your imagination to bring ideas to life, and allowing truth to take root in your heart. Use the phrase as a stimulus for prayer. To begin with, you could try praying one phrase for five minutes. For more on Lectio Divina see David Foster, *Reading with God* (London: Continuum, 2005), pp. 1–5; Jones, *Sacred Way*, pp. 49ff; Henri Nouwen, *The Way of the Heart* (London: Darton, Longman & Todd, 1990), pp. 69–71.

23 God uses this term to indicate the preciousness of his people (Deuteronomy 32:10; Psalm 17:8; Zechariah 2:8).

Chapter 9: Receiving Father Love

1 Exodus 4:22; Deuteronomy 1:31; 32:6; 2 Samuel 7:14; 1 Chronicles 28:6; Psalms. 68:5;103:13; Isaiah 63:16; Jeremiah 3:19; Malachi 2:10. In some of these it is personal, referring to individuals.

2 Isaiah 49:15; 66:13; Hosea 11:3–4; Luke 13:34.

3 John 4:24.

4 Robert Jensen, *The Truine Identity* (Eugene: Wipf & Stock, 2002), p. 16.

5 Robert Jensen, 'The Father, He . . .' in Alvin Kimel (ed.), *Speaking the Christian God* (Grand Rapids: Eerdmans, 1992), p. 103.

6 Deuteronomy 32:6.

7 The principal texts referring to spiritual adoption are Romans 8:14–23; 9:4; Galatians 4:4–7; Ephesians 1:3–5.

8 Tom Smail, *The Forgotten Father* (London: Hodder & Stoughton, 1992), p. 40.

9 Michael Lamb (ed.), *The Role of the Father in Child Development* (Hoboken: Wiley, 2010). The findings summarised here can be found in the relevant chapters by different contributors.

10 Many different aspects of God's love are discussed in L. Button, *Father Matters: Distorted Image of God* (Essex: HSP Publishing, 2010), pp. 22–54.

11 For more on boundaries see Henry Cloud and John Townsend, *Boundaries* (New York: Perseus, 2004).

12 For an excellent exposition of this passage see Tom Wright, *Paul for Everyone: The Prison Letters* (London: SPCK, 2002).

13 While some commentators argue that Ephesians 6:4 is addressed to parents in general, the most convincing

interpretation seems to be that this instruction is for fathers in particular. See Andrew T. Lincoln, *Ephesians* (Dallas: Word Books, 1990), p. 406.

14 Leanne Payne, *Crisis in Masculinity* (Eastbourne: Kingsway, 1985), p. 87.

15 Office for National Statistics (2021). https://www.ons.gov.uk/peoplepopulationandcommunity/birthsdeathsandmarriages/families/datasets/familiesandhouseholdsfamiliesandhouseholds, accessed 17 January 2023.

16 Office for National Statistics, *Divorces in England and Wales* (2020). https://www.ons.gov.uk/peoplepopulationandcommunity/birthsdeathsandmarriages/divorce/datasets/divorcesinenglandandwales, accessed 17 January 2023.

17 A number of these characteristics in fathers and their possible effects are discussed in Lisa Guinness, *In the Beginning* (London: Living Waters UK, 2009), pp.100–2; Floyd McClung, *Father Heart of God* (Eastbourne: Kingsway, 2007).

18 For a fuller treatment of the effects of 'father wounds', including the particular effects for women and men, see Guinness, *In the Beginning*, pp. 118–19, 137–8.

19 For more on the relationship between masculinity and human will see Payne, *Crisis*, pp. 106–7.

20 Exercise created by Dr Andrew Miller.

21 Smail, *Forgotten Father*, p. 41.

22 Nouwen, *Home Tonight* (London: Darton, Longman & Todd, 2009), p. 111.

Part 4: Practising and Sustaining Restoration

Chapter 10: Living Well

1 Luke 8:14–15; Ephesians 4:13; Colossians 1:28; 4:12; Hebrews 5:14; James 1:4.

2 This metaphor is used by Paul in his letter to the Corinthians (1 Corinthians 3:1; 14:20) and also by the author of Hebrews (Hebrews 5:13).

3 This language to distinguish between the public and private spheres of a leader is used by Simon Walker, *The Undefended Leader* (Carlisle: Piquant, 2010), pp. 27–37.

4 This is the title of an influential book by Jürgen Moltmann, which explores the significance of the crucifixion: see Jürgen Moltmann, *The Crucified God* (London: SCM Press, 1974).

5 For a fuller explanation of practising the presence of God, see pp. 24, 69 and 71; for more on Lectio Divina, see p.72; for more on Ignatian meditation see p. 12.

6 Sources of liturgy are from *The Book of Common Prayer* (Cambridge: Cambridge University Press, 2005). You can find the Church of England's Common Worship liturgy at https://www.churchofengland.org/prayerand-worship/join-us-service-daily-prayer. Liturgy also includes Shane Claiborne and Jonathan Wilson-Hartgrove, *Common Prayer Pocket Edition* (Grand Rapids: Zondervan, 2012); David Adam, *The Rhythm of Life* (London: SPCK, 2008).

7 For more on spiritual direction see Jeanette Bakke, *Holy Invitations: Exploring Spiritual Direction* (Grand Rapids: Baker, 2000); Gordon Jeff, *Spiritual Direction for Every Christian* (London: SPCK, 2007), pp. 13–15.

8 That is to say that Christians belong to the Church,

whether or not they actively participate in it: see Eugene Peterson, *A Long Obedience in the Same Direction* (Downers Grove: InterVarsity Press, 2000), p. 175; Dietrich Bonhoeffer, *Life Together* (London: SCM, 1954), p. 18.

9 Bonhoeffer, *Life Together*, p. 14.

10 Lesslie Newbigin argued that as we live out the gospel in community we demonstrate and interpret it to the world: 'I am suggesting that the . . . only hermeneutic of the gospel is a congregation of men and women who believe it and live by it': see *The Gospel in a Pluralist Society* (Grand Rapids: Eerdmans, 1989), p. 227.

11 For an excellent discussion on this theme see Richard Foster, *Celebration of Discipline* (London: Hodder & Stoughton, 1989), pp. 159–77.

12 Luke 22:18; 1 Corinthians 11:23–6.

13 Sacramental theology maintains that God is encountered through matter. A sacrament was defined by Augustine as 'the visible form of an invisible grace'. For a thorough exploration, see John Colwell, *Promise and Presence* (Milton Keynes: Paternoster, 2005). See also Leanne Payne, *Real Presence* (Grand Rapids: Baker, 1995), pp. 35–43.

14 Ibid., pp. 36, 41.

15 Some denominations require a priest to be present whenever communion is shared. Please feel free to ignore this suggestion if you are uncomfortable with it, or if it goes against the teaching of your church.

16 For practical help in praying the psalms see Dietrich Bonhoeffer's excellent little book, *The Psalms: Prayer Book of the Bible* (Oxford: SLG Press, 1982).

17 For more on this theme, see A. Voskamp, *One Thousand Gifts* (Grand Rapids: Zondervan, 2010).

18 Ireneus, *Against Heresies*, Book 4, 20:7.

19 Research published by the Children's Society in 2018 indicates that one fifth of fourteen-year-old girls in the UK had self-harmed that year: see https://www.childrenssociety.org.uk/good-childhood, accessed 17 January 2023.

20 Exodus 20:8, 9. The commandment to keep the Sabbath can also be found in Deuteronomy 5:12–15; Isaiah 58:13–14; Jeremiah 17:21–7; Ezekiel 46:1–12.

21 Tony Jones, *The Sacred Way* (Grand Rapids: Zondervan, 2005), p. 184.

Chapter 11: Dying Well

1 This was one of the texts read and preached on at Ruth's funeral.

2 Chris Johnson, *Dying Well According to John Wesley*, https://seedbed.com/dying-well-according-to-john-wesley/ (2012).

3 John Dunlop, *Finishing Well to the Glory of God* (Wheaton: Crossway, 2011), p. 89.

4 From the Anglican service for the Ordination of Priests.

5 Joseph McPherson, *Our People Die Well* (Bloomington: Authorhouse, 2008).

6 A phrase used by Henri Nouwen, *Life of the Beloved* (London: Hodder & Stoughton, 1992), p. 95.

7 Martyn Layzell, 'I Stand in Awe' (Integrity Music, 2001).

8 The seven final sayings of Jesus are often reflected on during the Easter season, and are here interpreted as principles for dying after the manner of Christ.

9 Henri Nouwen, *Our Greatest Gift* (London: Hodder & Stoughton, 1994), pp. 72.

10 Catherine Marshall, *Beyond Ourselves* (London: Hodder & Stoughton, 1961), p. 102.

11 Plotinus (204–70). Quoted by Augustine in *City of God*, Book IX.

12 N. T. Wright, *Surprised by Hope* (London: SPCK, 2007), p. 166.

13 Nouwen, *Our Greatest Gift*, p. 33.

14 Grace Sheppard, *Living with Dying* (London: Hodder & Stoughton, 2010), p. 124.

15 See also Romans 8:9–11, 23.

16 See Wright, *Surprised by Hope* for a thorough theological discussion on the shape of biblical hope.

17 Sheppard, *Living with Dying*, p. 76.

18 C. S. Lewis, *The Last Battle* (London: Bodley Head, 1956), p. 161.

19 Sheppard, *Living with Dying*, p. 79.

20 Nouwen, *Our Greatest Gift*, p. 61.

21 Ibid., p. 35.

22 Richard Baxter, *The Saints' Everlasting Rest* (FQ Classics, 2007).

23 This was later summed up in a short article by her husband. See https://talkingaboutdying.org/resources/good-heaven-after-death-what, accessed 17 January 2023.

24 Brendan Manning, *Ruthless Trust* (London: SPCK, 2002).

25 Thomas Chisholm (1866–1960).

26 Philippians 3:11, MSG.

Appendix 1: Ministering Restoration to
Individuals – In Conversation with Ruth

1 Ruth Carter Stapleton, *The Gift of Inner Healing* (New York: Bantam, 1977).

2 Duncan Buchanan, *The Counselling of Jesus* (London: InterVarsity Press, 1985).

3 Leanne Payne, *Listening Prayer* (Grand Rapids: Baker, 1994).

4 Signa Bodishbaugh, *The Journey to Wholeness in Christ* (Grand Rapids: Baker, 1997).

Appendix 2: Ministering Restoration in the Local Church

1 https://www.new-wine.org/events, accessed 17 January 2023.

2 https://www.healingprayerschool.org.uk/events-1, accessed 17 January 2023.

3 https://www.journey-uk.org, accessed 17 January 2023.